Outwrite

Outwrite

Lesbianism and Popular Culture

Edited by Gabriele Griffin

Pluto Press

LONDON • BOULDER, COLORADO

First published 1993 by Pluto Press
345 Archway Road, London N6 5AA
and 5500 Central Avenue
Boulder, Colorado 80301, USA

British Library Cataloguing in Publication Data
A catalogue record for this book is available from the British Library
ISBN 0 7453 0687 X hb
ISBN 0 7453 0688 8 pb

Library of Congress Cataloging in Publication Data
Outwrite : Lesbianism and Popular Culture / edited by Gabriele Griffin.
        200p. 22cm.
    Includes bibliographical references and index.
    ISBN 0-7453-0687-X. – ISBN 0-7453-0688-8 (pbk.)
    1. Lesbians' writings. American–History and criticism. 2. Women
and literature–United States–History–20th century. 3. Women and
literature–Great Britain–History–20th century. 4. United States–
Popular culture–History–20th century. 5. Great Britain–Popular
culture–History–20th century. 6. Lesbians' writings, English–
History and criticism. 7. Lesbians in literature. I. Griffin,
Gabriele.
PS153.L46094 1993
810.9'9206643–dc20   93-2991
                                                                  CIP

Designed and produced for Pluto Press by
Chase Production Services, Chipping Norton
Typeset by Stanford Desktop Publishing Services, Milton Keynes
Printed in Finland by WSOY

Contents

For
Katrin Zielke

Introduction

'We would have it otherwise/We on the margins'[1]

Outwrite: Lesbianism and Popular Culture was properly the idea of Anne Beech, editor with Pluto Press, who wrote to me after the 1991 Women's Studies Network conference and ought to be acknowledged here. When I then got in touch with one of the contributors, Carol Ann Uszkurat, about producing a chapter for this book she answered with 'Hurray!' and 'At last!' on a postcard, expressing her sense, repeated in her essay in this volume, that not much has been done on the intersection between the popular and lesbian cultural production. The same notion obviously informed Anne Beech's original suggestion and, to some extent, both are right.

Lesbian cultural production, including the production of lesbian popular culture, has proliferated in the last 20 odd years and so, perhaps only more recently in Britain, has commentary on this production. This commentary, when it has appeared in book form, has predominantly come in three guises: as sociopolitical comment on lesbian existence, as lesbian theory, and as critique of lesbian cultural production. Frequently, all three have been combined in one volume. In terms of recent publications, Julia Penelope's *Call Me Lesbian* (Freedom, CA: Crossing Press, 1992), Bonnie Zimmerman's *The Safe Sea of Women* (London: Onlywomen Press, 1992), Dianna Fuss's *Inside/Out* (London: Routledge, 1991), and Karla Jay and Joanne Glasgow's *Lesbian Texts and Contexts* (New York: New York University Press, 1990) are good examples of (the combination of) these different kinds of commentary.

As critique of lesbian cultural production these texts, and others like them, have often focused on writers and books with a place in mainstream and 'high' cultural canons to the exclusion of popular forms and modes of culture. Where 'the popular' is considered, it is often confined to one or two chapters on the subject within a volume which otherwise addresses what has already been or is in the process of becoming canonised. One consequence of this has been that the emphasis has remained predominantly (though not exclusively) on white middle class lesbians' work. Thus quite a lot of material can be

1

found on Radclyffe Hall's *The Well of Loneliness*, on the writings of Gertrude Stein and Virginia Woolf, on the poetry of Adrienne Rich, and on Jeannette Winterson's *Oranges are Not the Only Fruit*. Little, on the other hand, is available on Gale Wilhelm's novels, the poetry of Marilyn Hacker, the songs of Cris Williamson, or the plays of Sarah Dreher. And it is not enough to say that the former have some intrinsic cultural merit which the latter lack. Such value judgments tell us nothing about how and why a lesbian text acquires a place in mainstream/'high' culture, a complex issue which still needs to be investigated. However, the focus on lesbian cultural production has begun to shift away from the already enthroned towards an exploration of the range of lesbian cultural production available now, one very recent example being Sally Munt's excellent anthology *New Lesbian Criticism* (London: Routledge, 1992) which offers lesbian critiques on a variety of popular forms.

'We slant-written against the text of the world'[1]

In looking at *New Lesbian Criticism* and as soon as one considers the intersection between lesbian cultural production and the popular, one comes up against issues of definition.

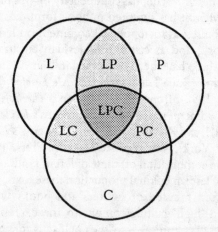

Key:

L = Lesbian
P = Popular
C = Culture

We may want to ask, what is meant by 'the popular'? We may want to consider lesbians as producers, representations in, or consumers of popular culture. 'Popular', obviously, is a relative term pertaining, among other things, both to what many people want, and to particular formulaic sub-genres and modes of production.

Lesbians as producers of popular culture

Lesbians produce texts which are popular predominantly with lesbians or liked by both lesbian and heterosexual audiences. The BBC version of Jeannette Winterson's *Oranges are Not the Only Fruit*, for instance, was popular both with lesbian and with heterosexual audiences, but it was not written as a formulaic text and its popularity across a range of audiences was facilitated by the popular medium, TV, in which it was re-cast. Its adaptation for TV, as Hilary Hinds has demonstrated, made *Oranges* a popular lesbian text (text here understood as anything that can be 'read' or interpreted).

Lesbians also produce popular culture by utilising formulaic patterns. These can be derived from sub-genres existent in heteropatriarchal culture such as the thriller, science fiction and the romance, for instance. Such an appropriation immediately raises the question of the relationship between lesbian versions of, say, the thriller, and dominant heterosexual culture, a question to some extent addressed in Paulina Palmer's essay in Chapter 5. One could argue that the use of these popular forms serves to counteract the absence of lesbians from much of heteropopular culture, undercuts the notion that heteropatriarchy 'owns' these popular forms, inscribes lesbians into popular culture and subverts some of the ideological conservatism inherent in formulaic texts by asserting the existence of lesbians and by thus questioning the stereotypes which govern much mainstream popular culture.

Last but not least, lesbians have developed at least one popular form of their own: the coming out story. Although concerned with the lesbian protagonist finding her sexual identity and situating herself in relation to her environment accordingly, the coming out story has roots in other forms of narrative familiar from dominant heterosexual culture, as Nicki Hastie demonstrates in Chapter 4. It can be related to 'myths of origin', quest narratives, and the *Bildungsroman*, but is yet a sub-genre all of its own because of the specificity of the coming to self in which the protagonist is engaged.

Lesbians represented in popular culture

We might want to suggest that all representation of lesbians in popular culture is a good thing because it gives lesbians a public platform but, where such representation operates within the mainstream, it is frequently problematic because it replicates stereotypes of lesbians produced within heteropatriarchal culture which derogates lesbians. Witness the controversy over the current mainstream film *Basic Instinct*, reviled by many lesbians for its portrayal of lesbians as pathological killers, but a box office hit with what one assumes must be a heterosexual audience. Jenny and Celia Kitzinger and Penny Florence take up related concerns in Chapters 1 and 7 respectively.

But stereotyping frequently occurs when lesbians are represented in popular form for a lesbian audience, too. Carol Ann Uszkurat discusses this issue in relation to lesbian romance. The defiant lesbian hero is, of course, a classic example here. Such stereotyping is, in part, a function of using formulaic models as such, which foster the repetition of types. But it is also associated with (re)producing types popular with lesbian audiences in search of both 'ideal' and 'real' versions of lesbians, whether as self or as other.

Lesbians as consumers of popular culture

In so far as the meaning of a text is constructed through the interaction of the text with its audience, it is impossible to dissociate the product from its consumer. Popular culture is produced with particular audiences in mind but the audiences are not entirely predetermined by the product. Lesbians consume both popular culture made for a specifically lesbian audience and popular culture made for a heterosexual audience. The possibility of reading with and reading against the text comes into play here. Popular culture made for lesbian audiences allows lesbians to read with the text; popular culture made for a heterosexual audience can be read against the grain.

While diverse possibilities of reading texts may be available in the abstract, this does not imply that audiences, lesbian or otherwise, will always respond in the 'politically/ideologically correct' way as Jenny and Celia Kitzinger indicate in Chapter 1. Such 'correctness', in any event, will depend on the particular position the reader is holding; what may be deemed appropriate by a separatist lesbian, for example, may not be seen in the same way by a non-separatist one. Popular culture tends to be consumed for pleasure, and pleasure is often a function of the recognition of the familiar – hence the formulaic aspect of the popular. What is familiar for women socialised into heteropatriarchy, such as particular kinds of power structures, is not necessarily what some lesbians might consider to be 'politically correct'. Witness the debates around lesbian pornography and lesbian SM. 'For women/perspective is more easily maintained,' suggests Audre Lorde in one of her *Chosen Poems* (p 78). I wonder. And: what perspective? As Adrienne Rich, putting together *An Atlas of the Difficult World*, states: 'where do we see it from is the question' (p 6). Precisely.

'We are your comment/We annotate, we say'[1]

We live in an age of diversity and fragmentation, a fact more easily understood on a theoretical than on a concrete level. One of the very positive aspects of the proliferation of lesbian cultural production over the last 20 years has been the recognition that 'lesbian' is not a unitary term. This recognition was given focus by Adrienne Rich's coining of the phrase 'lesbian continuum', a phrase once accepted but now, in particular because of its denial of the specifically sexual nature of lesbians' relations with each other, much disputed. The importance of this debate for lesbians is registered by the fact that virtually all the contributors to this book allude to it in one form or another. The lively discussion about differences among lesbians has gone hand in hand with lesbians encoding themselves increasingly diversely in their cultural production, not always in agreement with each other but always intent on making a statement about lesbians. Diversity has thus become a key term in lesbian cultural production and it is reflected in this collection which focuses specifically on the intersection between this production and the popular. It indicates the range of work which is being done by lesbians in relation to lesbian popular culture.

Diversity operates on a number of levels in this volume. Most basically, the chapters focus on different aspects of lesbian popular cultural production, covering representations of lesbian sex, lesbian romance, different ways of telling lesbian *her*story, coming out stories discussed as lesbian bibliomythography, lesbian thrillers, lesbian/feminist science fiction, lesbian cinema and the use of popular music in constructions of a sense of lesbian identity. Secondly, they reflect some of the range of differences in attitude among lesbians so that, for instance, Carol Ann Uszkurat takes a different view of the usefulness of psychoanalytic criticism for lesbian readings of texts than does Penny Florence. The relationship between lesbian and feminist cultural production is also implicitly under debate. Thus in the chapter on lesbian/feminist science fiction, Sonya Andermahr offers some reasons for reducing the difference between the lesbian and the feminist versions of the genre. In the context of lesbian bibliomythography, on the other hand, Nicki Hastie affirms the specifically sexual nature of lesbians' commitment to each other which makes that commitment different from other kinds of female bonding based on, for example, the politics of feminism. Carol Ann Uszkurat takes a historical view of the reception of lesbian romances of the 1950s and indicates the excluding influence which lesbian feminism has had on certain kinds of lesbian cultural production. Paulina Palmer, in contrast, indicates the liberating effect lesbian feminism has had in enabling lesbians to appropriate, inscribe themselves in and subvert dominant popular culture. Both Jenny and Celia Kitzinger and Penny Florence question the ideological bases of some of the representations of lesbian sex currently available.

These diverse issues and views are encoded in the different styles in which the chapters are written: the essays on lesbian romance, lesbian science fiction and lesbian thrillers all offer analytical surveys of these popular genres without extensively and overtly importing their authors into the text, whereas, at the other end of the spectrum, the chapter on lesbian biblio(mytho)graphy, possibly as a function of its being concerned with coming out stories and how they have changed over time, is both more experimental in style and intertwines authorial voice/experience and text-based analytical commentary. In this context, too, the use of pronouns varies. Some of the contributors use the first person ('I'/'we') prominently, others don't. More mundanely, perhaps, some chapters have extensive endnotes, others few or none.

All of this, I would suggest, is not a cause for concern but for cele-bration. Difference generates debate and dynamic; the ability to handle diversity is often one of the real strengths of those who have been or are marginalised within mainstream/dominant culture. It is this flexi-bility which ensures survival. Maintaining this, however, is not the same as saying 'anything goes', or that the choices made are not in some way significant.

In this context, one omission regarding this volume needs to be mentioned: there are no contributions by Asian or Black women, although texts by both are discussed. This absence is very much to be regretted. However, I did try. I wrote to several Asian and Black women, inviting contributions. They all replied promptly and con-structively, suggesting other suitable women who might be able to do the work, saying that they themselves had too many demands to deal with as it was to take on another project. I am not alone in this experience. In her introduction to *New Lesbian Criticism*, Sally Munt writes, 'The fact that all five Black contributors commissioned to write articles for this collection did not deliver reflects the pressure on the few to represent the many' (p xix). This absence of Asian and Black contributors is as likely to occur in a British context as in, say, the United States, as my chapter in this volume indicates. This does not, however, absolve us from the need to uncover and reconstruct the Asian and Black lesbian culture which exists in this society.

'The text is not all there is, Not all/There is, not all'[1]

For all the differences between the chapters, they have a number of important things in common. They foreground lesbian practice in the context of popular cultural production. They highlight diversity in lesbian positions and, as such, offer contributions to current debates in Lesbian Studies, lesbian criticism, lesbian theory and lesbian politics. They index the need and attempt to reflect critically on lesbian cultural history and affirm that this history is dynamic, not only as one constantly in the making but also as one being re-made over time.

One of the joys of the chapters is that they all critically detail diverse positions on the topic they are covering. They are neither politically naive nor politically defensive but tend to suggest that we need to find a position of commitment within the range of attitudes available to lesbians. In this respect they affirm, in the context of analysing lesbian popular culture, what Sally Munt suggests in relation to lesbian theory in the introduction to *New Lesbian Criticism*: 'Lesbian theory needs to endorse its own polyvocality, encourage dialectical exchange, and reject the defensive posturing of truth-games' (p xiv). And, as Julia Penelope points out: 'Easy generalizations about *all* Lesbians are impossible; each of us participates in heteropatriarchal culture to varying degrees. We make different social, economic, and political choices in the contexts of our backgrounds and experiences and our interpretations of them. But I cannot use that fact to avoid generalizing' (*Call Me Lesbian: Lesbian Lives, Lesbian Theory*, Freedom, CA: Crossing Press, 1992, p 39). Finding the balance between the general and the particular, the Lesbian and the lesbian, negotiating the triangulation between lesbian, popular and culture is what all the contributions in *Outwrite* are attempting to do.

P.S.

'The text is not all there is, Not all'

There are also the contributors, and I should like to take this opportunity to thank them for their hard work, their excellent time-keeping (especially of those who had to work to a tight schedule), their promptness in responding to queries and, most importantly, their interesting and thought-provoking contributions.

1 'Doing it': Representations of Lesbian Sex

Jenny Kitzinger and Celia Kitzinger

Heterosexual couples writhe about on the big screen in simulated orgasmic bliss, monopolise TV dramas and situation comedies with their marriages, adulteries and divorces, unashamedly flaunt their hetero-sexuality in shows like 'Blind Date', promote their 'bonking' fantasies in the tabloids, and fill women's magazines with their worries about con-traception, (hetero)sexual techniques and marital aids. Compared with this surfeit of representation of heterosexual coupling, images of lesbian sex are conspicuous by their absence.

Until 1961, the US Production Code specifically forbade represen-tations of lesbianism or male homosexuality. This meant that Hollywood rewrote original scripts, and even history, to ensure the exclusion of lesbian material – as witnessed, for example, by the 1950 *We Three* het-erosexualised version of Lillian Hellman's play, *The Children's Hour*, or Garbo's portrayal of a heterosexual romance to explain the abdication of the Queen of Sweden in *Queen Christina* (cf. Sheldon, 1987). Portraying lesbian sex, acknowledging its existence, was seen as dangerous – as if women might rush wholesale into lesbianism if they realised that it was an option. The attempt in the United Kingdom in 1921 to include lesbian practices in the category of acts of gross indecency failed because 'it was believed that such legislation would bring these practices to the attention of other women who had not ever heard, or even dreamed such things were possible' (Smith, 1991, p 134). Clearly it was felt that lesbian acts (like 'terrorist' ones) must be denied 'the oxygen of publicity' (Schlesinger, 1987, p xviii).

Explicit lesbianism is still censored today. Lesbian sex scenes were left on the cutting room floor in the filming of *Times Square*, and the lesbianism was all but erased from the screen version of Alice Walker's (1983) novel, *The Color Purple*. Caroline Sheldon's film *17 Rooms: What lesbians do in bed* – described as 'a light-hearted satire on voyeurism and prurience' (Davies *et al*, 1987) – was twice withdrawn from the 1986 British television Channel 4 series of lesbian and gay films 'on technical grounds'. Nor do lesbians feature much in contemporary media coverage of HIV and AIDS, in which 'women' always means 'heterosexual

9

women' – an assumption which is all the more striking given the explicit acknowledgment of differing male sexual practices. A heterosexual assumption is conveyed through, for example, advice to women to ensure that their partners are entirely heterosexual (a little difficult for lesbians!), and the message about condoms: 'every handbag should have one' (*The Guardian*, 28 June 1990). Even when lesbianism is acknowledged in the media, lesbian *sex* is not. A lesbian character introduced into the American day-time soap opera, *All My Children*, was not permitted (by ABC's Standards and Practices Division) to touch another woman in a sexual way, and a suggested dream sequence in which one of the characters was to fantasise about a lesbian sexual relationship was forbidden (Landau, 1984). In sum, lesbianism is underrepresented in the mass media, and lesbian sex is often invisible.

But then, perhaps invisibility is preferable to the alternatives. As we write, lesbian and gay activists are picketing Paul Verhoeven's $40 million thriller, *Basic Instinct*. This film features a beautiful bisexual killer who dispatches her victims with an ice pick during sex. Such images draw on a long history of representing women who have sex with women as predatory, crazed, psychopathic sadists. This history includes *Windows*, which features a lesbian who pays a man to rape her 'best friend' with whom she is secretly in love, and then becomes sexually aroused by repeatedly listening to a tape recording of the assault; *The Killing of Sister George* in which the protagonist is sexually excited by forcing her lover to eat cigars; the predatory behaviour of the lesbian character in *She's Gotta have It*; the BBC's version of *Portrait of a Marriage* which includes Vita's rape of Violet; and NBCs made-for-TV movie, *Born Innocent*, which showed girls sexually assaulting another 14 year old girl. When lesbian (and gay male) sexuality is represented, then, it has routinely been portrayed as dangerous and perverted, inextricably intertwined with violence and despair. Of 32 films with major homosexual characters (female and male) from 1961 through to 1976, a third of the gay characters commit suicide and half are murdered (Russo, 1986, p 32).

Probably the most widespread images of lesbians are to be found in heterosexual male pornography, and pornographic representations of lesbian sex are staple fare in tabloids carrying phone line advertisements with headlines like: 'Girls Who Play with P*ssy: Total uncut action of lesbians who unashamably [sic] play with each other for your pleasure', 'Leather Lesbians will let you watch for free', 'Lesbian Special: Hear the Moaning and Groaning of our Sexual Pleasure', and 'Dial an Orgasm: Licking Lesbians'. Lesbian sex is often represented as a form of 'foreplay', warming women up for men: lesbians are 'liberated' girls who enjoy all kinds of kinky sex, but whose lesbianism rarely withstands the arrival of the male on the scene. The sex scenes in many more recent 'positive' films seem unable to escape from this pornographic tradition: *Desert Hearts* 'with its steamy eroticism – lesbians depicted as eminently unthreatening romantic sex-kittens hungry to get their paws on each other' (Dobbs, cited in Grundberg, 1987); *Personal Best* with its 'heaving breast and thigh sequences, a film in which the heroine ends up in a safe heterosexual relationship' (Sheldon, 1987, p 91); and *Liana*, in which 'the camera does not identify with either of the two women but objectifies them both equally, acting as a voyeuristic onlooker and inviting the audience to do the same ... the distancing and objectification is intensified by the use of a blue filter and a whispered voice-over in French' (Whitelaw, 1987). Feminist film critic Laura Mulvey (1975) was among the first to point out the way in which the 'gaze' in such films is constructed from a 'male' point of view: such images 'invite women to consume them from a temporarily assumed male point of view' (Williams, cited in Straayer, 1984).

These images of lesbian sex as inadequate, predatory, or as a kind of kinky foreplay, are echoed in the daily treatment meted out to lesbians, both in terms of sympathy for our sterile, arid, loveless lives, and with the suggestion that 'all you need is a good fuck'. The common assumption is that only men can provide women with fulfilling sexual activity and that, at best, lesbian sex is a form of mysterious but titillating foreplay. They are also reflected in the common assumption that lesbian sexuality is in some way 'male', and that we, like men, have a voyeuristic relationship to other women's bodies. Under the front page headline, 'Dykes Go Ga-Ga Over Gabby', the *Daily Sport* (10 June 1992) describes how 'leering lesbians' are 'driven wild' by 'heaving knockers' at Wimbledon: 'coachloads of lesbo tennis fans will swoop on a top women's tournament next week. But instead of feasting their eyes on brilliant stroke play and well-placed balls, they'll be ogling at flashes of knicker and bouncing boobs'. We have both been offered pornography by men who expected us to join with them in admiring the images and, recently, a male relative showed us photographs of his yachting holiday with a bikini-clad girlfriend, and commented jocularly as we lingered over one of the snaps, 'You are meant to be looking at the boat, not the woman'. As Chris Straayer (1984) points out, 'lesbians have persistently been misassigned a male point of view by straight society'.

For many lesbians, however, the 'male gaze' is an alien perspective, and rather than experiencing pleasure at her exposure, identification is with the woman who is the object of the camera's gaze. Wendy Chapkis (1986, p 145) comments on the images in *Playboy*:

> The silicon-filled, airbrushed body of the Playboy Bunny not only serves as the fantasized Other, but also as a woman with whom I identify. I find myself resenting her and fearing for her. Her sexuality offers me nothing – it is an absence waiting to be filled. Her appearance is a signal of vulnerability and helplessness. Her beauty is a carefully constructed appeal to the boy protectors out there.

Many lesbians actively resist taking pleasure in the display of naked female bodies in the media and resent stereotyped portrayals of lesbian sex. Protesting against the sex scenes in films such as *Another Way*, Lis Whitelaw (1987) says: 'As a lesbian I do not want to be forced by the camera to behave in this voyeuristic way, turning other women into objects, nor do I want to be party to their arousal of men by means of the depiction of lesbian sex.' A common lesbian feminist response to mainstream/pornographic representations of lesbian sex has been to critique and boycott them. The attempt to introduce anti-pornography legislation (the Dworkin-MacKinnon ordinance) and the picketing of screenings of *Basic Instinct* are recent examples. Yet this kind of response is increasingly depicted as born of a naive and puritanical feminism, driven by pro-censorship and anti-sex impulses (cf. Segal and McIntosh, 1992). The more sophisticated and radical response to heteropatriarchal images of lesbians, it is now suggested, is actively to take pleasure from them.

Re-reading lesbian sex scenes

When we watch a film, read a book, switch on the TV, we are not passive receptacles into which media messages are poured. What we 'take out' of a text is not wholly determined by what the authors/producers 'put in'. Audience interpretations may differ from those of the author/producer; different audiences make different readings. Building on Laura Mulvey's psychoanalytic theories, de Lauretis (1987) argues that audiences can 'remake' films through bringing their social needs and historical understandings to any viewing experience. Audiences often actively engage with texts for their own purposes, and lesbians are 'particularly adept at ... construct[ing] our own destabilising readings' (Munt, 1992: xiii). For example, lesbians may 'find a lesbian subtext' in films not intended for us. Lesbians read our experience into female 'buddy' films and form a devoted audience to TV series which show women living or working together: *Cagney and Lacey, Prisoner: Cell-Block*

H, and *Golden Girls* have all become cult dyke programmes. Alternatively, lesbians may take pleasure in seeing the media try and fail to represent lesbian sex: lesbian feminist reviewers of *Personal Best* (a film written and directed by a straight man), 'expressed pleasure in watching the dominant media "get it wrong", in watching it attempt, but fail, to colonise "real" lesbian space' (Ellsworth, 1986 cited in Gross, 1991, p 37).

Audience interpretations also differ depending on *who* is doing the viewing/reading, and *when*. One of us (CK) remembers, back in the early 1970s, the pleasure of reading *The Well of Loneliness* (in which sex is described – about two-thirds of the way through – with the words, 'and that night they were not divided ...'), because – negative in so many ways, as this book is – it at least conveyed the fact that lesbians existed. Kate Alexander (1987) describes a similar experience: 'Twenty years ago the tragedy of Stephen Gordon's life inspired and haunted me. Now it infuriates and offends me'; and Peter Freer describes how when he watched the film, *Taste of Honey* as a young man 'the very existence of a gay character was a positive experience – I recognised myself. The same film, seen today, fills me with horror. Now I know I'm not alone; then I didn't' (quoted in Gross, 1991, p 37). There is no simple way of labelling images 'positive' or 'negative'. To see *any* acknowledgment of our existence feeds a hunger to see our lives reflected in the media. Lesbians desperately seeking images are an inventive, imaginative and energetic audience. We flock to cinemas in droves whenever word gets out about films with the smallest possible lesbian content, 'cruise the libraries' (Lynch, 1990) for books with lesbian content, stay up late to watch the 'lesbian kiss' on *L.A. Law*, phone each other up to say 'turn on the telly quick, there's a lesbian scene', and exchange gossip about the sexual proclivities of media 'personalities'. There is, apparently, pleasure to be derived even from such distorted, obscure and implausible reflections of our lives as are provided by the mass media.

This recognition of the complexity of audience relations with the media, this acknowledgment of our differing and changing relationships to books, films and TV programmes is important in understanding lesbian viewing, and is vital if we are not to fall into the trap of seeing ourselves (or rather *other* people) as passive consumers of media messages, or as automata ready to do the bidding of the propaganda machine.

However, the notion of the 'active' audience is sometimes used by theorists drawing on postmodernism and deconstruction to justify a total denial of any meaning intrinsic to a text. Audiences are presented as 'all powerful', able to read a book, film or TV programme in a multiplicity of different ways. The values which went into creating the text, the codes it contains, the dominant social context within which it exists are rendered irrelevant. Emphasising the plethora of possible readings, some writers argue that instead of, or as well as, experiencing *displea-sure* from oppressive images, and engaging in feminist critique, we can and should seek pleasure from them. Lesbians, then, can choose delib-erately to 'read against the grain' or 'between the lines'. However 'negative' the original representation, lesbians can recreate the image within our own framework. Instead of constantly criticising, refuting and denouncing oppressive representations of lesbians, we can use those images for our own pleasure. Responding to a critical review of *Personal Best*, Chris Straayer argues that both critique of and pleasure in male-produced images of lesbians have their uses: 'A feminist critique may be more combative but expends energy. A feminist reading usurps the oppressor's energy' (Straayer, 1984).

This can seem an attractive idea. Under heteropatriarchy, a system within which lesbian pleasures are specifically crushed and denied, anything which gives us pleasure, or from which we are able to 'take' pleasure (especially *sexual* pleasure) can seem like a Good Thing — even, inherently revolutionary. But there are, it seems, no limits to these allegedly lesbian feminist re-readings. Some feminists appear to be suggesting that even the use of heterosexual male authored pornogra-phy for lesbian pleasure can be subversive. According to Linda Williams:

> There was never any guarantee that girl-girl numbers originally con-structed for the heterosexual pleasure of masculine viewers could not be appropriated to different ends by different viewers ... [A] lesbian viewer who happened upon a pornography that was not marketed to her [might] enjoy these numbers despite their heterosexual frame. (p 253)

Similarly, Kobena Mercer (1992, p 125) argues that 'Lesbians and gays can consume heterosexual porn, and vice versa, by adopting intricate and shifting patterns of identification across gender and orientation.' In appropriating pleasure never intended for us, we are (allegedly) doing something radical. The implication of all this is that now a lesbian who orgasms poring over a copy of *Playboy*, or listening to 'XXX rated filth' on a male porn line, can be construed as engaged in a politics of subversion — 'acts of repossession' (Munich, 1985), 'a kind of cultural guerrilla warfare' (McIntosh, 1992, p 159). Once feminists saw it as a *problem* that some women derived sexual pleasure from male-identified sexual representations and, in particular, pornography: now it is seen as something to celebrate, an act of resistance.

The use of words like 'resistance' to describe audience uses of the media for our own purposes invests these readings with grandiose political implications. As Gitlin (1991, p 336) points out, 'resistance' stamps the audience's active interpretations and unexpected pleasures with 'a kind of dignity, even glory' by employing 'a vocabulary derived from life-threatening political work against fascism – as if the same concept should serve for the Chinese student uprising and cable TV grazing'. The vivid language of warfare, resistance, sabotage and subversion suggests that something radical is going on. But is it? Proponents of this view argue that, in refusing to accept oppression as *the* meaning of a text, we refuse complicity with the oppressor. In re-reading it, we reject the victim role. The problem is that sometimes texts *do* locate people as victims. We cannot afford the luxury of 'subversively re-reading' for our own pleasure texts with anti-lesbian (or sexist, racist, or anti-Semitic) content. In order to challenge oppression, we must be able to name it, must be able to identify oppression as the meaning of a text.

Feminists struggled for decades to name 'sexism' and 'anti-lesbianism'. We said that particular images of women – bound and gagged in pornography magazines, draped over cars in advertisements, caricatured as mothers-in-law or nagging wives in sitcoms – were oppressive and degrading. The deconstructionist insistence that texts have *no* inherent meanings, leaves us unable to make such claims. This denial of oppressive meanings is, in effect, a refusal to engage with the conditions under which texts are produced, and the uses to which they are put in the dominant culture. The 'de Man affair' offers a horrifying example of the dangerous consequences of this penchant for 're-reading' texts and having them mean anything the reader feels like. After his death, leading North American deconstructionist, Paul de Man, was exposed as having written for a pro-Nazi, anti-Semitic newspaper in his native Belgium during the Second World War: he had written in praise of 'the German revolution', advocated the deportation of Europe's Jews, and proclaimed the hegemony of Nazi Germany in Europe. Fearful that his exposure would signal the demise of deconstruction as a powerful academic movement, other deconstructionists leapt to his defence with the suggestion, from Derrida, that his late friend's infamous *Le Soir* article could be read as an implicit *attack* on anti-Semitism. As one critic of deconstruction put it:

> When Derrida and others interpreted [de Man's writing] as somehow a repudiation of anti-Semitism, they inadvertently proved the case

against themselves – by illustrating the ease with which deconstructive procedures could be used to fudge inconvenient truths ... Falling
into a trap of their own making, these critics obligingly furnished us
with an object lesson in the dangers of their interpretive method.
(Lehman, 1991)

The playfulness of deconstruction, its wilful 're-reading' of texts to
mean the opposite, begin to take on distinctly unpleasant overtones when
applied seriously to actual events in the real world. The dangers of this
interpretative method for lesbians' rereading mainstream representations
of lesbian sex is that this, too, can 'fudge inconvenient truths' and
obscure the fact that mass media representations do contain meanings
independent of playful (re-)readings and that these meanings are often
anti-woman and anti-lesbian. To take pleasure from such images then
becomes not 'subversion' but 'collusion'.

Finally, it is not only lesbians who read their own meanings into sex
scenes. Men make their own interpretations. Stills from *Personal Best* were
reproduced in *Playboy*, and some of the tabloids made a concerted effort
to construct a pornographic reading of the television version of *Oranges
are Not the Only Fruit*. This latter re-reading was in spite of the deliberate
attempt of author and director to produce a sex scene which 'wouldn't
be dirty raincoats or like *Desert Hearts* where the women appeared to
have "no hands"' (Winterson, 1990). Nonetheless, the tabloids antic-
ipated 'the fruitiest lesbian love scenes ever on British TV', employing
words like 'steamy' or 'torrid'. Reviewing the media response, Hilary
Hinds quotes *Today* as one of the worst offenders:

> According to a male friend, the lesbian love scenes in this drama are
> not nearly fruity enough. In order to fully fulfil the 'ultimate male
> fantasy' he says the actresses should have had bigger breasts.
>
> What we need, he adds, is a lot more tits. Samantha Fox and Maria
> Whitaker would be ideal.
>
> Had this transpired, I would have had to suggest a slightly different
> title for this excellent series: Melons Are Not The Only Fruit ...
> (*Today*, 25 January 1990 cited in Hinds, 1992, p 166)

This rather desperate attempt to force the serial into better conformity
with male fantasy by recasting and renaming it illustrates the potential
for *male* pornographic re-readings.

Recognising the dangers inherent in lesbian consumption of
mainstream representations of lesbian sex, and fearful of male appro-

priation of lesbian-generated images, one possibility is simply to refuse to collaborate with the production or distribution of lesbian sex scenes.

Refusing lesbian sex scenes

'Heterosexuals can see themselves and their relationships portrayed critically on film without feeling personally threatened; I don't think lesbians can' (Grundberg, 1987). The problem, for lesbians, is that the images are produced in the context of oppression, and it can feel as though the cost of media representations of lesbian sex hugely outweighs the benefits. Perhaps our best bet is to settle for positive portrayals of female friendships and to forget about graphic depictions of lesbian sex?

There are now many media portrayals of relationships between women as warm, supportive and intimate, and as contexts for personal growth, but not explicitly sexual: films like *Thelma and Louise*, *Bagdad Cafe* and *Salmonberries*. They might lead us to question how important it is to portray the sex between women rather than, or as well as, strong female friendships. Would such films really be 'better' for portraying lesbian sex? Because lesbian sex has been 'repressed', are we now duty-bound to ensure that it is 'expressed'? Part of the answer to this question must depend on the extent to which we see 'sex' as an essential, politically vital aspect of our lesbianism – and that, of course, has been a matter of considerable dispute amongst feminists.

Historian Lillian Faderman (1980) contends that, historically, women's 'passionate friendships' with other women, relationships which today would attract the label 'lesbian', often did not include genital contact. 'Whose interests does it serve', asks Sheila Jeffreys, 'to regard lesbianism solely as a sexual practice?'

> Lesbianism as a sexual practice is not a threat. If it were, then it would not be the stock in trade of brothels and men's pornography. Lesbianism as an emotional universe which provides an alternative to women from slotting into the heterosexual system, on the other hand, is a threat. It is then anarchic and threatens the organising principle of male supremacy. (p 24)

Such an analysis suggests that the portrayal of strong relationships between women should suffice.

But there *is* a difference between 'women-identified women' and lesbians. Many lesbians have criticised Faderman for watering down lesbianism, desexualising it. Sheila Jeffreys (1989: 22) concurs that some of the concern about the desexualising of lesbianism is well grounded, pointing out that, 'the uniqueness of lesbianism and the lesbian identity has been under threat from the concept of sisterhood ... Women who simply have "best friends" who are women share neither lesbian oppression nor lesbian experience'. Indeed, friendships between het- erosexual women, far from being part of a 'lesbian continuum' (Rich, 1980), are seen by some theorists as essential in propping up hetero- patriarchy by making relationships with men tolerable for women:

> The motivation for heterosexual woman-bonding is analogous to that of a battlefield hospital: to get the casualties fit and well so that they may be sent straight back to fight – not to rescue combatants from the horrors of war or to protest war itself ... Thus the oppressed collude with the oppressor, patching up the harm done by him, and keeping it secret, private 'women's business'. (Wilton, 1992)

The celebration of female bonding in buddy movies, then, is not *nec- essarily* 'pro-lesbian' or even 'feminist'. Many of these films make it quite clear that the protagonists are still enthusiastically committed to sex with men, and decisive limits are placed upon the possibility of sensual contact between the women: Thelma and Louise are permitted to kiss each other only just before they deliberately drive over the edge of the Grand Canyon. Moreover, some of these films (including *Julia, Bell Jar* and *Girl Friends*) contain anti-lesbian scenes designed to reassure the viewer that love between women does *not* imply lesbianism (cf. Char- bonneau and Winer, 1981). In *Julia*, for example, an unpleasant young man, a stray acquaintance of Lillian's introduced solely for this scene, accuses Lillian of having an affair with Julia. Since he is distasteful, we are expected to recoil with horror from the prospect of a lesbian liaison, and to reject his 'dirty' insinuations. Lillian immediately responds to the 'insult' by hitting the young man and overturning the table at which they are sitting. Her reactions make the scene doubly pernicious in that, as film critics Claudette Charbonneau and Lucy Winer (1981) point out, we are shown a strong woman, unafraid to express her anger against a man, but doing so in order to deny the extent of her commitment to women. Beneath the feminist facade of these films lies an insidious anti- lesbianism. In sum, buddy movies do not represent lesbian realities – or do so, at best, in a partial and fragmented way. They are not 'lesbian films' minus the sex scenes.

Believing that heterosexual women's friendships are different from commitments between lesbians, and that sex is an important aspect of lesbianism, we are loathe to accept that refusal of representations of lesbian sex scenes is the only viable political position. We would like to see representations of passionate *lesbian* relationships and politics. We want media images which address *lesbian* rather than simply female reality, and which do not erase the sexuality of lesbianism. perhaps the answer is to write our own?

Re-writing lesbian sex scenes

Producing our own representations of lesbian sex inevitable runs the risk of male co-option. We cannot guarantee lesbian-only circulation. Men can, and will, consume our images for their own purposes: postcards by lesbian photographer, Della Grace, are on sale in Soho along with male porn, 'alternative' lesbian film showings are often accompanied by the heavy breathing of the men in the cinema with us, and bringing lesbian sex 'out into the open' exposes us to further male invasion and scrutiny. Considerations like these lead some lesbians, like Sybil Grundberg (1987), to 'deplore this instinct for self-exposure – to declare publicly what lesbians (supposedly) do in bed. We are under no compulsion to answer the porn industry with an approved soft-core porn of our own.'

We think these are reasonable concerns. However, as Adrienne Rich (1989) says, 'everything we write will be used against us/Or against those we love'. Many lesbians (including us) are reluctant to give the threat of the 'male gaze' the power to censure our own representations of our lives. Representations of women are always at risk of pornographic interpretations from men – however remote such readings may seem from the intent of the producer. In a particularly disturbing example of a pornographic reading, journalist Tom Bussmann, writing a few years ago in that bastion of liberal values, *The Guardian* (26/27 August 1989), referred to the photograph (by Nick Ut) of Phan Thi Kim Phuc: one of the most powerful images produced during the Vietnam war, it depicts the nine year old girl running screaming and naked from her napalmed village. He suggests that this qualifies her to become 'a well-paid centrefold'. If even this image of human suffering can be re-read into sexual innuendo, then there are *no* images we can produce as women or as lesbians which are not vulnerable to male pornographic interpretations. We would not countenance the suppression or censorship of Nick Ut's photograph simply because some men read it with a pornographic male gaze, and we would not want to suppress lesbian generated images for the same reason: we want honest representations of lesbian sex in all their complexity. As Anna Livia (1987, pp 74–5) suggests, many feminists now insist that 'as our lives must be lived in open defiance of male opinion ... so our writing will honour only its own purpose, and if men have a little wank on the offshoots, so the world is full of little wankers.'

What does concern us, however, is this. If we construct lesbian representations of lesbian sex, how do we know that we have done so *as lesbians*, and from 'a lesbian gaze', as opposed to adopting a male gaze and utilising the conventions of male pornography? Simply claiming that they are 'by women, for women' doesn't solve the problem. There is a well-established practice of 'boudoir portraits' in the United States in which women pay to have themselves photographed (usually by female photographers) in soft-focus, wearing little more than a pout and a G-string. The photographs are often intended as presents for male lovers, but are also seen as raising women's 'self-esteem' ('better than sitting on an analyst's couch for an hour', Karina, in Burgess, 1989), and as enabling them to live out their fantasies ('I work in a male-dominated area and I have to tread a fine line to keep my femininity and yet be strong. This was my release, kind of like a fantasy', 'Kathy', in Burgess, 1989). The resulting photos are indistinguishable from the images in *Playboy*.

How are lesbian representations different? Barbara Smith (1988, p 180) claims that simply the fact that some images are 'by lesbians, for lesbians' is a radical step in itself.

> Pornography for lesbians stands representation theory on its head, because here the gaze is *not* male or masculine, there is no sharp distinction between object and subject because, being female and lesbian, the participant observer can either inhabit the 'gap' or directly participate in the proceedings, but in either case she cannot completely be detached from what is portrayed.

Nonetheless, Barbara Smith admits that 'what is called pornography for lesbians, at present *appears* little different to straight male pornography'. Others have made the same point about lesbian strip shows: 'the result looks just like a heterosexual performance' (Duggan, quoted in Tyler, 1991, p 56). Lesbian representations of sex have the problem of differentiating themselves from the 'girl-girl numbers', already staples of heterosexual pornographies and sex shows. This problem can be addressed only by exploring the specifics of what marks a representation as lesbian, constructed through a 'lesbian gaze'.

Mary McIntosh argues that 'making feminist "pornography" and declaring ourselves as sexual beings is not simply something that we do for our own pleasure, using such freedom as we have gained; it is also a way of undermining all the oppressive things that sexuality has meant for women in the past.' (McIntosh, 1992, p 167). But, like 'boudoir' photography, lesbian pornography can also reinforce those oppressive meanings. Many lesbians believe that it does. The feminist bookstore, Sisterwrite, in London refused to stock *Love Bites* (a book of lesbian erotica by Della Grace, published by Gay Men's Press!) or the lesbian porn magazine *Quim* (which reproduces Della Grace's photographs), because the material is 'violent and could cause offence to some of our customers'.

The two issues of *Quim* which we have seen (Summer, 1989; Summer, 1991) are heavily reliant on the traditional pornographic paraphanalia of sadomasochism: whips, chains, studded belts, black leather boots, stiletto heels, corsets, Nazi-style caps, fists and pierced nipples. Far from 'transgressing' traditional representations, they reinscribe them: the dominatrix, the bound woman on a rack, the huge (albeit detachable) dick. The fantasy of 'transgression' appears, too, in the lesbian photographic exhibition, *Stolen Glances*. The claim is that photographs (eg, by Morgan Gwenwalk and Jill Posener) of women in stereotypical pornographic poses, women in black leather or fur, bodies distorted by corsets, posed and exposed to the camera, 'appropriate the visual codes of pornography precisely in order to highjack heterosexual sites and customs' (Boffin and Fraser, 1991, p 14). They argue that lesbians who use traditionally fetishised garments and materials are challenging the status quo: 'the lesbian artifice of leather, silk and make-up uses it as the bricolage of a dominant culture it challenges by subverting a language we had thought was familiar, but which is now made strange' (Boffin and Fraser, 1991, p 58). (But meanwhile Hollywood goes on prescribing compulsory heterosexuality, and leather and fur – derived from killing animals – remain expensive commodities, fetishised by the porn and advertising industries.) We cannot see any difference between the cages in which lesbians dance in the London lesbian club *Venus Rising* and those in which women dance provocatively for men in the heterosexual London club, *Night of the Living Ultra Vixens*. All the trappings of sadomasochism are commonplace on the heterosexual scene among middle-aged business men (cf. *Sunday Express*, 7 June 1992). Nor is the allegedly 'transgressive' fascist symbolism beyond the bounds of social acceptability in today's repressive right-wing climate. 'Nazi Chic' (Norman, 1992) is part of contemporary fashion: a Chelsea boutique decorates its carrier bags with a Nazi double-headed eagle, framing Hitler's aphorism, 'The strength of the country is in its youth', and T-shirts are on sale in London with a giant swastika on one side, and the words 'Keep Britain Tidy' on the other. So when lesbians appropriate the symbols of domination, just what is being transgressed?

Part of what is 'transgressed' is, of course, feminism itself, with feminists characterised as censorious, moralising 'thought police'. In lesbian pornography, feminist ideas are routinely 'sexualised, depoliti- cised, burlesqued' (Carola, 1988, p 170) and lesbian producers and consumers of pornography present themselves as 'bravely struggling against the censure of powerful, reactionary, moralistic prudes, puritans and feminists' (Carola, 1988, p 169). The name *On Our Backs* – a lesbian porn magazine in the United States – is a parody of the feminist pub- lication *Off Our Backs*: its motto, 'the lesbian is the lust of all women condensed to the point of explosion' parodies the famous phrase from radical feminist Anne Koedt, substituting 'lust' for the original 'rage'. The sexualising and depoliticising of feminism is hardly unique to lesbian pornography. The woman reading the recorded message on one of the male porn lines assures the listener that she is a radical feminist, has broad shoulders, cropped hair, wears dungarees, works on a building site, and hates 'male chauvinist pigs', before revealing for male pleasure titillating details about her sex life with a barmaid. The new UK het- erosexual women's porn magazine, *For Women*, is explicit in its anti-feminism. Like so much that is presented by lesbian pornographers as exciting, deliberately shocking and outrageous, the apparent eroticism of anti-feminism is part of a very stale formula.

Also 'transgressed' in these depictions of lesbian sex is the stereotype of female (or lesbian) sexuality as gentle, diffuse, egalitarian and rooted in the context of a caring relationship. This idealisation of lesbianism has been a problem, and several writers have argued that the (mid 1970s) spate of sisterly and sanitised positive images can leave (particularly young) lesbians with no representation or validation for their own negative expe- riences of lesbian sexuality or relationships (Lewis, 1992). Certainly the new pornographic lesbian images disrupt that sanitised version. But so too do books like *Naming the Violence* (Lobel, 1986), which deals with abuse and battering in lesbian relationships, and *Against Sadomasochism* (Linden et al, 1982) in which women explore and seek to understand their own sadomasochistic fantasies and activities. The difference between violent sex scenes in pornography such as *Macho Sluts* (Califia, 1988) and those in, say, Kate Millett's (1985) *Sita* is not so much in the degree of abusiveness they reveal, or the extent to which they function as a 'turn on', as in their political purpose. Kate Millett's book graph- ically describes the power games women play through sex in order to disturb and unsettle; she critiques what she offers us. By contrast, *Quim* and *Macho Sluts* revel in the sexual power discrepancies they depict, refusing to express negative opinions about *any* form of sexual expression. In the launch issue, *Quim* quote sex therapists Margaret Nichols and Jo

Ann Loulan: 'It is more important at this stage in history to support women being sexual, however they are sexual, than to judge which aspects of their sexuality are non-patriarchal and which are male-identified' (Nichols); 'Some members of the lesbian community foster homophobia by trying to establish "politically correct" ways in which lesbians may express their sexuality ... Our beds are not large enough to hold our families, politicians, society and the lesbian community' (Loulan). We fundamentally disagree with both these therapists. Simply celebrating lesbian sex – by which lesbian pornographers mean all the sexual things that women who call themselves lesbian do (including sex with men) – is not enough. Our sexuality is *always* influenced by the world in which we live and affects that world: sometimes 'pleasure' needs questioning.

The two of us take pleasure in (some) representations of lesbian relationships and lesbian sex. One of us (CK) has participated in the production of photographic images of lesbian sex to illustrate a chapter on lesbianism written for our mother's book, *Women's Experience of Sex* (Kitzinger, 1986). We are not 'anti-sex', nor against representations of sex *per se*. But we agree with Susan Cole when she says she has come to understand that she is 'against sexual pleasure *as pornography and mass culture construct it*' (her emphasis). We would say, with her: 'I no longer believe that the words "sexuality" and "diversity" must be uttered in the same breath. I differ with those who defend sexuality no matter what its content' (Cole, 1989, p 107). We find implausible the idea that the lesbian erotica of *Quim* and *Macho Sluts* are transgressive of heteropatriarchal norms, and we do not believe that pleasure in representations of sex is in and of itself radical. We are not *opposed* to pleasure (on the contrary, we like it very much when we can get it!), but we do find 'pleasure' an extraordinary emphasis for feminism as a political movement. As Sheila Jeffreys (1990, p 264) says, commenting on the Sex Issue of the magazine *Heresies* (1981) in which 'sex was defined simply as the possibilities for pleasure':

> An issue on housing would not be expected to focus on interior decoration at the expense of looking at homelessness. An issue on women's work would probably not just focus on individual fulfilment but on the issue of exploitation. It is inconceivable that an oppositional group of socialists would set themselves up to say that there has been altogether too much gloom and doom about oppression, now was the time to talk about fashion, interior decoration, eating out and so on ... [I]t is only in the area of sexuality that individual pleasure has taken precedence over the ending of oppression.

'Pleasure' should not be an unquestioned rationale, overriding all other considerations. Sexual excitement cannot be taken as inherently radical, nor can our 'pleasure' be assumed to be an unproblematic criterion by which to assess images of lesbian sex. Lesbian pleasure is not constructed in a heteropatriarchy-free zone, and sexual arousal can bypass or undermine our critical faculties. There is nothing 'pure', 'unsullied' or inherently revolutionary about the lesbian orgasm. Taking pleasure in sex scenes which enact power struggles or which play with the symbols of fascism may reflect the measure of our complicity in our own and other people's oppression. '*Even in play*, to affirm that the exertion of power over the powerless is erotic, is empowering, is to set the emotional stage for the continuation of that relationship, politically, socially and economically' (Lorde, 1982, p 68). We believe that critical representations of such activities are fine: uncritical celebrations of them are not.

We believe that debates about how to represent lesbian sex need to address all the levels of production of meaning: the process of initiation of lesbian images (who pays for them, who directs the action or participates in it, for what purposes are they produced?); the content of the images (codes and symbols); and the audience readings. We would not wish the ubiquity of the male pornographic gaze to lead us into self-censorship. We do not want to serve up only coy and acceptable images of lesbians with cats and pot plants, the kind heterosexuals would approve of, like the Saatchi advertisement made for *Out on Tuesday*. Lesbian sex is not always pretty, or sweet. Nor do we wish to deny the passion of lesbian desire. But we do think that the current emphasis on the active lesbian audience re-reading male porn for their own 'revolutionary' purposes, and the celebration of sadomasochism in lesbian porn is misguided and dangerous.

If we are to explore and create representations of lesbian sex, we need to address clearly the social construction of our sexuality, its political meaning and content. The challenge for lesbian writers, film producers, actors, poets, photographers and artists is *not* simply to produce images which turn us on, or which 'invert' traditional male sexual codes: rather, we would like to see the invention of new ways of exploring sexuality, which challenge and deconstruct (instead of simply affirming) desire as it currently exists. Just as many women artists working in the latter half of the 1970s in Britain and North America explicitly rejected direct or symbolic representation of the female body, arguing that its meanings were already over-determined by multiple imaging in mass media and artistic traditions, so lesbians need imaginatively to reach beyond the cliched symbols of mainstream sexual fantasy and porno-graphy. Mary Kelly's *Post Partum Document*, for example, recognising the problem of trying to produce direct representations of motherhood given cultural uses of 'madonna with child', instead poses motherhood as a complex production of social and cultural meanings which it is the task of the artist to deconstruct. The explicit purpose of such work is to 'disrupt the expected pleasures' offered by the subject matter and its usual treatment in visual art, in order to engage the viewer in an active process of critically considering how such conventional meanings are made. 'A painting of a mother changing her baby's nappy would be easily overlooked as kitsch, but not so with dirty nappy liners annotated and placed within a discourse that needs work to be unravelled and refuses to place the figure of the mother on view' (Mulvey, 1976 quoted in Kramarae and Treichler, 1985, p 350). Art critics were appalled by the *Document*: 'A painting of a mother looking at her naked baby is one thing ... infant shit on the wall something else indeed' (Oakley, 1982 in Kramarae and Treichler, 1985, p 350). Maybe lesbians need to consider such ways of exploring the passion, concreteness and contradictions of lesbian sex.

We would also like to suggest the possibility that, at this moment in history, the pursuit of lesbian erotica is not the most urgent of our struggles, and that changing the political and social conditions within which images of lesbian sex are produced is an essential prerequisite to the creation of more liberatory images. Then, and perhaps only then, can we create and view representations of lesbian passion and desire, which are affirmative, challenging, and truly transgressive:

> I remember a scene ... this from a film I want to see. It is a film made by a woman about two women who live together. This is a scene from their daily lives. It is a film about the small daily transformations which women experience, allow, tend to, and which have been invisible in this male culture. In this film, two women touch. In all ways possible they show knowledge of what they have lived through and what they will yet do, and one sees in their movements how they have survived. I am certain that one day this film will exist. (Griffin, 1976)

Acknowledgment

We would like to thank Sue Wilkinson for useful discussions and helpful comments on an earlier version of this chapter.

2 Mid Twentieth Century Lesbian Romance: Reception and Redress

Carol Ann Uszkurat

Introduction

According to Barbara Grier, Ann Bannon's *Odd Girl Out* was the second best-selling American paperback in 1957.[1] That is pretty amazing because *Odd Girl Out*, a *lesbian* romance, was published in the 1950s, the era of McCarthyism, which is associated with particularly repressive attitudes towards lesbians and gay men. As Lillian Faderman suggests:

> At first glance it is surprising that it was in the 1950s, in the midst of the worst persecutions of homosexuals, that the lesbian subculture grew and defined itself more clearly than ever before ... (*Odd Girls and Twilight Lovers*, p 159)

This growth registered in a flood of lesbian paperback fiction which hit American drugstore bookstands in the 1950s and 1960s. Ann Bannon's so-called Beebo Brinker series,[2] lesbian romances featuring Beebo as a recurrent protagonist, belong to this 'golden age' of lesbian writing but, because they are considered pulp fiction, Bannon's novels as well as other lesbian romances have received little critical attention hitherto. I want to redress this balance, in the first instance, by stressing the need for these texts to be understood as forming part of the expansion of lesbian culture(s) in this century. This involves a consideration of the socio-historical background against which the lesbian romances of the 1950s and 1960s emerged. Further, I want to suggest some reasons for the minimal attention given to this paperback writing by lesbian feminist critics. Finally I want to examine the possibilities and limitations inherent in utilising analyses gleaned from critical readings of hetero-sexual romance, on the one hand, and from the application of psychoanalytical theory, on the other, for a review of lesbian romance of the mid twentieth century.

Romance publishing and lesbianism

The background to the American publishing boom of romance fiction has been well documented by Janice A. Radway (*Reading the Romance*,

Verso 1987) and others who have offered a variety of explanations for the popularity of heterosexual paperback romance. They all take particular note of the expansion of the publishing industry after the Second World War. In the years leading up to 1970, heterosexual paperback romance was big business, with publishers capitalising on increased literacy and leisure. They operated 'on the assumption that a book can be marketed like a can of beans or a box of soap powder' (Radway, p 391). The market itself 'fell increasingly under the sway of vast communications conglomerates' (Radway, p 351). In her list of takeovers of the 1960s, Radway mentions Random House, Fawcett and Doubleday, all of which produced lesbian paperbacks as one of their 'lines', as indexed in Barbara Grier's *The Lesbian in Literature* (Naiad, 1981). First published in 1967, and reprinted with updated information several times since then, this book lists lesbian paperback romances alongside more 'literary' works. Neither Radway nor other writers on romance, however, have as yet produced publishing data for lesbian romances.

The Ladder, a lesbian magazine produced by one of the first lesbian organisations in the world, the 'Daughters of Bilitis',[3] was instrumental in disseminating information about the existence and content of these texts. Throughout the 1950s and 1960s, a regular feature in *The Ladder* drew readers' attention to a selection of lesbian paperback romances available on mail order from the magazine. It offered reviews like the following:

Meet Marilyn by Sloane M. Brittain
Interwoven plot with many characters includes a highly constructive lesbian relationship which emphasises permanence and reliability in personal life. The love between Marilyn and Liza is well told and evenly balanced with the rest of the book. Sympathetic without maudlin approach – and one of the better paperback treatments. (Gene Damon, *The Ladder* vol 6, Feb 1961, p 2)

By providing these concise reviews, *The Ladder* informed a growing readership about lesbian romance paperbacks. How and where had this readership arisen? The answer to this question takes us into the history of mid twentieth century American lesbian/gay consciousness, by which I mean the state of mind whereby same-sex relationships were re-cast out of a negative mould into one of civil rights within a growing sub-culture.

The sociohistorical context

Recent lesbian/gay historical research has uncovered the growth of the homosexual community in post Second World War America, the war having acted as something of a catalyst for this growth:

> The war uprooted tens of millions of American men and women, plucking them from families, small towns and ethnic neighborhoods of large cities and depositing them in a variety of sex-segregated, non-familial environments. (John D'Emilio, 'Gay Politics and Community in San Francisco since World War II', p 459)

Coming from backgrounds which in various ways upheld heterosexuality as the norm, many conscripts – female and male – found themselves in a space and context within which it was possible to express and/or encounter other options concerning sexuality:

> For some it simply confirmed a way of living and loving they had already chosen. For others, it gave meaning to little-understood desires, introduced them to men and women with similar feelings, and thus allowed them to 'come out'. (D'Emilio, p 459)

As one woman soldier put it:

> Well, there we were in Japan, all these kids. We were twenty, twenty-one and MacArthur had said he wanted American women in Japan so that Japanese women could see what free American women looked like. I'm sure that what he meant was not the five hundred dykes who got off that boat. And I mean, *dykes*. We had an all-woman band and they were all in men's band uniforms. We had girls night home, one night a week, where we were all dancing and drinking, falling in and out of love. (Pat Bond, 'Tapioca Tapestry', p 166)

The ruptured world of work and gender in Second World War America also meant that women in general and lesbians in particular were better able to finance their socialising. This provided much needed economic clout:

> For lesbians it was particularly important that women were given the opportunity to make a living wage. This meant they could live independently of men. (Weiss and Schiller, *Before Stonewall*, p 32)

Like the single-sex environment for conscripts, the material conditions of work also added an impetus to the growth of lesbianism amongst the civilian workforce:

> The war years were characterised by living environments that were temporary and sex segregated. Hotels and dormitories catering for working women ... sprang up in the cities. In these female settings, away from families, friends and small town mentality, many lesbians discovered their sexual preference. (Weiss and Schiller, *Before Stonewall*, p 33)

As the growth of organisations such as Matachine and Daughters of Bilitis throughout 1950s America demonstrates, not all such 'preferences' ended with the war.[4]

The growth of these lesbian organisations also indexes the possibility of an increasing lesbian readership and a gradually spreading sense of defiance of heterosexist norms among lesbians. Against the description of the organised civil rights based homosexual movement of the 1950s and 1960s as reflecting the 'accommodationist, conformist spirit of the Eisenhower era' (D'Emilio, p 460), both the beat movement for men (Barbara Ehrenreich, *The Hearts of Men*, pp 24–8) and the butch/fem dichotomy for women have been considered forms of social protest. Madeline Davis and Elizabeth Laposvky Kennedy, who interviewed role playing lesbians who lived through the 1950s and 1960s, argue that:

> ... the community's growing public defiance was also related to its increased concern for enforcing role-appropriate behaviour in the fifties. Butches were key in this process of fighting back. The butches alone, or the butch-fem couple, were always publicly visible as they walked down the street, announcing themselves to the world. ('Oral History and the Study of Sexuality in the Lesbian Community', p 440)

The idea of lesbian role play as 'the community's resistance to oppression' is backed up by a lesbian who lived through this period, Joan Nestle, who maintains, 'In some sense Lesbians have always opposed the patriarchy; in the past perhaps most when we looked most like men.' (*A Restricted Country*, p 106)

What is the connection between this and the existence of lesbian paperbacks? In a rare look at one of the writers of that time it has been suggested that the works of Ann Bannon:

... provided a public point of identification for women coming to terms with their own lesbianism in their search for recognition. According to Joan Nestle, 'buying an Ann Bannon book in the 50s was tantamount to coming out to yourself'. (Diane Hamer, '*I Am a Woman*: Ann Bannon and the Writing of Lesbian Identity in the 1950s', p 51)

Lesbians appear to have read this text as part of an emergence of a positive lesbian identity in post-war America.

But during the rise of the second women's liberation movement, which took an increasing interest in lesbianism throughout the 1970s, lesbian romance was ignored. The main focus of published critical attention tended to be on two types of writing, either more 'classical' forms of writing or the lesbian feminist fiction that has appeared in recent years. What was it that prevented lesbians from looking at a crucial part of their own cultural history?

Anti-romance lesbian feminist reception

I would suggest that the answer to this question is, at least in part, associated with the rise of lesbian feminism from the late 1960s onwards and the attitudes towards pre-liberation movements' lesbianism promoted by some lesbian feminists. Thus, in a paper given at the Women's Studies Network conference in London in 1991, I argued that severe limitations come into play when an attempt is made to read any kind of popular lesbian fiction with perspectives informed by radical feminist and/or lesbian separatist theory. Other kinds of lesbian analysis are emerging now, but my interest here is to consider why lesbian romance paperbacks have been ignored for so long. In 'Process, Politics, Perspective and Meaning' I argued that the precepts of certain strands of lesbian feminist thinking offer no positive way of looking at romance, let alone lesbian romance. I want to suggest three reasons for this.

My first point concerns the way in which the lesbian feminism that emerged in the 1970s viewed pre-women's liberation movement lesbianism. Coming out in the 1970s and actually proclaiming a lesbian identity with pride was no easy step to take. In this country, for example, Maureen Colquohoun found herself ejected from the Labour Party when she 'came out'. Further, the media did not provide anything like the nowadays limited but at least noticeable profile increasingly afforded to lesbian and gay issues. This low and often negative media profile, along with the shame wrongfully associated with a sexual orientation that is not heterosexual, were both challenged by the emerging lesbian feminist and gay movements. However, especially in the case of women's liberation, this involved a scotching of 'bad old days' in favour of 'enlightened new' ones. All that had been lesbian before the rise of these perspectives was brought into question. Lesbian role play in particular was criticised.

Feminism in general provided a critique of the heterosexual demarcation of gender-assigned roles. This had a direct bearing on the way in which lesbian butch/fem role play was consigned to the dustbin of unsound practices. In contrast to the current re-visioning of lesbian role play by women like Joan Nestle, the 1970s saw the growth of a lesbian politic that was keen to assert lesbianism in what were regarded as more positive ways. Along with this went a disdain for the whole of the subculture that had struggled into existence prior to the women's liberation movement. Even lesbians who had moved within those circles were encouraged to reject their past on these new political grounds.

> We lesbians from the fifties made a mistake in the early seventies: we allowed our lives to be trivialised and reinterpreted by feminists who did not share our culture. The slogan 'Lesbianism is the practice and feminism is the theory' was a rallying cry, but it cheated our history. (Joan Nestle, *A Restricted Country*, p 105)

The texts under consideration, lesbian romances of the 1950s, were produced at a time that was seen as deserving little or no respect.

This leads me to my second point. There was, I would suggest, a definite link between the politics of lesbian feminism of the 1970s and the lack of critical regard dished out to pre-Stonewall popular paperbacks. As lesbians came out and/or into the American academe, they not only infused their courses with the emerging lesbian feminist perspective but also used academic models which they remoulded to fit hitherto ignored lesbian literature. In academic literary terms, feminists sought out long lost women writers and pleaded the case for their significance within a canon of their own. Published in 1977, Elaine Showalter's *A Literature of Their Own*, which assessed the writing of 'British women novelists from Brontë to Lessing', provided a guiding light for those critics who were out to redress the gender balance in literary studies. In 1979, Sandra M. Gilbert and Susan Gubar added *The Madwoman in the Attic* to this enterprise. It examined 'the woman writer and nineteenth century literary imagination', focusing on writers like Emily Dickinson, Mary Shelley and George Eliot with a critical lens that aimed to discern repressed feminist anger lurking in their texts.

Similarly Black, Black lesbian and lesbian critics added their voices to a clamour that called for an end to the silences specific to their groups. In arguing that all women, irrespective of race and sexual orientation, could produce great writing these critics, despite their differences, rarely stopped to question the concept of 'great' writing itself. Rather, the interest was in literally canonising those women whose writing could be re-categorised as some kind of feminist 'classic' belonging to a tradition of great women's writing. The title of Barbara Christian's book *Black Women Novelists: The Development of a Tradition 1892–1976* highlights this. One reason, I would suggest, why lesbian romance paperbacks have been left out in the critical cold for so long is that the legacy of searching the 'classics' rewrote itself into lesbian scholarship at the expense of more popular forms of lesbian writing.

Much attention has been paid to Gertrude Stein and the expatriate lesbian modernist Paris school, the sexual ambiguity of writers like Virginia Woolf and other writers' work that can be read for some kind of lesbian sub-text. In 1980 Lillian Faderman published her literary and historical research into the writing of lesbians since the Renaissance, *Surpassing the Love of Men: Romantic Friendship and Love between Women from the Renaissance to the Present*. Although it was a much needed lesbian intervention, the book has been criticised for its very middle class focus in terms both of the women and of the writing Faderman examines. Looking back at *Surpassing* from the 1990s one critic has noted that 'The focus on white, middle class and upper class women limited the usefulness of the book' (Estelle B. Freeman, 'Missing Links', p 15). This emphasis is very much in evidence when Faderman appraises the lesbianism evident in the writing of Gertrude Stein, who is mentioned twelve times in the index. There is only scant mention of the mass of lesbian paperbacks produced in the 1950s and 1960s, and that is dismissive. Those texts are condemned for 'presenting the lesbian as a poor suffering creature' (Faderman, *Surpassing*, p 392). Even in her recent work, *Odd Girls and Twilight Lovers*, which offers a contemporary history of lesbianism, Faderman spends little time on these texts. Despite the fact that the title of this book is taken from titles of lesbian paperback novels, they are afforded little regard in her study:

> Of course the characters of the lesbian pulp novels almost always lived in shame and with the knowledge that, as the titles often suggested, they belonged in 'twilight', 'darkness' or 'shadows'. Self hatred was requisite in these novels. (p 147)

Faderman does, however, note that lesbians could 'peruse the pulps for their romance and eroticism' (p 147), a point on which she does not dwell and one to which I shall return later. Suffice it to say that Faderman's academic perspective on what constitutes lesbian writing worthy of attention has little, if any, leaning towards popular culture. And here she is not alone. In 1981, for example, Bonnie Zimmerman published an article that, as the title suggested, aimed to produce 'an overview of lesbian feminist criticism'. Rather than assessing the kind of 'out' lesbianism presented in popular lesbian paperbacks from before the 1970s, however, Zimmerman suggested that Rossetti's 'Goblin Market' or the relationship between Lucy Snowe and Ginerva Fanshawe in *Villette* might reveal a lesbian subtext. Similarly, the Afro-American lesbian critic Barbara Smith in 'Towards a Black Feminist Criticism' (1977) argued a tight case for a lesbian reading of Toni Morrison's novel *Sula*. The emphasis in all these cases is on subtext. My aim here is not to dismiss such a focus but to stress how skewed the critical lens has been, directed as it was away from more popular forms of lesbian writing. Black lesbian criticism can justifiably point to a lack of available texts specifically by and for Black lesbians before 1970. However, not all other critics who seek to map out and critique lesbian writing have such an excuse because of the mass of popular lesbian romance that was produced.

Recent lesbian feminist literary criticism has continued to hoist the flag for 'great' lesbian writers. In the United Kingdom the 1980s ended with a collection of lesbian essays which emphasised that, in researching any aspect of lesbianism, problems will arise concerning 'the standard of proof' (Lesbian History Group, eds *Not a Passing Phase*, p 7). This collection provides discursive essays on the possible lesbianism of Charlotte Brontë and of George Eliot. Women who were incontrovertibly lesbian and who wrote pulp fiction in the 1950s and 1960s – paperback writers like Ann Bannon and Valerie Taylor – do not get a look in.

Similarly, two recent books from America gave short shrift to more popular writing. Offering an extended overview of lesbian writing in the 20 years between 1969 and 1989, Bonnie Zimmerman has this to say about the kind of writing that existed before the rise of the contemporary women's movement:

> In the pulp romances of the fifties and sixties, with Ann Bannon's Beebo Brinker series as a representative example, lovers come together and drift apart in the dismal mob-run bars and closet like apartments of New York City. (*The Safe Sea of Women*, pp 79–80)

Karla Jay and Joanne Glasgow's 1990 collection of lesbian feminist criticism, *Lesbian Texts and Contexts*, has a marked focus on the rich and privileged end of the lesbian writing spectrum. Writers like Djuna Barnes who moved in well heeled Parisian circles at the turn of the century, along with those already well established in the canon but up for lesbian grabs, like George Eliot and Virginia Woolf, are discussed. In the course of one tantalisingly short contribution, Lee Lynch offers an ambivalent assessment of the lesbian pulp of the past:

> Their ludicrous and blatantly sensational cover copy were both my signals and my shame. Valerie Taylor's *The Girls in Three B* and Randy Salem's *Man among Women*: these books I would savor alone, heart pounding from both lust and terror of discovery, poised to plunge the tainted tome into hiding. ('Cruising the Libraries', p 43)

In general, however, the emphasis remains on the canon and veers away from any significant focus on the popular literature of the past. The same can be said of the ingeniously entitled *What Lesbians Do in Books*, which has its emphasis on a lesbian literary history rather than on the pulp products of the past. Radclyffe Hall is lined up with Virginia Woolf, and the metaphysical poetry of Katherine Phillips dictates the flavour of the collection. The one contribution that addresses a popular form of writing is on contemporary lesbian detective fiction and assesses it from a radical feminist perspective. In terms of white western lesbian literature, this is typical of a critical lens that has assiduously avoided engaging with the lesbian romances that began appearing in the early 1950s.

It is not surprising that the published academic record of lesbian feminism followed in the footsteps of both Black and white feminists placing women's writing onto the 'classics' agenda. Towards the end of the 1970s, however, some feminists began to analyse more popular forms of writing. Taking perspectives from the growth of Cultural Studies which made room for popular fiction, heterosexual feminists, as I shall show later, offered appraisals of popular heterosexual romance. Why was this mantle not taken up by lesbian feminists? So far I have offered two reasons for the anti-lesbian romance stance of lesbian feminist criticism: a political antagonism towards lesbianism before lesbian feminism emerged, and the academic leanings of lesbian feminist critics themselves have meant canon building rather than an analysis of lesbian popular culture.

The third reason I wish to discuss will suggest why lesbian feminism did not enter the critical arena created by feminist readings of heterosexual romance. That this did not happen, I would suggest, is because of the negative way in which radical/lesbian feminism viewed popular culture as an insidious bogey man out to brainwash women.

Both the initial and prevailing radical feminist readings of popular culture during the 1970s were infused with deep suspicion. In a feminist reification of the kind of orthodox Marxist/Frankfurt School that proliferated in the 1960s and popularised concepts such as 'mass/false consciousness', radical feminists rewrote 'dominant order' to mean 'oppressive patriarchy'. Mary Daly in her 1978 worldwide bestseller *Gyn/Ecology* argued that:

> Spinsters can find our way back to reality by destroying the false perceptions of it inflicted upon us by the language and myths of Babel. We must learn to dis-spell the language of phallocracy, which keeps us under the spell of brokenness. This spell splits our perceptions of our Selves and of the cosmos, overtly and subliminally. (p 4)

Denied reality by false perceptions, women were characterised as subliminally controlled into a state of brokenness. This concept of a false consciousness for women was very much added to when another book suggested that:

> Because woman is represented as one who craves sexual sadism, violent male sexual aggression both equates with and is confused with love and romance. False notions have been created in the mass consciousness in order to justify and legitimize behaviour based on these notions. (Kathleen Barry, *Female Sexual Slavery*, p 184)

Lesbian feminism split from feminism in the mid 1970s before feminism had engaged with the new thinking in Cultural Studies which questioned the view that woman could simply be constructed as the victim of patriarchy. That the decade ended with a lesbian feminist coining of the term '*compulsory* heterosexuality' is an apt demonstration of the extent to which lesbian feminism was tied to the crucible of radical feminist thought. More recently, radical lesbian feminist Celia Kitzinger has both continued the argument against romance itself and demonstrated an ongoing refusal to even acknowledge other ways of engaging with subject/society relations:

> Various feminist critiques of romantic love present it as an objectifying and individualistic construction of the patriarchy which functions as a means whereby men have justified their dominance over women. 'Romance, like the rabbit at the dog track, is the illusive, fake, and

never-attained reward which, for the benefit and amusement of our masters keeps us running and turning in safe circles' (Jones, 1970) … (*The Social Construction of Lesbianism*, p 117)

Note the date of the quote Kitzinger chooses to back up her own assertions – 1970 – when the initial analysis of popular culture as a prime determinant of (false) consciousness was very much part of the feminist agenda.

As the 1970s drew to a close, socialist feminism was becoming more and more prepared to address the nuances, influence and construction of popular heterosexual paperback romance. What, if anything, can lesbian criticism glean from the way heterosexual romance was assessed?

The 'straight' and narrow

One important thread that runs through the readings of hetero romance is an emphasis on psychoanalysis as a means of tying in popular romantic narratives with the relationship a woman is expected and encouraged to make with a man. Replacing the conditioning of patriarchy with the scripted subject, these readings construct women as being at the mercy of a more subtle indoctrination. What critics of hetero romance tend to do is add to the feminist evaluation of Freud's work which questions the initial dismissal of psychoanalysis as biased, sexist and both anti-women and anti-lesbian. Instead, emphasis is placed on the argument that the human subject is born with the capacity to be sexual but is socialised into heterosexuality. This revolution in feminist thought was first proposed by Juliet Mitchell, who argued that there is 'a permeation throughout Freud's work of the notion of bi-sexuality: the presence in both sexes of the inclinations of the opposite sex' (*Psychoanalysis and Feminism*, p 312). This view flew in the face of those perspectives which had condemned Freud as a sexist patriarch. Instead, psychoanalysis itself was seen as containing a fundamental challenge to strict gender roles:

> … both sexes are born into the desire of the mother and as, through cultural heritage, what the mother desires is the phallus-turned-baby, *both* children desire to be the phallus for the mother. Again, *only the boy can fully recognise himself in his mother's desire.* Thus *both* sexes repudiate the implications of femininity. Femininity is, therefore, in part a repressed condition … (Mitchell, *Psychoanalysis and Feminism*, p 404)

And so, the argument goes, the woman can only get back to mother with the attainment of the phallus/baby. From this perspective, the very feminine protagonists of romance can be seen as agents against repression, out to engage actively in their destiny by getting their man. Both the texts and their readers thus become not the conditioning and the duped respectively, but are now seen as part of a process of negotiating back to a rightful state.

That patriarchy has, for various reasons and in various ways, made the position of women subservient, is not ignored in such readings. Psychoanalysis adds the dimension of desire and actually attempts to address the question: what do women want? Whereas early radical feminist accounts of romance had found desire to be a concept which *oppressed* women into subjugation, these readings offer romance as the kind of writing and reading matter which uses sexist expectations as an arena for dealing with a myriad of women's/gender-related issues.

In 1979, Ann Barr Snitow, one of the first critics to give romance serious consideration, was highly critical of the fact that the women's movement had 'left this part of female consciousness largely untouched' ('Mass Market Romance', p 161). Taking such texts seriously meant turning away from a judgmental analysis of culture as formative in a reprehensible way. Instead, interpretations were brought into play which allowed the female subject to be seen as having a measure of power within the narrative. In looking at popular texts ending with a woman in a man's arms, romances themselves were cited as part of the means towards that end, but not in simplistic Marxist terms of women being conditioned into inevitable subjugation by these narratives. Rather, the narratives were seen as part of a dialectical struggle between desire in a broad sense and heterosexuality. In their various ways, critics highlighted the obstacles which were both provided and overcome by narratives that formed part of the journey toward the woman/man scenario. Time and time again, critics define desire by picking up on the kind of feminist psychoanalysis which mushroomed in the mid 1970s. Theorists like Dorothy Dinnerstein and Nancy Chodorow are used as the analytical hook on which to hang readings of popular romance. Not surprisingly, analysis that sought to dissect woman/man relations is both limited and highly problematic when looked at for transferable models that might offer some means of reading lesbian romance.

The work of Janice A. Radway, which utilises feminist psychoanalytical theory, becomes problematic when considered from a lesbian perspective. In her research Radway turns to Chodorow's work because this theoretical model seems easy to apply both to the pleasure and to the restoration offered by romance narratives according to their readers. One important plank in Radway's analysis of romance reader response involves readers being able to:

> … relieve tensions, to diffuse resentment, and to indulge in a fantasy that provides them with good feelings that seem to endure after they return to their roles as wives and mothers. (*Reading the Romance*, p 95)

The apparent ability of such reading both to highlight and to compensate for what is unsatisfactory in real life leads Radway to categorise romance as 'compensatory literature' (p 95). Precisely what is compensated for and what is being restored takes the critical investigation into the arena of psychoanalysis.

In *The Reproduction of Mothering*, Chodorow uses Freudian object relations theory to give a feminist version of how a child is socialised into gender. Boys, Chodorow argues, will identify with a working father who is absent from the home more often than the mother. Seemingly ignorant of the materialist dynamics that take the working-class mother out to work, she maintains that the father/work and mother/home scenario leads the lad into an estranged relationship from the man who must be his role model. The boy must dissociate himself from all that is female so that he can successfully be socialised into the dominant male role. Whereas the boy is so constructed as to become aloof from mother/woman so that he can seek union with a woman, the girl is made into an extension of her mother. She is socialised into seeking motherhood, the safe site of nurturing and the place where she, unlike the boy, is never made to feel at gender odds. Desire for the male enters female consciousness as the route back to the nurturing that in adult life can only be experienced by doing whatever is necessary to become a mother. It is this desire that 'finally produces in a woman a continuing wish to regress into infancy to reconstruct the lost intensity of the original mother-daughter bond' (Radway, *Reading the Romance*, p 136). Chodorow looks at what this desire means in terms of contemporary gender relations and proposes that women desire babies because they cannot produce safe, secure nurturing with a man who has been socialised into non-caring masculinity. Women have no option but to reproduce mothering.

Like Freud, Chodorow identifies the mother as the first object of desire and, like Mitchell's reading of Freud, she argues that this is a desire which society is out to eradicate. Radway explains how Chodorow details women's psychosexual needs:

Because women move out of their oedipal conflict with a triangular psychic structure intact, not only do they need to connect themselves to a member of the opposite sex, but they also continue to require an intense emotional bond with someone who is reciprocally nurturant and protective in a maternal way. The homophobic nature of the culture effectively denies them the opportunity to receive this from the hands of someone who resembles the woman responsible for their memory of it. (*Reading the Romance*, p 140)

The Chodorow proposal that women 'need to connect themselves to a member of the opposite sex' has been roundly criticised by Adrienne Rich for being dismissive of lesbianism ('Compulsory Heterosexuality' in *Desire*, p 216). More recently this position has been taken to task because for Chodorow:

... lesbianism is virtually dismissed with the pre-emptive opinion that 'lesbian relationships do tend to re-create mother-daughter emotions, but most women are heterosexual'. (D. Fuss, *Essentially Speaking*, p 48)

Add to this the opinion that a homophobic culture prevents women from turning to each other and you have an analysis that effectively diminishes the lesbian option – and not only in terms of woman to woman relationships. The emphasis that Radway places on Chodorow's feminist psychoanalytical theory leads her to stress that, because women cannot have each other, so to speak, they recreate what they had with the first woman they knew by having a baby. So, we may well ask, what does that make a lesbian who wants a baby – greedy? My point here concerns the way that a predominantly heterosexual lens, which sites itself in psychoanalytical models of reading, can beg questions around assertions which leave lesbian experience out in the cold. It also places severe limitations on any hope of transferring such models onto an assessment of lesbian romance. This is especially so when, as Radway proposes, the pleasure of reading romance is tied up with compensating for absences in heterosexual experience. Hardly the kind of comfort required by a lesbian reader of lesbian romance! If the models being applied address only heterosexual relations, it is no wonder that none of the critics who choose to reassess popular romance look at the lesbian equivalent.

I have demonstrated how one such critic, Radway, provides an analysis of romance which is of little critical use for the reading of lesbian romance, thus adding to the long critical silence on the latter. A brief look at some other critics reveals other pitfalls. Snitow, for instance, partly premises her reading of romance on the Dinnerstein assertion that women are 'less able to give way to simple physical delight without a sense of total surrender' ('Mass Market Romance', p 157). In relation to texts that identify heterosexual heroines as 'in a state of constant passive readiness' ('Mass Market Romance', p 158) this theoretical perspective makes sense. In reading for a subconscious subtext, Tania Modleski argues that because these texts go to 'extremes to neutralize women's anger and to make hostility bearable' they testify 'to the depths of women's discontent' (*Loving with a Vengeance*, p 58). Rosalind Coward offers a psychoanalytical reading which revolves around the belief that popular romance can be seen as 'regressive' because it is 'directly reminiscent of infantile fantasies.' Hence the powerful pull of heroine toward hero is explained as a replay of the 'adoration of the father by the small child' (*Female Desire*, p 191).

All these are pronouncements on the state of heterosexual play, but in terms of lesbian sexuality, what do such perspectives offer? It is, I would suggest, difficult to transcribe 'passive readiness' onto lesbianism. Even concerning butch/fem relationships, too often condemned as a mere replica of the worst excesses of active/passive heterosexual relational practice, recent research has proposed a more complex model of inter-action. Based on interviews with lesbians who lived through the period 1940 – 60, one study maintained that 'Within this framework of butch-fem roles, individual lesbians *actively* pursued sexual pleasure' (M. Davis and E.L. Kennedy, 'Oral History', p 433). In terms of lesbian paperback romances which explore butch-fem relationships, the active/passive dynamic is not easily transferred. When lesbian protagonists relate outside of roles, such a project becomes an impossibility. The two women in Patricia Highsmith's *Carol*, for example, start as heterosex-ual and on the outside of any lesbian social scene. Even those narratives that play out a relationship between a heterosexual woman and a lesbian do not necessarily clothe protagonists in roles. A moment from *Three Women* by March Hastings provides a pertinent example. The young and feminine Paula, engaged to be married, has accepted drawing lessons from her fiancé's aunt, Bryne. Despite the fact that Bryne keeps her lesbianism secret, Paula is attracted to the older woman, who is rep-resented in womanly terms. This moment in the narrative precedes their making love for the first time. In a scene highly charged with eroticism, Bryne offers to model for Paula:

Bryne pulled the sweater over her head, revealing the hollows of her cleanly shaven armpits. The warm odor of her perfumed body floated on the air. She dropped the sweater carelessly and started to raise her slip. Paula clutched the easel, paralysed by the thing that was happening to her. Her stomach contracted with waves of unfamiliar sensation she could not name. (March Hastings, *Three Women*, p 64)

Note the absence of collar, tie and suit! Later in the narrative Paula considers this: 'Neither she nor Bryne was trying to imitate the other sex. In a group of fifty women, could anyone pick them out as Lesbians?' (p 170). My point is that when desire works between women it is difficult to transfer models that seek to explain the desire of women for men. What place here for 'the adoration of the father'?

But what of the way in which heterosexual romances have been read as a significant indication of 'the depth of women's discontent' with the state of heterosexuality? One potential problem with considering this – especially in the psychoanalytical terms employed by Radway – is that it would be possible to propose a reading in which a woman runs back to a mother figure rather than toward the father figure. Although I place myself open to charges of classic Freudian 'resistance' I, for one, would want to reject this use of psychoanalytical theory. Transfixing lesbianism into a regressive mould diminishes conscious agency and confines this adult and vibrant form of sexuality to the realms of the immature. As to whether or not these lesbian texts can be read as a critique of heterosexual practice is another question.

Overt discontent with marriage, for example, forms part of one of Valerie Taylor's lesbian romances. The thoughts of Mrs William Oldenfield go beyond the pages of fiction when she pronounces on her heterosexual lot in life:

Maybe if you did the housewife bit for ten or fifteen years you got used to it. Maybe a fifteen-minute bedding twice a week, without active participation, came to stand for sex. A pretty prospect. (*Return to Lesbos*, p 29)

Although the sentiments are unmistakable, there are problems in highlighting them as a comprehensive critique. There are, I would suggest, as many inherent dangers in citing heterosexuality as wrong in itself as there are in the more usual project of diminishing lesbian experience and/or finding it morally reprehensible.

So far I have been indicating some of the limitations of attempting to translate aspects of heterosexual romance readings onto lesbian experience and texts. I want to take the problem of applying a psychoanalytic lens to lesbian romances two stages further, first considering the complex, ambivalent and changing relationship that exists, to date, between lesbianism and psychoanalysis, and then looking at what happens when the lesbian critic appropriates psychoanalytical perspectives for a reading of the romances of one of the best known lesbian pulp writers, Ann Bannon.

Lesbianism and psychoanalysis

I begin with the case 'against' as that, historically, was the initial stance. The negative reception of psychoanalysis by lesbian feminism – a line of thinking that continues to this day – helps to explain the extended silence around popular lesbian romances. If lesbian feminism is antagonistic towards psychoanalysis, it is hardly likely to take anything from readings of popular heterosexual romance which rely heavily on such perspectives, especially as lesbianism has often found itself maligned and treated as a disorder by a theoretical frame that is concerned with the 'heterosexual-as-the-normal' orientation. The spill-over from personal experience into political position is an understandable one.

As early as 1964 Judy Grahn was fighting back in her own words with 'The Psychoanalysis of Edward the Dyke' (*The Work of a Common Woman*, pp 26 – 30), a savage and satirical attack on definitions that 'treated' lesbianism with electric shock and aversion therapy. Lesbians had no problem in agreeing with the condemnations heaped on Freud's head in texts which identified the discontents of twentieth century western women. Betty Friedan, Kate Millett and Germaine Greer were all critical of psychoanalysis. Their consensus offered a dismissal of both the man and his followers on the grounds that the theories were rooted in patriarchal values that were out to secure woman in a subordinate and domesticated place beneath man.

In 1974 Juliet Mitchell offered a Marxist feminist reading of Freud that flew in the face of this initial critique by championing the man for suggesting that the human subject is open to following several paths due to a bi-sexual predisposition. As socialist feminists started to take the polymorphous into their perspectives, lesbian feminism was splitting away from the women's movement to form an enclave of its own. Fuelled by a concern for women who get a raw deal at the hands of men, they continued to see psychoanalysis as an area you enter at your peril. The early 1980s work on child sexual abuse did much to underwrite the initial contempt felt by many radical/lesbian feminists. Critically examining the famous case of Dora, Jane Rondot pointed out:

Freud harps back to masturbation and incestuous infantile desire to explain away a further childhood symptom which became chronic – 'dyspnoea' or chronic asthma. According to Freud, Dora's breathlessness occurs because she overhears her father panting during intercourse (although Dora's parents were estranged, Freud is assuming that Dora's father insists on his 'conjugal rights'). Isn't it more credible that Dora's 'symptom' of breathlessness is linked to sexual abuse which may have included fellatio? ('Hysteria or Resistance: The Great Freudian Cover-Up Part II', p 24)

This radical feminist mistrust has remained part of the ideological fix of lesbian feminism, but it has been increasingly challenged in the 1990s. The 1990 lesbian edition of *Feminist Review*, 'Perverse Politics: Lesbian Issues', embraced psychoanalytical perspectives as an area that could be appropriated by lesbians – not a proposal that went down well with all radical lesbian feminists:

> Power, pleasure and degradation: what is depressing about these articles is how little of what they offer us is new. The writers rely on traditional Freudian psychology ... (Davina Cooper and Didi Herman, 'Turning Us Off', p 18)

I quote this for several reasons. First, it shows a radical lesbian feminist willingness to dismiss any kind of 'pleasure' that lies beyond their own political perspective. As I have argued this is one reason why lesbianism before 1970 has been so royally disregarded by radical lesbian feminists. Secondly, by expecting something 'new' it reveals a resistance to the subtle ways in which meaning can be discerned as being made within cultural studies. Last but not least, it demonstrates the depth of feeling that runs counter to those lesbians who wish to engage in psychoanalysis. How appropriate is this position? Do we have nothing 'new' to learn here? I raise these questions not as some adjunct to my main argument. Rather, I raise them because one of the very few readings of lesbian romance to date has come from a critic who openly engages with the theory: Diane Hamer. How successful is she?

Identity and lesbian 'pulp'

In view of the meagre and negative reception afforded the lesbian paperbacks produced during the 1950s and 1960s, what Diane Hamer has to say on the subject comes as a welcome change. In taking the writings of one of the authors of the time seriously, Hamer offers the opening of a positive critical space that is long overdue. Warmly received as a piece that cites Bannon's writing as a 'critique of sexuality' which explores 'desire and sexual identity as historical entities', this essay would appear to provide the comprehensive context necessary for an assessment of lesbian romance (Sally Munt, 'Review Essay', p 97). For me, however, problems arise when the historical perspective is over-shadowed by a focus on lesbian identity. Also, 'romance' as it is conceptualised in these openly lesbian texts is discounted by Hamer, because she rightly notes the lack of formula which, according to het-erosexual feminists, is evident in heterosexual romance. This leads to a dismissal of any comparison with Mills and Boon because 'such a parallel is questionable in terms of generic conventions' (Hamer, p 50). But is there not room to consider how exactly 'romance' was part of the lesbian culture of the 1950s and why? I leave this question open because my main concern here is to focus on the way in which an emphasis on identity alone ignores other perspectives.

As regards history, Hamer is careful to remind us of the moral climate of the time:

> The fictional fantasy world Bannon created through her novels was not separate from, but formed part of the reality of being lesbian in the 1950s. Bannon herself was swamped with requests for help and advice about lesbianism from isolated women desperate for information ... (Hamer, p 51)

In a pertinent footnote we are informed that:

> All the correspondence she received from women she subsequently destroyed for fear of discovery by her children – a classic example of the way in which lesbian history can be lost to us in the necessary bid for secrecy. (Hamer, note 20, p 73)

As regards the medical model that so plagued lesbians like Judy Grahn throughout this period, Hamer is quick to identify one Bannon character that reverses the more usual outcome:

> Vega's identity is based on a denial of her lesbianism, a denial that drives her first to drink and then to insanity, at which point her family section her to the local psychiatric hospital. (Hamer, p 53)

The informative aspects of Bannon's five novels are contextualised as a means by which 'the reader is guided through ... lesbian social codes and mores' (Hamer, p 52). But for Hamer the texts offer more than the nuts and bolts of the hidden social scene that Bannon set out to make familiar to interested lesbian readers. On the agenda, as perceived by this reading, is the discursive entry into lesbian identity.

> There is more than one way to become a lesbian, and Bannon, by constructing fictional biographies for her lesbian characters, produced a new knowledge about how one arrives at a lesbian identity. (Hamer, p 70)

There is no doubt that Bannon took a variety of definitions of lesbian identity by the horns and challenged negative pathological and biological assessments thereof. The treatment of the Vega character quoted above is an apt example. Problems arise, however, when the psychoanalytical/identity approach become dominant. Sexual identity is then foregrounded at the cost of other crucial aspects of the texts. Looking at lesbianism as 'identity' is not a new enterprise, and Hamer herself picks up on the text that was first visited with this particular perspective, *The Well of Loneliness*. Jonathan Dollimore has pointed out that:

> *The Well*, as Jeffrey Weeks and Sonja Ruehl have argued, helped initiate a reverse discourse in Foucault's sense: lesbians were able to identify themselves, often for the first time, albeit in the language of their oppressors. (*Sexual Dissidence*, p 49)

Similarly, Hamer's emphasis is on the making of a lesbian identity through a variety of routes that she finds in these texts. With the spotlight on the invert Stephen Gordon and Beebo Brinker, a butch protagonist, Hamer proposes that 'in a sense the dilemma of gender identity faced by them is not dissimilar to that which confronts every girl according to Freud's account of the oedipus complex' (p 57). At this point her analysis becomes suspect, because it seems contrary to the many-faceted angles at play at the time these texts were produced. The introduction of psychoanalysis has the often noted propensity of leaving a range of contexts, complexities and specificity behind. When Hamer suggests that 'every woman's feminine identity is only ever precariously established, resting upon the repression in their unconscious of girls' early masculine drives ...' (p 57), I find myself raising two questions: first, I am troubled by the conflation of all women into one scenario: secondly, I find myself concerned that this single scenario ignores differences of circumstance within and across time.

The idea that the psychoanalytic paradigm can speak of all women's experience has long been a bone of contention within feminist thought. In assessing the limitations of sealing all women into any one philosophical theory, Jean Grimshaw reminds us that:

... the divergences in the lives of women and in feminist thinking mean there is no non-contested or isolable paradigm of female values or priorities which can be seen as the source for feminist philosophical thinking. (*Feminist Philosophers*, p 259)

In attempting to transfix Bannon's lesbians within a re-oriented Freudian paradigm, more material considerations within lesbian romances and during that time are likely to be ignored. The butch role, for example, could be read as an assertive grab for masculine privilege at a time when mores concerning feminine appearance and passivity were rigorous. If all women take on the butch role to merely re-enter (or never leave!) the door marked 'early masculine drives', then history ceases to matter. The very different reasons behind 1950s role play and the reappropriation of such roles in the 1980s are lost in a free floating paradigm which, ironically, seeks to anchor socio-sexual lesbian behaviour to one point of origin.

Where Hamer is most useful is in her positing of lesbians as fighting with and against predominant definitions of lesbianism current at the time. The emphasis on sexual identity, however, allows a slipping away from other aspects also important in Bannon's texts. What of the woman who has to deal with other identities? J.R. Roberts, in an annotated bibliography that lists writings by and about Black lesbians, makes a brief but telling reference to Bannon's *Women in the Shadows*:

In her attempt to survive and succeed, Tris, a minor character in this fifties' pulp lesbian novel, denies both her lesbian identity and her Black heritage. (p 30)

Any reading of the lesbian identity of this character must, surely, bring into play issues of race, for example, and how that identity line is handled both inside and outside of that 1959 narrative.

In relation to economics and work Bannon's texts have much to say concerning the ramifications of lesbianism during the 1950s. Beebo Brinker, for example, finds herself out of higher education and without professional qualifications because of her lesbianism. Laura does not return to college because her heart is broken by a lesbian love affair. Tris, mentioned above, considers herself more liable to gain credence and employment as a dance teacher if she passes as Asian rather than admitting herself to be Afro-American. Such crucial aspects are left by the wayside if the focus is reduced to the psychoanalytical.

If these texts are to receive the comprehensive reception they deserve, then there is room to approach them from several vantage points.

Engaging with definitions of sexual identity is one of several important aspects. In this chapter I have attempted to indicate what aspects need to be considered if the mass of lesbian paperback romances are to be assessed comprehensively. Throughout I have both identified and argued against the over-long critical silence that these paperbacks have been afforded. By placing them in the historical conditions out of which they arose, I have tried to indicate the place these texts should hold as part of a lesbian and gay history. In addressing the critical silence from lesbian feminism – especially the radical kind – I have raised questions around the legitimacy of not critically embracing an invaluable part of a popular lesbian culture. The analysis offered of the heterosexual bias within both the subject matter and interpretation of feminist readings of romance has demonstrated the pitfalls in any attempt to transfer models used for readings of heterosexual romance.

As I have tried to show, the employment of psychoanalytical perspectives comes unstuck under a lesbian lens. Although lesbian appropriation of such perspectives has opened a valuable critical space for debate, I remain unconvinced that the interpretive ball should stay in the singular court of lesbian sexual identity. We are, after all, talking about a vast number of texts, authors and readers which emerged during a period in which heterosexuality held the high moral ground in law and attitudes without the benefit of the open networks, overt political perspectives and support available today. Both the production and reception of lesbian romances at and in their time offer fruitful areas for research. Earlier I quoted Faderman and Nestle on what lesbians could be said to have obtained from these texts at the time of their production. Listening to these readers would unlock a barrage of contexts and would go some significant way towards constructing a critical site that covers culture, history *and* identity. My own tentative work in this area has already provided me with a sample of British lesbian reader response that differs according to variables like class.

Moves to address lesbian popular culture today need to be complimented by a willingness to assess what kinds of popular culture existed for lesbians in the past. By looking at why this has not happened in the case of the lesbian romances produced in the 1950s and 1960s, I have tried to add to initiatives in this area which seek to address the varied paths that same-sex sexualities have had to negotiate.

3 History with a Difference: Telling Lesbian *Her*stories

Gabriele Griffin

Lesbians are still, as *Hidden from History*'s subtitle suggests, in the business of 'reclaiming the lesbian past' because, to quote Marcy Adelman from the introduction to her *Not a Passing Phase*: 'How [can] we envision our futures if we [don't] know our past … ?' (p 10). One might argue that at this stage in the reclaiming of lesbian *her*story, all writing by, on and for lesbians fulfils this function of bringing to light what has been hidden from view and as such constitutes *her*storical texts. *Hidden from History*, concerned with the history of homosexuality, is – significantly, it seems to me – edited by one female professor of English and Women's Studies and two male professors of History, projecting itself as a work by academics two of whom are historians. Discovering lesbian *her*story in the context of history as an academic discipline is *one* way in which that story can be presented. However, there are other ways in which such a history, lesbian stories, can be told. It can emerge from texts (which themselves may be/come the sources for historical investigations) that do not have the status of academic history books and, indeed, where people are marginalised from mainstream cultures, their sense of their history and identity will often be indexed in texts which exist outside academe. In this chapter I want to look at some such texts in order to highlight how lesbians document themselves. The texts in which lesbians encode their stories bear relations both to the dominant and to the popular cultures within which they come into being and I want to consider some of the issues involved in those relations. History is not just a matter of reclaiming the past; it is also a way of recording the present and I shall therefore briefly discuss lesbian texts in relation to that present.

Being counted

One popular way of presenting and disseminating history is through books of lists, designed both to inform and to entertain. They continue a tradition of 'rational recreation' which in current culture finds one

outlet in the many varieties of quiz games offered for popular entertainment. Books of lists are declarative; they assert a body of knowledge
which is not intended either to be queried or verified. Their importance
lies in their display of cumulative knowledge. In 1990 Dell Richards
published one such book entitled *Lesbian Lists*.[1] Richards's use of a
popular format, a book of lists, is interesting because books of lists are
about quantity: they testify to the need to see things in terms of recur-
rences (so many people having done *x*, or one person having done *x*
so many times, for instance), reinforce the notion that quantity counts
and, most importantly perhaps, indicate that there exists a cumulative
knowledge that can be disseminated in quantitative form. What, on one
level, *Lesbian Lists* is saying is that there are lots of lesbians, that lots of
information about lesbians is available, and that this information can be
packaged in terms of numbers.

The lists concerning lesbians which Richards provides fulfil what
Martha Vicinus and her co-editors of *Hidden from History* describe as the
first stage of 'work in women's history: filling in gaps left by traditional
historians with women's stories' (p 12). Thus one can find out about
'7 Lesbian Musicians, Composers and Opera Divas' (p 46), and about
'10 Amazon Treatises' (p 79). Offering information on lesbian *herstories*,
Lesbian Lists is useful as a resource which might well appeal to lesbians
beyond academe because of the popular format which it utilises. It offers
one answer to a need described by Joan Nestle:

> We need to know that we are not accidental, that our culture has
> grown and changed with the currents of time, that we, like others,
> have a social history comprised of individual lives, community
> struggles, and customs of language, dress, and behaviour – in short,
> that we have the story of a people to tell. ('Voices from Lesbian
> Herstory', p 110)

At the same time, books of lists, it seems to me, in some respects
continue a tradition of display of *curios*, eliciting the question, wonderingly
uttered, 'Did you know that ... ?' and inviting the reader to contem-
plate their content with surprise, pandering to the reader's desire to
marvel. Richards's section on 'Amazon Queens and Other Exotics', for
instance, by its very title seems to stimulate such wonder. To the
extent that the entertainment value of books of lists is a function of such
a display they bring to the surface the issue of difference and how,
culturally, difference is encoded and dealt with. Readers may marvel
at the specificity of the body of knowledge displayed in a book of lists
and/or at the quantitative dimension of the information. Both affirm

a divide between what is taken for granted and what is considered extraordinary. You do not marvel at the ordinary. In this respect, books of lists continue a tradition in History (with a capital H) of privileging that which is not ordinary; they can therefore fall prey to the accusation of conservatism in a preserving as well as a political sense of the word.

However, *Lesbian Lists* not only fills in gaps and thereby establishes a lesbian *herstory*; it also, like all history, has the function of constructing a sense of continuity, of affirming that there are stories to tell which will provide a map of lesbian 'culture, history, and personalities' through time and across space. What *Lesbian Lists* is read for, then, depends on the reader, who may come to it for information, entertainment, or affirmation. Books of lists have diverse and possibly problematic roles within their cultural contexts. It is therefore interesting to look, briefly, at the responses *Lesbian Lists* elicited which, themselves collected into a list of '5 Women Who Love Lesbian Lists and What They Each Say About It', self-referentially introduce the book. That list provides an indication concerning the projected readership of *Lesbian Lists*. The five women cited are all established lesbian authors, known, one assumes, to a lesbian readership if not to a general one. This seems to suggest that the book is intended for lesbian readers familiar with lesbian writing. Emphasis is on '[presenting] lesbianism in all its wonderful diversity' (p 14), and what these five women's responses to the book indicate is the extent to which *Lesbian Lists* is regarded not merely as a form of entertainment, but as a *herstory*-building block which preserves and passes on knowledge of a lesbian nation. Thus Judy Grahn is quoted as saying that the book 'makes clear that we have a culture of our own, with its own political history, its own philosophy, and its own cosmology'. Lee Lynch's comment is: 'I started reading *Lesbian Lists* for fun. Then it dawned on me: this book is a resource and a validation. We can never record too many facts about lesbian culture; the act of listing is one of handing down, of passing on, a joyous *we are*!'

In the context of cultural visibility, lesbian discourse is young, so young that all articulation is immediately duosemic, signalling both the possibility of utterance (as in itself a source of jubilation) and (the celebration inherent in) the making of a trace, the construction of an i-dent-ity, the imprint that makes visible self to self and self to others. Such celebration of a coming-into-being goes together well with some of the lists offered by Richards such as the one of '9 Poetic Chinese Terms for Female Genitalia from Han Dynasty Marriage Manuals (206 BC – AD

26)' (p 159) but sits less easily with '6 Countries with the Harshest Penalties against Lesbianism' (p 212). Indeed, it is the presence of these two types of lists – those that affirm and those that point to the undermining of lesbian existence – which makes this book into more than one of 'great fun' as Greta Schiller, director of the film *Before Stonewall*, is quoted as saying. By highlighting diverse material, including the legal and political conditions of lesbian existence across countries and cultures ('5 of the Best Countries in Which to Live – from a Legal Standpoint – if You Are Lesbian' and '12 US States Where Lesbian Acts Are Still Illegal', pp 215, 217), *Lesbian Lists* creates a *her*story of lesbian living which gives cause for celebration as well as for concern. It continues a tradition of lesbian presentation which details lesbian existence by simultaneously foregrounding the 'ecstasy' and the 'agony' of lesbian lives.

One celebratory aspect of *Lesbian Lists* is the fact that Richards decided to concentrate on lesbianism before 1970, because including 'the whole spectrum of contemporary lesbianism … would have filled volumes' (p 14), a sentence which highlights the proliferation of lesbian texts over the past 30 years. Historically, this proliferation is associated with the women's liberation movement of the late 1960s and early 1970s, which helped women gain a public and politicised platform, and thereby enhanced women's visibility in society significantly. Included in *Lesbian Lists*'s list of '9 Non-Fiction Books Every Lesbian Should Own' (p 53) is one book which offers a history of the emergence of lesbians in the women's liberation movement, Sydney Abbot and Barbara Love's *Sappho Was A Right-On Woman*.

'Before' and 'after'

Sappho Was a Right-On Woman is a key text in lesbian *her*story for me, because at the level of content as well as of form it is a representation of a critical change in the cultural and social visibility of lesbians which occurred in the context of the women's liberation movement of the late 1960s and early 1970s. To understand this change, it is necessary to look at *Sappho* in greater detail.

In its construction of lesbian history, *Sappho* owes much to popular cultural products such as magazines and TV programmes. It may be that this is related to a notion relevant to the 1960s and early 1970s expressed in Suzanne Neild and Rosalind Pearson's *Women Like Us* that if you wish to 'promote homosexuality' you should do so in a format that will remind readers of mainstream cultural production and therefore not upset them. In *Women Like Us*, Rachel Pinney says about Esmé Langley (who founded the lesbian magazine *Arena 3*, first published in January 1964):

> ... I was absolutely horrified that she didn't look like something straight [sic] out of *Vogue*. If you're going to sell a thing like lesbian, you've got to look like *Vogue*. (*Women Like Us*, p 26)

Sign of the times! The front cover of my copy of *Sappho Was a Right-On Woman* shows two tanned, manicured women's hands with red varnished nails, reaching out and touching each other in what is not so much a vigorous handshake or passionate firm grasp but rather a delicate, ceremonious courteous contact of the fingers, possibly the prelude to a raising of one hand by the other for the purpose of kissing the hand. This posture of the hands also serves to show off the ring with the woman's symbol on one of the hands. It is only this symbol which marks this representation's difference from advertisements for handcream, soaps, or jewelry, thus establishing a link to mainstream cultural representation and possibly also suggesting that the difference between the women in these ads (aimed as they are at a heterosexual market) and lesbian women is small – again, a point frequently made in the late 1960s.

Inside the covers of *Sappho*, too, echoes of popular cultural products can be found. Thus like one of those advertisements on supposed self-improvement products that one can find at the back of magazines, *Sappho* as a text is divided into a 'before' and an 'after' section but, instead of being captioned 'before' and 'after', its two parts are entitled 'What it was like' and 'Living the future'. 'What it was like' is a rather curious read, looked at from the 1990s, not because of its content with which many lesbians will feel very familiar but because it describes the life of the lesbian (and the use of the singular, 'lesbian', and of the definite article 'the' is deliberate here) prior to the women's liberation movement in terms reminiscent of wildlife programmes. Indeed, reading this section one would not be surprised to find a subtitle like 'Lesbians: Their habitats, habits and haunts' for that is how the section on 'What it was like' presents itself.

The sense of lesbians being described as a rare species is in part a function of the *style* in which the first section is written. 'Lesbian', for example, is used as a unitary concept, generically, in the singular and often combined with the definite article. Verb forms tend to be in the present tense and indicative (the favoured form for suggesting 'universality'). In consequence, phrases like 'the lesbian does ...' or 'the lesbian is ...' occur frequently in the first section of *Sappho*. Statements like the following are typical:

Perhaps dressed in dark tones or in black, in the fashion of old gay custom, the Lesbian blends into the environment, camouflaged like other life forms that develop protective coloration in hostile environments. By day she must contain her feelings in a dark closet; but protected by the night she feels she can allow her lightest moods to emerge. (p 70)

In its first section *Sappho* which, one has to remember, was published in 1972, presents the lesbian as a rare (and endangered) species ('Less is known about her – and less accurately – than about the Newfoundland dog' p 13) whose every aspect of life is one hazardous fight for survival. Issues such as holidays (p 48) and office clothing (p 49), for example, that one might find addressed in women's magazines as part of the 'how to be a better ...' campaign, are here tackled as concerns which represent hurdles in the lesbian's life, governed by guilt, self-hatred, isolation and loneliness as it, supposedly, is. This, it is suggested, was the lot of lesbian women before the women's liberation movement.

The representation of lesbians as women paralysed by negative feelings about themselves and by their sense of isolation is, of course, a common phenomenon, especially in lesbian texts dating from before the 1960s. It has become part of the mythology of lesbian history, a function of the fact, as Joan Nestle puts it in 'When The Lions Write History', that 'for many years, our only social existence was on the pages of medical, psychological, legal, and religious texts – all dedicated to proving our pathology' (p 179). This is underwritten by texts like *Sappho* which, while taking an entirely sympathetic line towards lesbians, continues the tradition of Radclyffe Hall's *The Well of Loneliness* by pathologising lesbian existence. In the 'What it was like' section of *Sappho*, lesbians are portrayed as singular – in every sense of that word – living apart from and even in ignorance of a lesbian community. Literary texts such as Radclyffe Hall's *The Unlit Lamp* (1934) are pertinent examples of the same phenomenon. Other, later, texts detail the lesbian in similar terms. Witness Rosemary Manning's first autobiographical text *A Time and A Time* (1971). And in *Oranges are Not the Only Fruit* (1985) the protagonist only realises that other women in the community in which she lives are lesbian too when one of them 'comes out' to her (p 106). Even then this revelation is met with amazement: 'What on earth was she talking about? Melanie and I were special' (p 106). The representation of the lesbian woman who experiences herself as isolated from a lesbian community is a significant part of lesbian history. She is a part of the pathologised past of lesbians as well as the pathologised present in which AIDS has become one new means by which isolation can be enforced.

Historically, a change from the lone lesbian's being the dominant, indeed virtually the only (represented) version of lesbian existence, to its being one among many other kinds of depiction of lesbian life occurred, as *Sappho* documents, in the context of the women's liberation movement. Lesbians' 'fight for survival' was, at that time, transported onto the open platforms of feminist activism and the second half of *Sappho* offers an account of lesbians' struggle in the United States to gain acceptance within the all-female, nationwide organisation NOW (National Organisation for Women), a three-year struggle (1969–71) which involved women like Rita Mae Brown, Susan Brownmiller, Betty Friedan and Kate Millett. This struggle, which moved lesbian women from the shadows and the twilight into the limelight, highlights a point of transformation in the visibility of lesbians, signalling the emergence of a sustained documentation of lesbian *her*story into western culture. Perhaps the most important achievement of the women's liberation movement of the 1960s was that it once more[2] made visible women as an organised section of society with a political agenda. As one of its central concerns this agenda focused on the establishment of women's independence from men. The drive towards female autonomy, according to *Sappho*, united lesbian and heterosexual women because:

> We were Feminists before we were Lesbian activists, and we know that both Feminists and Lesbian activists fight to become self-reliant; both find dependence on men unnatural. The common political goals of the two groups make sexual preference an unimportant difference. (p 16)

However, this seemingly 'unimportant difference' soon became a source of conflict[3] among the women involved in NOW as the term 'lesbian' was used as a label and, more to the point, a form of abuse against all feminist activists irrespective of their sexual preferences. In their manifesto 'The Woman identified woman' (1970) Radicalesbians made the issue explicit by stating that 'in this sexist society, for a woman to be independent means she can't be a woman – she must be a dyke' (*For lesbians only*, p 18). As Audre Lorde in 'Scratching the Surface: Some Notes on Barriers to Women and Loving' eloquently indicated, the same charge was levelled at Black women, not just for wanting to be independent of men but for wanting to bond with other women. And Kate Millett stated at a press conference on 17 December 1971:

'Lesbian' is used as a psychic weapon to keep women locked into their male-defined 'feminine role'. The essence of that role is that a woman is defined in terms of her relationship to a man. A woman is called a Lesbian when she functions autonomously. Women's autonomy is what Women's Liberation is all about. (*Sappho*, p 124)

The debate about the specificities of female autonomy (was it a purely economic matter as initially envisaged?) in the context of women's sexual identity raised the issue of women's allegiances with each other/with men and necessitated a re-viewing of what the women's movement was supposed to be about. It led to a recognition that:

the women's movement has to be about sexuality. Otherwise, it's just another civil rights movement and that's not dealing with the problem women have to face. If sexuality is at the base, then Lesbianism is totally relevant. (*Sappho*, pp 128–9)

This relevance was acknowledged in a re-visioning of the concept of 'the lesbian'; a re-valuing of the term 'lesbian' took place which moved that appellation from one of abuse to one of pride. The 'political lesbian' emerged, described in *Sappho* in three different ways as:

1. a woman who becomes a Lesbian as a result of Feminist theory [and who] sees Lesbianism as a separatist, alternative life-style;
2. women who live a total commitment to women, even though they have never had sexual relations with women;
3. a Lesbian who is politicised, that is, she has analysed her situation in society according to the theory of sexism and the nature of sex roles. (*Sappho*, pp 152–3)

What I want to highlight here are not the various definitions of the phrase 'political lesbian' offered, with which many lesbians may well (dis)agree, but the fact that the women's liberation movement made women as a significant part of society visible, that the women only spaces it helped to create provided a context in which lesbians could be(come) visible and that the struggle concerning the status of women with diverse sexual orientations within the women's liberation movement *moved women on* from considering themselves in relation to men to thinking about themselves in relation to other women *and* that this process, finally and importantly, led to a debate about what it means to be lesbian. Its most significant outcome was the recognition of diversity among women, a diversity which is encoded in Adrienne Rich's much debated phrase 'lesbian continuum'. *Sappho* to me is a key text because it charts the move from seeing lesbians in unitary terms – 'seeing' being the wrong verb here as invisibility was the order of the day within that context – to lesbians becoming visible and being regarded as diverse.

Getting on

The enhanced visibility of lesbians from the 1960s onwards resulted in an increased visibility of lesbian cultural production. Thus documenting themselves, lesbians generated the material from which their stories would emerge and through which they and their history would be sustained. Despite the fact that the lesbian cultural production of the early 1970s signalled the diversity of lesbian existence as first overtly addressed within the context of the women's liberation movement, the 'canon' of lesbian writing which gradually emerged and which, it would seem, was dominated by and addressed itself to white, mostly middle class lesbians, did not immediately take direct account of the diversity among lesbians which registers race, class, ability, and age, for instance, as significant factors in lesbian existence. Thus – to remain with just one of these factors: age – texts like *Desert of the Heart* (1963) and *Rubyfruit Jungle* (1973) have consistently had more critical attention than, for instance, *Sister Gin* (1975) and *Memory Board* (1987). One significant difference is that the first two texts constitute novels of self-discovery which detail the emergence of a lesbian identity, a coming out to oneself and others. Such texts have proved perennially popular. This is easy to understand: these texts frequently mirror lesbian readers' own histories of finding their sexual identity, their trials and tribulations in coming to terms with their lesbianism and coming out. They can also offer the lesbian reader an idealised version of herself, especially when – as in *Rubyfruit Jungle* or *Oranges are Not the Only Fruit*, for example – the protagonist is constructed as successfully fighting for the expression of her sexuality against the odds, taking on and triumphing over a heterosexist establishment which seeks to (re)form or extinguish the lesbian protagonist's sexual identity. These texts, however, replicate, as do many texts which centre on romance, a phenomenon commonly found in heterosexist cultural production, namely, that the dynamic of the narrative is provided by a young female protagonist whose mobility is determined by what seems to be the only and the most significant choice she has to make, that of aligning herself with an appropriate partner/sexuality. I do not wish to decry the importance of making that choice or of its being culturally represented but I want to underline that this emphasis of focus on the young (20 – 40 year old) up and coming (out) protagonist in pursuit of a suitable love (object) first undercuts the possibility of representing the diversities of lesbian existence and, secondly, replicates the heterosexist assumption (there grounded in the notion that women will ultimately remain economically and therefore in all other ways dependent on men) that the only significant moment in a protagonist's life is the point of partner/sexuality choice.[4] Yet, as is acknowledged in *Sappho*:

> For Lesbians, independence and responsibility for self are lifelong realities and not merely interim needs between support by father and support by husband. (p 135)

One issue forgrounded by lesbian oral history as documented in *Women Like Us* and *Long Time Passing* is that lesbian life styles have been different from middle class heterosexual women's lifestyles in that – unlike the protagonists of Jane Austen's novels – lesbians who have chosen not to marry but to make a life of their own, sometimes on their own, have had to support themselves in every respect. As an inevitable effect of this, their lives have been dynamic in that they have frequently moved geographically and occupationally as well as relationally. Lesbians have had a mobility which many heterosexual women until quite recently have not enjoyed and this mobility, which is and remains a possibility throughout lesbians' lives, is not acknowledged where the focus is only on the young female (on the verge of) finding her partner/sexual identity. For this reason, *Sister Gin* is another key text for me in that, early on in the current surge of lesbian cultural work, its focus was on the changing relationship of two middle-aged women, partners of 20 years' standing. *Sister Gin* topicalises older lesbians and, perhaps even more importantly, sexual desire for the older woman who, not glamourised *á la* Marlene Dietrich, is seen as attractive as and beyond an aged and aging body. Su's love and need for the 77 year old nearly deaf Mamie Carter, which develops into a sexual relationship, constitutes an emphatic denial of the notion that sexuality is only for the young. The women in *Sister Gin* are very different from the protagonists of much lesbian popular cultural production: they are well over 40, fat, wrinkled, struggling with diets, alcoholism, joblessness, the desire to leave their partners. Their portrayal, however, does not – and this is where the text is significantly different from some writing on lesbians of the early twentieth century – cast them in the role of victims of a heterosexist society but presents them as subjects to/of life changes in which they make choices which have positive as well as negative effects. The breaking of the taboo about love between older people as a 'suitable' topic for presentation in *Sister Gin* goes hand in hand with an extended discussion about another, related taboo topic, the effects of the menopause on one of its protagonists. This, too, makes *Sister Gin* a key text for me, for it registers the diversity of physiological experiences in women's life cycles, many of which are still not thematised either in lesbian work or in other kinds of (mainstream) cultural production.

(It is perhaps worth noting here that much more has been done for the visibility of older lesbians in recent years in the context of oral history and various forms of documenting lesbians lives than in 'literature'. We might want to ask ourselves why this is the case and to consider what the cultural, social, and political factors might be which determine lesbian cultural focus.)

Finally, *Sister Gin* is a key text in lesbian history for me because it engaged *in 1975* the issues of race and of class which more recently have formed part of the wider debate on lesbian diversity. Su, its protagonist, in struggling to become a writer, tries to find out what voices she can inhabit. Her experiences as a reviewer of books have told her that being a woman does not create an automatic bond among women. She recognises that Black women need a voice to speak their experiences. In what seems like an interior monologue Su has a Black woman, Miss May, speak to her:

> Now you know how you were feeling when those books put you in them. They let you move around a little while and then go on out the door. You didn't say anything but pretty soon you got a Sister Gin to say it for you. Haven't I got as good a claim to that sister as you? (p 206)

But what sister? As the actual protagonist of *Sister Gin*, Miss May, says to Su: 'It's a mighty funny use of the word family when we don't share nothing but the bottle. I hope we're not fixing to use sister that way' (p 214).

Ultimately, Su faces her *alter ego* Sister Gin's, verdict: You just can't speak for Miss May, that's all. Let her go out the door. And she doesn't need you to hold it for her, either (p 215).

This stance is also taken by Black women. In 'Scratching the Surface ...' Audre Lorde writes, '... if we do not define ourselves for ourselves, we will be defined by others – for their use and to our detriment', and she pleads for recognition of 'the notion of difference as a dynamic human force, one which is enriching rather than threatening to the defined self' (p 45). Similarly, bell hooks' writing in the 1980s has forcefully argued for Black women's need to project their own voices. *Sister Gin* makes visible women who, within much lesbian writing, especially of the older canonised variety, are invisible: older women, black women. It problematises their lives and the subject positions one might adopt in relation to them, which is why *Sister Gin* is a key text in lesbian *her*story for me.

Beneath 'The Quilt'

One way in which lesbian history can be reclaimed is, of course, through the (re)publishing of lesbian texts. This is particularly important in the context of documenting diversity – texts by white, middle class, English speaking lesbians are easier to come by in Britain than lesbian writing originating in other cultures and yet these latter texts are crucial for developing lesbian history within the multi-cultural society that Britain is. The text that I therefore want to speak of here is the short story 'The Quilt' by the Indian writer Ismat Chughtai. Reading this short story made me aware of the fact that I know nothing about the representation of lesbians in Asian Indian cultures and when I looked through some of the more recent publications on lesbian existence and lesbian feminist criticism, such as *Hidden from History* (1989), *Lesbian Texts and Contexts* (1990) and *New Lesbian Criticism* (1992), there was nothing about Asian Indian lesbian writing, although Black lesbian writing tends to be more extensively discussed. *Hidden from History* in particular addresses homosexuality across a range of cultural and historical backgrounds. An Indian woman working on short stories by female Indian writers told me that in her culture lesbianism is a taboo topic. Yet, at the same time, here is this short story, 'The Quilt', which, though only published in English in 1991, was first published in India in 1944. The story, according to its translators, provoked a scandal and Chughtai was tried for obscenity, not unlike Radclyffe Hall for *The Well of Loneliness*. The existence of 'The Quilt' would suggest to me that there must be more material of this kind available in Indian languages, that there – as elsewhere – there is a lesbian *her*story hidden from view.

'The Quilt' is the story of the relationship between an Indian woman and her female servant.[5] It is told by the Indian woman's niece who, as an adult, remembers a week she spent with her aunt while still a child, sleeping in the aunt's room and discovering something going on beneath the aunt's quilt, namely, the aunt's lesbian relationship with her servant Rabbo. The aunt, who was not allowed to leave the house and was sexually spurned by her much older homosexual husband (whose 'household revolved around the boy-students' (p 8), develops an entirely sensual/sexual relationship with Rabbo who spends all her time massaging, scratching and bathing the Begum. When the servant is away for a day the Begum enlists her niece to service her physical needs. The child, who adores her aunt and is proud to be of service, finds herself suddenly terrified by her entry into sexual terrain as the aunt becomes excited by the niece's touch.

One of the most interesting aspects of this short story is that it leaves unresolved the attitude of the narrator, the Begum's niece, to lesbianism. Veering between the two perspectives of the narrator as adult and the narrator as child, the story indicates both a fascination and a horror with lesbianism. Men are presented as posing no threat as sexual predators for women – the Begum's husband's preoccupation with boys is described as 'a strange hobby' but not to be compared to the 'disgusting sports' such as breeding pigeons which other men engage in (p 8); the narrator derides her own mother's dislike of her mixing with boys who are nothing but 'my own brothers and their puny little friends'. The Begum's 'patronage', on the other hand, is described as 'more terrifying than the fear of the world's worst goondas [ruffians]' (p 17). The Begum's (ab?)use of the child's delight in serving her aunt by tending to her body raises, for a reader of the 1990s, the issue of sexual child abuse, and the effect of the experience on that child remain unexplained. Her fear of the aunt's patronage notwithstanding, however, the narrator keeps faith with the Begum in not telling of her relationship with the servant; she remembers with excitation the events of her childhood ('My mind begins a mad race into the dark crevasses of the past; memories come flooding in' p 7); and she suggests that Rabbo's entry into the Begum's house was the point when the Begum 'started living' (p 8), a phrase the narrator might not have used if she was homophobic. The narrator's own sexual preferences as an adult remain undisclosed – one is left with the image of, on the one hand, one adult woman, the Begum, finding sensual and sexual satisfaction with her female servant, and on the other, the female narrator's obsession with having witnessed this.

'The Quilt' offers a glimpse of the possibility of a tradition of lesbian writing by Asian Indian women of which little seems presently available in Britain.

Celebrating lesbian unions

If the (re)discovery of lesbian texts is one means of creating lesbian cultural history, the documenting of lesbian life styles is another. Increasingly, texts serving this purpose have begun to surface and *Ceremonies of the Heart: Celebrating Lesbian Unions* is just one of these. It describes and shares with the reader ceremonies of lesbian commitment, combining a historical account of lesbian unions with 27 descriptions of individual contemporary ceremonies of lesbians' commitment to each other, most of which took place in the 1980s. These individual accounts are organised so that domestic photographs – snapshots of most of the lesbian couples from their day of celebrating their relationship with each other – precede a narrative in which the couples in the first person, either singular or plural, describe their story: how they met, how friends and family responded, how they decided on the ceremony, what they did 'on the day' and how this influenced their subsequent life. Reading this book is in some respects like meeting a stranger on a train who takes out a photo of her and her partner on their 'day of union' (in the book some call it 'wedding') and then tells you all about that event and the relationship. First one looks at the photos, then one is told about the women in the photos, and then one goes back to the images, trying to 'match up' narrative and photo. Do these women 'look like' their narratives? Do these photos confirm what the narratives tell us?

The photos focus on the women as couples. Some photos, like the one which has been used for the cover of the book, but also the one of Anna and Deborah (p 131), portray the couple in conventional wedding photograph terms, dressed as bride and bride or bride and groom, one taller, the other shorter, looking into each other's eyes or kissing, togetherness signalled by arms around each other. For the most part, the couples occupy the foreground and there are no other people in the photo. In some cases, a child is bound into the union by occupying the place between the couple who tend to look either at each other or at the camera, all smiles. The fact that these photos are, in the main, snapshots taken by amateurs for the purposes of 'private consumption' rather than photos set up by professional photographers for 'public consumption' is revealed in the composition of the photos. Quite frequently the women are cut off at the thigh for example (eg, pp 173, 191, 199). Occasionally, the photos are blurred (eg, p 159). The background to the photos tends to give the impression that it was simply there rather than chosen. These could, in fact, be the photos of any of our friends. A dialectic between the personal and the public is thus set up, augmented by virtue of the fact that the photos appear in a book to be bought by the general (lesbian) public. The personal element is intensified by having the first person narratives which provide contexts for the photos and thus rescue them from being anonymous incidents witnessed by someone's camera, to acquiring a 'personalised' meaning fashioned through the narrative.

This 'personalised' aspect is given yet another public dimension by the fact that all the photos stem from the day of the celebration of a specific lesbian union, that they all focus on a similar event, a particular culturally engrained ritual which, at a given point in a relationship, many people engage in. The experience recorded here is thus at the same time both specific to and special for two particular individuals, and reflective of a cultural practice engaged in by many people. It testifies both to 'the diversity of forms lesbian couples [create] to honor their relationships' (p vii) and to the 'great similarity in the spirit reflected in the history of women's bonding and in the current accounts of lesbian ceremonies of union' (p xi). This is revealed, among other things, in the issues involved in the setting up of these ceremonies as described by the couples. They are very similar, starting with whether or not a ceremony should be held at all, what form it should take, who should be invited, what having the ceremony would/does mean, and so on. The narratives are also similar in that they all offer a happy resolution of the story of the couple: they met, they fell in love, they stayed together and made a long-term commitment to each other, encapsulated in the union photo.

One of the issues raised by and in these narratives is the relationship between the celebration of lesbian unions with similar ceremonies, weddings, in heterosexual contexts. Most of the couples feel the need to comment on that relationship and most of them discuss their own, friends' and families' views on this question. Anna and Deborah, the couple who, as far as this book is concerned, had the ceremony closest to a traditional heterosexual church wedding, offer a number of inter-esting comments. Anna starts with an oppositional stance: 'we felt that this was something we supposedly couldn't have because of being gay, and I think it was the opposition that made us want such a traditional ceremony' (p 132). She also says that being gay meant that they approached the ceremony from a very different stance to heterosex-uals so that they 'kept the words about traditional roles out of the ceremony' and 'no one was giving anybody away' (p 133). Her line that 'Being two women we are not bound to the traditional roles of society.' is interestingly countered by her partner's sense that one needs to 'acknowledge and support those feelings' which are residues from a past in which she 'grew up as a traditional little girl' (p 134). This raises the question of the extent to which one can move beyond or leave behind the social and cultural contexts which shaped one's early life – contexts that for many women in their thirties, forties and fifties now were, for the most part, heterosexual patriarchal ones. For the women in this book, feeling 'the need for a public statement of some kind about our commitment to one another' (p 94), an overt process of negotiation between past and present is undertaken. Their ceremonies are not necessarily or inevitably ones of 'appropriation' – the trysting ceremonies, for example, have a long-standing cultural tradition outside heterosexual society. Perhaps the issue is one of rejecting the notion of 'cultural ownership' whereby one group 'owns' particular rituals, marking them as theirs by only allowing some people to participate in such rituals.

Ceremonies of the Heart, like *Sister Gin*, highlights *diversity* among lesbians in a number of ways. It is encoded in the range of different ceremonies the women engage in to celebrate their unions. It is also foregrounded through the varied racial backgrounds of the women who are presented in the text. As one of them who describes herself as 'a blend of Asian–Pacific people' says: 'To tell my story is to say that Asian–Pacific lesbians and gays exist ...' (p 90). And it is highlighted by the fact that women of quite a wide age range are shown, women in their fifties as well as women in their twenties. There are lesbians who have been 'out' for many years, lesbians who have come out only very recently, lesbians who have been lesbian all their adult lives, lesbians who were in heterosexual relationships for some of their adult lives, and so on. The one area in which there does not appear to be much diversity is class and professional background. Most of the women depicted are middle class, working in education, the social services, counselling, therapy and other similar professions. This highlights the fact that texts like *Ceremonies of the Heart* are, in some respects, self-selecting concerning the women they are likely to present. It is not possible, within the context of this chapter, to discuss the implications of that self-selectivity in terms of what it might say about the couples' attitudes towards ritual, spirituality (it *is* interesting to note for how many of the couples there is an important religious component to their ceremony), alignment within a wider social context, etc. There is no clear indication in the introduction how the editor selected or came to know about the couples she included, but many of these couples' professional situation is not unlike that of the editor and her partner. What this indexes, of course, is the fact that different people have differential access to cultural production. The possibility of articulating yourself, presenting yourself in print, is limited to a small number of people who know how to and wish to access the public forum reached by being in print.

Lesbian Studies

Many of the women who access public fora via being in print are women
who either have had or are in advanced education. As they produce texts,
as both lesbian cultural production and a body of knowledge about this
production has grown, so commentary on it has been generated and one
result of this has been the gradual emergence of Lesbian (and Gay) Studies
– at least at the level of concept – in education. As I write this chapter
the Second Lesbian and Gay Studies conference is about to take place
in London, signalling that in the 1990s Lesbian and Gay Studies will be
one of the areas of academic concern on the British educational agenda.
The fact that it is only the *Second* Lesbian and Gay Studies conference
indicates how new this subject is in British education. This is unlike the
situation in the United States where Lesbian Studies has had an albeit
somewhat contested place in education curricula for more than a
decade, as the book *Lesbian Studies*, edited by Margaret Cruikshank,
testifies. With that book, first published in 1982, this chapter in a sense
comes full circle, for *Lesbian Studies* replicates, in the context of
education, what *Sappho Was a Right-On Woman* detailed at the level of
politics, namely the emergence of the lesbian/Lesbian Studies within
the context of feminist politics/Women's Studies.[6] As Cruikshank
states in the introduction:

> ... the concept of 'lesbian studies' is fairly new. It means both the
> grassroots cultural work which tells us who we are and the more
> formally organised *courses* on lesbians which now exist in a few
> women's studies programs in women's centers. (p ix)

The current situation in Britain is not unlike the one described here;
apart from one or two courses like the MA in Sexual Dissidence at Sussex
University and some teaching of Lesbian Studies in the context of
adult education as detailed in Jean Milloy's and Rebecca O'Rourke's
The Woman Reader, for example, in education in general lesbian cultural
production tends to be presented and subsumed in the context of
women's studies or women's writing courses.

The problems associated with this situation are well documented in
Lesbian Studies. Thus the issue of whether or not students and teachers
should come out in circumstances where their academic progress and
careers might be affected is raised. In a manner not unlike that of
Sappho Was a Right-On Woman, the first section of *Lesbian Studies*,
'Lesbians in the Academic World', offers narratives of closeted lonely
lesbians who eventually come out and live happily ever after. It is also

worth noting that Barbara Smith, one of two Black women discussing lesbian literature, states about her and her colleague's situation: 'I think it's ... significant that the two people who taught these Lesbian lit. courses had *no* interest whatsoever in having careers in the university.' ('Lesbian Literature: A Third World Perspective', p 62) Smith also raises another issue relevant to lesbian studies, the question of Third World lesbians – who teaches them (as cultural producers and as students)? As Smith says:

> ... there are virtually no women of color who are out as lesbians who are in a position to teach courses in universities ... There are Third World Lesbians, but very few have the wherewithal to be able to teach a class at a university. There are also Third World Lesbians who do teach at universities who are not out or who are not feminists. ('Lesbian Literature: A Third World Perspective', p 62)

Although this is a statement made ten years ago about teaching Third World lesbian texts in the United States, what is said is clearly true of Britain today (1992).

Similarly, in 'One Out of Thirty: Lesbianism in Women's Studies Textbooks' Bonnie Zimmerman suggests that:

> most women's studies texts have problems integrating lesbian material into their structures because lesbianism is ghettoized: a lesbian perspective is not presented on the variety of social, cultural, and political issues explored by women's studies. (p 129)

This is not quite the case in relation to recent women's studies texts from Britain, such as Jane Aaron and Sylvia Walby's *Out of the Margins* or Terry Lovell's *British Feminist Thought*, or indeed recent texts from the United States such as Elizabeth Weed's *Coming to Terms*. In all of these, chapters on lesbian studies topics can be found. This may be because women's studies, like lesbian studies, has emerged later in British education than in US education and that, as a result, its trajectory is somewhat different from that in the United States, offering an accelerated and compressed version of the development of its counterpart there. However, although the establishment of women's studies in British higher education (where to date there is still only one undergraduate course in women's studies) coincides much more closely than it did in the United States with the emergence of lesbian studies, it is also, in my experience, the case that lesbian studies material is not automatically included in women's studies contexts, even where one might expect it to play a prominent role. On the MA course in women's studies in which I am involved, oral history, for example, is raised as an important issue, yet the discussion of the importance of oral history projects in terms of the subjects/objects they focus on does not include a lesbian perspective. One of the key texts used, Sherna Berger Gluck and Daphne Patai's *Women's Words* which is an excellent text, while giving much (needed) space to Black and Third World women's issues, has nothing to say about a lesbian perspective, despite the fact that there are a number of established lesbian oral history projects by now and despite the fact that J.R. Roberts in 'Black Lesbians before 1970: A Bibliographical Essay', for instance, states that '… the creation and collection of numerous oral histories of older Black lesbians is most crucial in creating a collective history of the twentieth-century Black lesbian life' (p 103).

This, of course, raises the question of difference once more, the question of plurality, unity and fragmentation as highlighted by the relationship between women's studies and lesbian studies. In 1992 in Britain, lesbian studies is beginning to differentiate itself from women's studies just as lesbians differentiated themselves from the general women's liberation movement as part of establishing their profiles in a wider cultural context. Such differentiation without doubt results in enhanced visibility. Simultaneously, it raises the question of the position and role of lesbian studies within a general cultural and educational context.

Visibility good?

Compared to the situation in Britain even just a decade ago, lesbian cultural production has a much greater presence and profile now. Despite the fact that many lesbian writers in the introductions to their texts proclaim the absence of this or that material on the relevant shelves, it is also true that more writing by and about lesbians is available now. It is now possible to expect bookshops like Sisterwrite and Silver Moon to carry a large amount of stock of lesbian writing; many so-called alternative bookshops too, like Blackthorn's in Leicester and Mushroom in Nottingham (to name just a couple outside London), devote as much shelf space to lesbian as to feminist writing. Lesbian writing has increased and diversified. There are not only novels and poems but plays, documentary material, manuals on lesbian etiquette and lesbian sexuality, theories of lesbian existence, journals and magazines for lesbians and much more. The printed page apart, there is *Out on Tuesdays* on TV, lesbian film, lesbian art, lesbian music. The London Lesbian and Gay Film Festival (whatever one might think of their selection of films) tours around Britain. Some of this work has reached mainstream culture, most spectacularly perhaps *Oranges are Not the Only Fruit*.

In a variety of ways lesbians are thus enscribing themselves into culture and making history, producing the material which signifies the accumulation of a body of knowledge of lesbian lives and the possibility of giving it cultural expression. However, this does not mean that lesbian work is necessarily easily available. Even where texts couch themselves in popular formats as, for example, *Lesbian Lists* does, this does not mean that they are available in the relevant section of any of the popular book-buying places such as railway stations or W.H. Smith. This may not matter for all the women who have access to various forms of cultural production, who, for example, go to alternative bookshops or arts centres, or can afford to pay for books, magazines, videos and the like. It does not speak to or of the women who exist outside that particular frame, who do not partake in culture in that sort of way. One could, of course, argue that this is a problem in the making of any history, that there are always individuals or groups of people who are represented by their absence or silence. But in the context of lesbian history, which is the one I am concerned with here, the situation is exacerbated by the fact that a voluntary censorship on the part of the agencies controlling cultural dissemination exists in relation to lesbian cultural production which means that lesbian work is not as widely available as it should and could be. A lesbian in search of her story still has to know where to look to find herself represented.[7]

4 Lesbian Bibliomythography

Nicki Hastie

No 'writing' exists that is not in fact a reading of former writing, an anthology in part, an appropriation of prior texts. ... The situation of a woman in some version of that-culture-in-which-we-all-exist may be described as the desirous reader. She is the reader desiring something, some thing not yet there, perhaps partially there, fleetingly there, oppositionally there, reductively there; if there, perhaps unread, and unread is unseen, unheard. The desirous reader chases this woman among words, these women among words. She reads them in, she reads them out. (DuPlessis, 1990, p 120)

Lesbian readers are 'desirous readers'. The absence of visible, knowable lesbian women in our early development, especially for women growing up before or in ignorance of the women's liberation and gay liberation movements, may mean that we turn to stories for sustenance. The reader makes expeditions into literature desiring something which will tell of her existence. Lesbian history is created by alternative reading: reading oneself in, where before were only lies and silence. We have to seek out our origins in order to be seen and heard. We tell stories which both derive from and help to maintain a collective lesbian 'myth of origins'. Lesbians have found a form for the lesbian personal voice through the coming out story; these stories (for the story is different for every one of us) are the basis of 'the lesbian myth of origins, the explanation of how we came to be as lesbians, how our consciousness formed and our identity developed' (Zimmerman, 1983, p 244). Lesbian readings and story-tellings are a process of naming ourselves: we who have been unread, unheard, falsely named, and I want to travel these personal journeys to show how this self-naming becomes possible. Stories which describe this process – the personal narrative or life-story, frequently referred to as the *Bildungsroman* (the 'literary' name for this type of formation narrative) – hold a special place in lesbian culture.[1] I see lesbian readers as desirous readers when actively seeking out sources of knowledge which can help us to 'write' our very own stories of development. I am fascinated by the reading process in the coming out process,

68

in the material we use/appropriate in order to be able to create our own stories.[2]

I am very lucky in that I was always encouraged to read. I grew up in a house where books were respected and treasured. I was never told that the hours I spent alone reading were a selfish and lazy way to spend my time.[3] I read, and lived and fell in love between the covers. It wasn't problematic for me to imagine 'the neatly twinned worlds of Passion and Literary Empathy'. I have taken this phrase from Christine Crow's novel *Miss X or The Wolf Woman* (p 11). This is a text which makes me want to shout out (come out) in public praise of what I privately crave.[4] In many ways *Miss X or The Wolf Woman* is a study of the desirous reader's progress and the process of reading for/with desire. Arriving at *Miss X*, I hope to journey through both fictional and critical/theoretical lesbian writings which suggest that how one becomes a 'lesbian reader' can itself be explored as a lesbian 'myth of origins'. With acknowledgments to the title of a recently published anthology of critical writing (Hobby and White, 1991) about lesbians as writers, readers and literary characters (a welcome sequel to the well-worn question 'what lesbians do in bed'), I am interested in examining 'what lesbians do *with* texts', which will of course include elements of what lesbians do *in* texts.[5]

Desirous readers: bibliophiles and bibliographers

Every text has a textual source behind it, usually many, although one in particular may be suggested or named explicitly. The process of writing frequently reveals the writer as reader. This is often the case in autobiographical narratives and autobiographical fiction.[6] Women who hope to contribute to the building of lesbian and/or Black and/or feminist history must also weave a history of textual sources within their 'writing' to ensure a continuity and sense of identity for oppressed cultures. This intertextuality acknowledges that our personal histories are anthologies of larger histories. The desirous reader becomes at once bibliographer, anthologist, anthropologist, etymologist and literary critic.[7]

Reading can sometimes provide the first glimpse of lesbian culture or community, the first connection. I considered myself at first to be a 'passive reader', feeling powerless because I couldn't see any community outside of my front door, could only struggle to imagine where or what this community might be. I didn't understand that I was already mapping out my journey, but I was beginning to sense the necessity of telling stories. I wrote a poem which helps me to recognise now the importance of reading in my own coming out story. I want to repeat the poem here for it is a significant moment in my *Bildungsroman*, a point when I deliberately and self-consciously acknowledged inherited materials in order to tell my own story.

Because nothing's easy I make
Escape routes
And bury my dreams under piles
Of other's dirty laundry
In the surreptitious corner of a page
From some master chronicle of my development.
They become part of my awakening
But are acted in darkness,
Not to save the face of modesty
But because the imagination has
No one on which to rehearse.
The creation of understudies and fill-ins;
The endless devotion to, and fascination with,
Fictional explosions.
Mentors, great protectors, spring from the page
And the street to queue in great numbers
As the wheel of transference makes its rounds.
There is adoration abound; no shortage of energy.
All this role-playing and closet aspiration
Call it desire; call it love –
Just because my love lies unacknowledged and undisclosed –
It was alright for Rossetti, though she had
Her 'offending' poems erased from celebratory collections.
Such burning desire enflamed her verse
But no merit – lovers unfamed;
And my books and my idols have no love for me
If they never do see my purpose.

I *was* the 'desirous reader' reading eagerly and avidly, consuming anything I thought might make reference to same-sex love. I wanted to make up for decades, if not centuries of censorship. I had a way of scanning a page or an entire book, some parts appearing more instantly entertaining than others, able to sense the printed word 'lesbian' even before my eyes could properly focus. At least, that's how it felt. This went totally against my self-defined ethic of reading every word, thinking the act of skip-reading somehow to transgress against the laws of literature. In my early days as a lesbian reader I seemed to be finding new definitions of behaviour, functioning as detective and, when picking up clues, shifting angrily between the benches of defence and prosecution. I might have overlooked Christina Rossetti if it had not been for her brief, yet shocking (to me), mention in Jeni Couzyn's introduction to *The Bloodaxe Book of Contemporary Women Poets*. In this instance I was alerted to a 'crime', committed by Rossetti's brother who, on editing her collected poems, 'extracted from the work half a dozen poems which, from their titles, appear to have been love poems addressed directly to women' (Couzyn, p 25). Reading this in 1986 at the age of 17, it became imperative to read out/in and write in/out the truth.[8]

'Becoming a lesbian reader' (Hennegan) before my experience in the 1980s entailed different expeditions, and the task was certainly far more difficult for women in the pre-1970 era, before a 'lesbian feminist' ideology promoted open debates about women and sexuality. But these earlier journeys through culture in search of clues to existence/origin still became journeys into literature.[9] Finding out can be at the same time exhilarating and terrifying. I wonder how many women have started with the dictionary, anxiously looking up the word 'lesbian', 'terrified, elated, painfully self-aware, grateful it was there at all' (Grahn, p xii). Seeing the printed word is a stamp of authority, inclusion in the patriarchal 'rule-book', some proof of existence.

One excellent location of source materials is the library. The voyage to the library, intent on self-discovery, has been described as 'an archetypal journey for the emerging lesbian' (Zimmerman, 1992, p 39). Libraries are a primordial scene of lesbian activity. No wonder I spent so long in the library aisles, shyly smiling at the women, staring meaningfully and for inspiration at the shelf labelled 'Sexual Politics'. (At least I had that; not yet one proclaiming 'Lesbian'.) I like Helen Taylor's bracketed aside in her essay about readers' responses to the romance genre: 'I think female librarians are key figures in many women readers' lives' (p 69).

Once inside the library or bookstore, settling into the role of investigator, the reader practices a method of selection, not according to any criteria of literary merit, but a 'reading for love' (Stimpson, 1991) which may fulfil personal satisfactions. Alison Hennegan describes her selective bibliographic practice as:

> that mysterious process whereby the searching eye rapidly and unerringly isolates those elements – identified in a particular publisher's colophon, in chapter headings, in an author's photograph or coded biographical note, in the identity of a series editor, in the cumulative

effect of a writer's previous publications listed in the front – which suggest that this book might repay examination. (pp 166–7)

She speaks also of a sensation akin to 'a pricking of my thumbs' (p 166) as an indication of a text's potential. A curious form of water-divination, perhaps: identifying the source. The 'L'-diviner (playing my own game of mythopoeic punning). Personal accounts from other readers reveal a similar skill. Maureen Brady 'still wander[s] through a bookstore or library, intuition channel open, until … led to the right book' (Brady, p 50). Lee Lynch began her journey at a similar time to Alison Hennegan (late 1950s/early 1960s), Lynch in the United States, Hennegan in Britain. Lynch writes of her 'gay antennae':

> I was driven, searching for my nourishment like a starveling, grabbing at any crumb that looked tasted, or smelled digestible … [The words she discovered] are the words which taught me who and what I was, which frightened and comforted me, which gave me my own life's work. (p 42)

She would 'cruise' the libraries, lustful, recording her favourite passages on index cards as reference/source material for her future writings. A passion for her future writings. A passion for reading enabling her own (w)rites of passage.[10]

My story makes connections with these accounts, yet is privileged by the passing of time. Lynch ends her story hoping that the proliferation of openly lesbian-identified texts in the 1990s will mean 'no little Lee [need] ever suffer again' (p 47) through isolation and loneliness.[11] I like to think that Alison Hennegan played a part in helping me to come out through her efforts to make writing 'come out' (p 189). Unlike Hennegan, whose journey through literature extended from Homer to Enid Blyton, I was able to move more swiftly through the library shelves, searching for a publisher's distinctive black-and-white striped spine: the familiar cypher of The Women's Press.[12] Here, if I didn't always find what I was looking for, I at least knew I was very close.

I don't mean to suggest by collating these personal narratives in this way that I support a theory of a universally-shared 'lesbian intuition'. There isn't a single definition or essence of 'the lesbian', but there are mythologies which help women to explore questions of identity and identity politics.[13] Every culture has its own mythology which illustrates how that culture has developed, lives and will grow. A mythology is a collection of stories we use to explain and guide our existence. The journey for Black women is very different from that of the white woman, requiring a reading of Black texts and cultures and a confrontation of both racism and homophobia. In *Zami: A New Spelling of My Name*, Audre Lorde writes myth and history for Black women and Black lesbians as she examines her relation with 'Black identity' and 'lesbian identity'.[14] *Zami* is Audre Lorde's personal reclamation of Black history and myth. Educated in the Western ethnocentric traditions of American schooling, Audre grows to resent the history she has been taught which excludes Black culture. It is through her mother's stories about her homeland, the Grenadian isle of Carriacou, that Audre begins her journey for sources which speak her own existence.

The female librarian enters Audre's life when still a very young child. Mrs Augusta Baker is the children's librarian who teaches Audre to read, a 'deed [that] saved [Audre's] life, if not sooner, then later, when sometimes the only thing I had to hold on to was knowing I could read, and that that could get me through' (p 22). And yet,

> All our storybooks were about people who were very different from us. They were blond and white and lived in houses with trees around and had dogs named Spot. I didn't know people like that any more than I knew people like Cinderella who lived in castles. Nobody wrote stories about us, but still people always asked my mother for directions in a crowd. (p 18)

Audre recognises that her mother is a very powerful woman, somehow quite different from any other women she knows, and 'that is why to this day [she] believe[s] that there have always been Black dykes around – in the sense of powerful and women-oriented women' (p 15).[15] Audre's mother tells stories which present an alternative vision of the world. Telling stories is survival, investing one's own perceptions of the world with legitimacy in the act of denying the authority of one story alone. Carriacou offers its stories: 'How Carriacou women love each other is legend in Grenada, and so is their strength and their beauty' (p 14). With this story Audre develops (both 'reads' and 'writes') a mythological history for Black women which Audre recognises that her life continues, and a new source of strength for Black lesbians in the name 'Zami. A Carriacou name for women who work together as friends and lovers' (p 255). *Zami* is Audre Lorde's 'biomythography', for as she explains, it 'has the elements of biography and history of myth. In other words, it's fiction built from many sources'.[16]

These autobiographical accounts are 'coming out stories' which emphasise the centrality of reading to self-development. They neither present lesbians as sick and sinful nor 'idealize [lesbians] out of the human

race' (Brady, p 56). This is very important to me, and engaging for myself
as a reader. The journeys into literature taken by Alison Hennegan, Lee
Lynch, Maureen Brady, Judy Grahn and Audre Lorde were stimulated
by the desire for literary manifestations of selfhood, a quest for identity
and a historical basis for that identity. They engaged in the creation and
affirmation of symbolic identities which could be self-validating in the
face of an oppressive dominant culture seeking to keep their 'readings'
of culture unread, and therefore unheard, invalidated. Minority and
oppressed groups wishing to develop their own culture have tended to
favour the process of adopting and restructuring the *Bildungsroman*
genre, for it is a generic form which legitimises the development of, or
struggle with, definitions of 'identity'.[17] The traditional *Bildungsroman*
takes the form of a journey or quest towards the total development of
the personality, a growth process leading to the cultivation of the
mature self which is defined by the protagonist's successful integration
into society.[18] Through the coming out story, 'the first basic tale of all
lesbian communities' (Zimmerman, 1992, p 34), lesbians attempt to
rewrite oppressive mythologies, appropriating genres and texts in order
to create a vision of alternative society. Since texts began to be marketed
specifically for a lesbian audience, proudly self-designated 'lesbian'
fictions have been able to function as coming out stories for the reading
audience, offering not only the author's story, but also a source of development for the reader's story: a shared coming out. '[B]uying a gay book
… could be your first act of coming out, the salesclerk the first person
to behold you with "suspicious homosexual material"' (Jay, 1978,
pp 29–30).

   Some books are 'pathfinder books' (Brady, p 51). I mean by this that
they become exemplary texts, significant 'bookmarks' in lesbian history.
The Well of Loneliness is one; *Rubyfruit Jungle* another. Both are examples
of the *Bildungsroman* genre. Interestingly, *The Well of Loneliness* and
Rubyfruit Jungle are probably the two texts with a lesbian theme best
known to a non-lesbian audience, making it easier for lesbians to locate
them in libraries or bookshops. Perhaps as many women begin with
knowledge of Radclyffe Hall's *The Well of Loneliness* as search for
meanings in the dictionary.[19] This text is now an (in)famous lesbian icon,
the title popularised by the 1928 obscenity trial which ordered the
book to be destroyed.[20] *Rubyfruit Jungle*, published in 1973, by which
time a lesbian audience had become discernible, did not seek a lesbian-
only readership and was marketed towards a mainstream audience (as
it still is).

Jonathan Dollimore (p 52) agrees that *The Well* and *Rubyfruit Jungle* are the two best known lesbian novels. He draws attention to Rita Mae Brown's reading of former writing, namely *The Well*, in her own writing of *Rubyfruit Jungle*. Brown doesn't need to name *The Well* for its influence to be recognised – at least, that is, by a reader 'in the know'. I want to use the connections that Dollimore indicates between the two novels to explore some of my thoughts about 'mythologised' lesbian texts.

Exposing some lesbian mythologies

The first 'authoritative' piece of critical writing I read on the lesbian coming out story as a re-vision of the *Bildungsroman* was Bonnie Zimmerman's 1983 essay 'Exiting from patriarchy: the lesbian novel of development' which provided the phrase 'myth of origins'. In that essay, Zimmerman surveys literature published in the late 1960s and during the 1970s, literature which seems to point either to a tragic end for the lesbian or to a completely idealised future. Zimmerman examines *Rubyfruit Jungle* in her essay, grouping it with the idealised texts. In them, lesbian heroes[21] are imagined escaping from all patriarchal constraints, leaving behind the territory of patriarchy much as the traditional *Bildungsheld* or hero of the *Bildungsroman* leaves the intellectually and socially restrictive life in the provinces to make his way in the city. (Compare Zimmerman, 1983, p 254 and Buckley, pp 17–18.) What the lesbian hero escapes to, or into, is the 'Lesbian Nation': an utopian political separatism within a lesbian community far enough removed from patriarchal territory to mean 'male cultures, male law, and male power can no longer touch [her]' (Zimmerman, 1983, p 256). The myth of exit from patriarchy and entry into 'Lesbian Nation' is a symbolic return journey to a 'homeland' that is the mythologised reincarnation of the island of Lesbos.[22] (Sappho is primary source material for the lesbian. Picking up the dictionary again in search of 'evidence' we are alerted to that other 'myth of origins': 'Lesbian: of Lesbos ... island in Aegean Sea, home of Sappho' (*Concise Oxford Dictionary*). This inheritance underlines the importance of naming the source.)

Yes, I need Sappho.[23] And yet I'm not happy with the 'Lesbian Nation' ideology. I'm not denying that such visions of the idealised community are needed and eagerly consumed by readers. They nourish the imagination and encourage relaxation away from the pressures of daily living. They also represent a political optimism present in the 1970s and the birth of a new kind of writing which could openly celebrate lesbian sexuality. The story of the heroic dyke who is tough, proud, and free from patriarchal constraints is an historically significant textual source. But it is on this same point that I lose patience with 'Lesbian nation'. Imagining that the coming out/coming home journey frees the lesbian hero from patriarchy ignores the *historical* passage which has made the Sappho story available to modern lesbian readers and writers – the textual sources, both written and oral, which are rooted in patriarchal culture (even if this means, as it frequently does, the lesbian reading must occur between the lines). The ideologies of this 'Lesbian Nation' beyond 'patriarchy' seem to deny the nature of the Sapphic inheritance. Only fragments of Sappho's poetry survive today. Far more is known of Sappho from debates held by (male) scholars of ancient Greek language and culture. These have secured her fame, if not always favourably for the modern lesbian. Lesbian mythmaking may attempt to overturn the patriarchal domination of culture and language (Zimmerman, 1992, p 21), but it cannot escape patriarchy.

Monique Wittig is one theorist engaged in imagining the 'lesbian community'. She asserts that there is no way to express the lesbian 'self' in the heterosexist tradition of language, but the truth is that lesbians have to, and do, find personal voices through what may appear, at first, to be alienating forms.[24] We may create language from silence, from incoherent whispers, but this is not a new language, just an alternative way of telling. Wittig's theories support the ideal of the 'Lesbian Nation' because Wittig imagines the lesbian inhabiting a 'free cultural space'. This idealised vision assumes a superior status for lesbians and also tends to 'homogenize lesbians into a single harmonious group and to erase the real material and ideological differences between lesbians' (Fuss, 1989, p 43). These assumptions also appear in *The Well* and *Rubyfruit Jungle*. However much *The Well*'s Stephen Gordon is constructed from the negative and stereotypical opinions of nineteenth-century sexologists, she remains peculiarly saint-like. In sacrificing her love for Mary, Stephen's struggle is imbued with Christ-like significance. The language of superiority is adopted again in *Rubyfruit Jungle*. As Dollimore (p 53) suggests: '[Molly Bolt's] resilience, and sheer incorruptibility in the face of exploitation, discrimination, and poverty are saint-like ... echoing *The Well*.'

I find I have a less-easily defined relationship with *Rubyfruit Jungle* than with *The Well*, even though Molly Bolt, the hero of *Rubyfruit Jungle*, insists on a positive self-defined sexuality. I don't think lesbian critical writing has yet had a chance properly to stand at a distance from Rita Mae Brown's 'pioneering' novel. *Rubyfruit Jungle* has certainly added a powerful example to the lesbian mythical 'hall of fame'. It has gone through many reprints and is marketed by its mainstream publisher as 'the ultimate word-of-mouth bestseller ... about growing up lesbian in America – and living happily ever after'.[25] Does today's reader feel cheated by this claim? I did, finally succumbing to the 'Molly Myth' in 1990, and seeking out my own copy for a first reading. Molly Bolt has been 'hyped' – mythologised – right out of her context within the novel. She explodes from the pages, uncontainable, and also unknowable. Mythologising Molly reinforces her position in 'Lesbian Nation', for when her historical grounding is removed she seems to enter an imaginative 'cultural space', but equally it reveals 'Lesbian Nation' as myth or fantasy. I don't know any lesbians who could follow Molly there.

It is important to understand that, although mythologies can sometimes offer a point of reference and encourage our existence, at other times myth turns into the oppressor. Myths 'are used to legitimate power relationships, to justify cruelty, injustice and an existing social order ... Mythologies have a tendency to divide essences into opposites' (Duncker, 1991, p 205). To use myth to universalise experience, 'to homogenize lesbians into a single harmonious group' is dangerous for everyone. Molly Bolt was an exemplar for lesbians in the 1970s, but for me only a victim of 'heroinisation',[26] or 'heroisation', as I prefer to call it. Since Bonnie Zimmerman's 'Exiting from patriarchy' essay, lesbian 'writing' has challenged the assumption of these coming out stories that 'Lesbian Nation' is a possibility for all women-loving women and their seeming denial of other socially and culturally determined factors.[27] The move is towards a recognition of diversity or 'lesbian nations' and a theorising of 'lesbian identity' which can take into account differences among women. *Zami* clearly voices cultural difference, challenging the complacency of the white woman's inheritance. Audre hears the texts of Afrekete and Zami, not Sappho.

The coming out process, a lifelong process of telling stories which create and express origins (Jay, 1978, pp 28–30), needs also to have its beginnings examined. Pinpointing some kind of beginning to the coming out process enables a recording of historical and political moments through which the individual has travelled: 'knowing how long a woman has been "out" [and where she came out] ... can often tell you a great deal about what she knows about lesbian life, what her frame of reference is, what kind of world she came out into' (Jay, 1978, p 28). I understand also that not only has the coming out a historical and cultural significance, but so too has the reading experience within the coming out process. Had *Rubyfruit Jungle* been my first introduction to a positive lesbian character, I would have cheered ecstatically.

Zimmerman (1986, p 211) has written: 'lesbians may ... question whether the incarnation of a "politically correct" but elusive and utopian mythology provides our only appropriate role model.' If other myths have been adopted to replace the ideal of the 'Lesbian Nation', as Yvonne M. Klein suggests, they appear to have learned a lesson and taken on a personal significance which shrugs off the search for lesbian 'authenticity' and superiority. These are myths inspired by the individual's personalised reading experience or her own imagining of the 'para-canonical library'.

A reader in lesbian fiction

Miss X or The Wolf Woman appears to take up the challenge of theorising alternative mythologies. In *Miss X or The Wolf Woman*, the lesbian reader's coming out story (*Bildungsroman* crossed with personal 'bibliomythography') comes of age. I agree with Zimmerman that lesbian fiction is growing up (1992, p 210), but I don't think we have 'outgrown' or 'gone beyond' (p 209) the coming out story, for the simple reason that in our lives we are never fully 'beyond' making that step of coming out. The form of the coming out story is continually revised, but it's one myth of origins we can't let go. *Miss X* stands out in my personal development because it reconsiders many of the questions and mythographies I have met in my own reading, and seems to offer itself as a theory of reading lesbian fiction. Here is a coming out novel which self-consciously reviews its place in and as lesbian fiction.

Miss X plays obsessively with textual sources, anxious to reference, cross-reference ('X'-reference), and to trace the etymology of significant words. The myth of origins has jokingly run wild, the lesbian reader now 'frantically seeking the source of the source' (p 203). Both the coming out novel and the mystery/detective novel are parodied. And the experience of reading *Miss X* begins itself to resemble a parody of the lesbian's early developmental search for clues to lesbian existence, having to seek out or make sense of often unlikely or coincidental connections. *Miss X* depends upon connections or cross-overs ('X'-overs), both in terms of structure and meaning. One of the text's clearest themes is a love of literature (p 152), Mary Wolfe as the intra-textual 'desirous reader' interconnecting with the extra-textual 'desirous reader', myself.

In *Miss X*, the protagonist's reading informs the narrative to an unusual extent in that her reading experience not only assists in shaping and explaining specific episodes of her personal development, but also gives shape to the text itself. Mary tells her story by ingesting myths, fairy tales and fantasies. This is fiction visibly constructed from many sources. Writing from a distance, Mary has her 'Blue Books' to guide her memory of the earlier developmental experience. In these notebooks Mary recorded 'my "private" thoughts and feelings of the moment, together with numerous quotations ... designed ... to relate to my recent personal eXperiences to the great InterteXtual Literary Storehouse of the Past' (pp 78–9). She is acknowledging her literary inheritance as *I* did in grey notebooks, enabling me now to date and re-live my earlier reading experience.

Miss X is, in part, a version of the apprenticeship novel conveyed through confessional form. Mary Wolfe is the schoolgirl developing sexual awareness, discovering a mentor in her headmistress and falling in love. 'Miss X' is of course a pseudonym, for Mary is aware that her's is an illicit desire. The headmistress is not the first object of Mary's desire. A case of mistaken identity during a reading of Racine's *Phedre* prompts Miss X to believe she is the one Mary loves. Unable to tell Miss X that she is wrong for fear of hurting her, Mary begins to desire Miss X alone, labelling her original love for Miss P 'a mere schoolgirl crush' (p 16). The subjects taught by Miss X (French) and Miss P (Classics) are significant. These are both a source and the influence upon other sources contributing to the story-telling of *Miss X or The Wolf Woman*. Passion and literature, both Classical and French, are closely linked in Mary's development. Baudelaire's poem, 'Les Femmes Damnees', in *Les Fleurs du Mal* is her first introduction to 'the forbidden fruits of Lesbos – women as ravenous wolves in the desert' (p 1). Her favourite Classical Greek myth is Homer's voyage of Odysseus which influences the structure of her own narrative as a journey.

At the beginning of the novel the reader is told that, apart from Baudelaire, the only other source Mary has read on the subject of lesbianism is 'that queer, twisted novel, *The Well of Loneliness*, by Radclyffe Hall, its language oozing with the very concepts it purports to condemn' (p 1). Like many other readers in the 1950s she comes across it surreptitiously, disguised in a brown paper wrapper in Miss X's flat. It is a significant source, for Mary expresses her first acknowledgment of her own lesbian sexuality in terms of entry into 'The Well', (both literally and symbolically, p 70) and later, out of despair, writes a poem with the same title as Hall's novel. Later, also, Mary's description of *The Well* will be turned against her as criticism of her own novel, *Miss X* (p 151).

Although the young Mary has limited access to 'lesbian writing', the older Mary, writing from a distance, betrays her knowledge of the historical treatment of the lesbian in literature. Describing a love which began in the 1950s, *Miss X or The Wolf Woman* borrows from psychoanalytic concepts dominant in that decade (Zimmerman, 1991, p 52). Psychoanalysis: one of the enemy sources in the history of oppression, but a starting-place for many lesbians, seeking explanations for themselves both voluntarily and under force. The novel opens with a visit to an analyst and this same passage is repeated at the very end. This isn't a vindication of psychoanalytic theories, however. Mary pays only one visit to the analyst and *Miss X or The Wolf Woman* is a testimony to the alternatives she has found. As a lesbian writer/reader, Mary develops a theory which is 'One up on the *OediPUS(s) CompleXXXX*' (p 205): the coming out process of writing itself. Telling her own story, she is empowered:[28] 'Writing is not ... a mere one-way diagram, but something which helps to release the X-factor or unknown' (p 220); 'Writing had given nothingness a name' (p 221).

In coming out stories, names are of vital importance, their significance being that the 'author' names herself. Mary finds that naming herself is a difficult process, precisely because the materials she inherits have either attempted to condemn lesbianism as both disease and perversion or to 'authenticate' lesbian experience. Thus she realises: 'Helping us transcend the merely personal, Myth ... can elevate us on its golden horns to the heights of [the] Universal' (p 60). It is the task of *Miss X or The Wolf Woman* to use myth in order to return to 'the merely personal', free then 'to explore uncertainty, ambiguity and vulnerability' (Wilson, pp 34–5). Mary tries on the persona of the Victim, Outlaw and Rebel, at times imagining herself the writer of a didactic tract in 'Defence of HomoseXuality' (p 152) and the opponent of oppression in general. She is the 'Voice in The Wilderness' (p 15), crying out for compassion, like the voice of Stephen Gordon at the end of *The Well* begging acceptance of God who has exiled her from the Edenic Paradise.

In a self-consciously ironic passage, which serves to distance *Miss X or The Wolf Woman* from the 1970s feminist confessional narratives which tended to avoid comedy and mockery (Wilson, p 36), Mary conflates 'The Wilderness' with the 'Lesbian Nation'/Paradise image. One morning Miss X and Mary Wolfe break free from school and find sanctuary on 'the sandy hillside we all called 'The Wilderness', tangled with rose-bay willow-herb, bracken, broom and scrub ... to snatch what fleeting pleasures of 'Mother Nature' we could' (p 29–30). Zimmerman shows (1992, pp 41–5) how an insistence upon the 'naturalness' of lesbianism in lesbian novels means that many lesbian love scenes take place outdoors, close to Mother Nature, especially in the utopian novel, where women are assumed to have a close relationship with nature. Mary's 'Wilderness' is 'Edenic' for a while ('Could it possibly be the lure of forbidden fruit which emboldened my companion to wager such perilous capers?' (p 30), but this is quickly exposed as a false imagining. No escape from patriarchy occurs.

Mary's search seems to be growing warmer as she encounters Monique Wittig. Note the shared initials. At least now Mary may find out how women 'manage' without the phallus (p 77). Mary's friend, Annabel, introduces her to Wittig, and the introduction of Annabel alerts the extra-textual reader to another level of 'reader' within the text. Mary 'tests' out her 'unfinished' novel on Annabel and Pin, her sister, by reading it aloud to them. Annabel is immediately critical, and, armed with her own reading of (lesbian) feminist theory, attacks Mary's prolific use of myth in similar fashion to Duncker (1991): 'Politically it's eXtremely suspect, you know. Universal time, universal consciousness, never mind the eXclusions, and not a chance in hell of ever getting things changed' (p 149). Annabel reminds Mary of the difficulty of overcoming our own potential to be the oppressor: '*Our* minds are just as much prey to the Phallocentric dichotomies of Patriarchal Discourse as theirs, you know,' and, rejecting an escape from patriarchy, she suggests that the challenge must be to 'develop our own New Rhetoric, capable, since we must still fly in it, of hijacking the plane of Patriarchy from within' (p 151).

To prove to Annabel that no theory is perfect, Mary accepts the 'hijacking' advice, only to show her that patriarchal myths can be implemented in the discovery of lesbian knowledge. Mary makes a dramatic re-invention of the story of Osiris. Osiris is savagely slain by his brother, Set, but 'travels the world over to *find the fourteen scattered pieces of his mutilated body ... in order to stitch them back together again and turn Osiris back into a god*' (text's emphasis, p 66). According to Mary's *Dictionary of Myth*, however, 'there was one small but allegedly vital piece still missing': the phallus. Mary, like Isis, is the travelling detective desperately trying to connect those 'pieces' in her own story. *Miss X or The Wolf Woman* is divided, not by chapter, but into fourteen sections, given the title 'Pieces'. Mary's vital missing fourteenth piece bears no relation to the phallus, though. The lost or hidden 'piece', the unknown or 'X', is actually 'the lesbian body', also the title of Monique Wittig's 'lesbian classic', *Les Corps Lesbien*. Making the final (fourteenth) connection involves an understanding of the erotic desire which is possible between two women; the discovery of a commitment of 'skin, blood, bone and breast and all' (p 201). The connection I discover here is with Stimpson (1988, p 97); see note 15. It must be contagious, this need to collect and connect the 'pieces' (sources).

Miss X or The Wolf Woman invites the extra-textual reader to play detective (p 193). This reader has her own responsibility in, and to, the text. The novel demands a 'substantial relationship with readers' (Miner, p 16), and acknowledges that it needs me, the reader, as much as I need it, a source to keep lesbian questions and identities alive in fiction. The reading experience is one of insecurity, and that's deliberate. A series of contradictions and inconsistencies, and a labyrinthine structure, ensure that the reader cannot come to rely on one reading or inter-pretation alone. There can be no 'authentic' reading. Annabel condemns the use of myth and yet she does not examine Monique Wittig's 'essentialist' lesbian mythology. She teaches Wittig's novels as examples of the 'Lesbian Feminist novel' on her Women's Writing Course, but just what is this elusive 'Lesbian Feminist Novel'? And which of the two M.W.s best grapples with this question? *Miss X or The Wolf Woman* anticipates its readers' criticisms, creating a space for dialogue and debate within the novel through its layers of 'readers'. Annabel is a 'lesbian reader', even though Mary (and I was tempted in that direction myself) first believes her to be a 'homophobic reader'. Further inconsistencies become apparent. The text seems to favour the printed textual source and to desire intimacy with a private reader (book in hand) because of its

> eXciting typographical eXperiment in which the keystone, 'X', [is] constantly eXposed, constantly reminding the Reader in turn not only of Miss X herself, but of the power of detached imaginative invention working through language, which ... proves the confident Self-presence of that other Miss X, the Author herself. (p 146)

However, Mary's significant coming out when she reads *Miss X* aloud at the end of the 'Tenth Piece' transforms the text into an orally trans-mitted source. 'Giving tongue' to her own words.

These ironic twists and turns ('Xiasmus') have a purpose. *Miss X or The Wolf Woman* is a novel about authorship and identity. It is about finding a way to tell the coming out story, to name the 'author'/'writer', without stemming the flux of identity. It represents one of the main con-tradictions in lesbian and gay culture, described here by Richard Dyer (p 200):

Lesbian/gay culture has always had for the sake of political clarity to include assertions of clear images of lesbian/gay identity, but it has also always carried an awareness of the way that a shared and necessary public identity outstrips the particularity and messiness of actual lesbian/gay lives. (p 200)

There isn't a single 'lesbian identity', no exemplar, no archetype.

'X' is for secrecy, the pseudonym, a mark of censorship and silencing, and a reason for anger and affirmation; and 'X' is, at the same time, a symbol for what is ambiguous, uncertain, currently without definition. *Miss X or The Wolf Woman* explores in a quite innovative way the whole history of lesbians choosing, or being forced to use, pseudonyms. From the introduction of the Miss X figure who could have any name, including 'Nobody' ('pseudonym' of another of Miss X's lovers, also escapee from the cave of the Cyclops, the Cave of Oppression, (p 199)), a tension between the concealing and the revealing of identity is set into play. Mary is herself a 'Miss X', the subject in process. Her name needn't be 'Mary Wolfe' at all. The 'or' in the novel's title is an example of this same weaving of pseudonym, not an 'either/or', though, which assumes the language of opposites, more like a 'both/and' (DuPlessis, 1986, p 276),[29] just as the 'author' is 'Mary Wolfe' and 'Miss X' and more. For one of Mary's 'pseudonyms', turn to the front cover: 'Christine Crow', 'something jazzy and alliterative ... with the same kind of ... triumphantly self-devouring relationship between the two parts as ... in "Mary Wolfe"' (p 178). I am reminded of Alison Hennegan's close scrutiny of printed texts, searching for 'lesbian' clues. The reader must look again at the cover, and also at the fly-leaf, where the disclaimer Pin suggests for the book when it is published (p 204) is actually repeated. The novel's very own intertextuality.

The personal mythology in *Miss X or The Wolf Woman* is *The Wolf Woman* mythology. This takes over from those other identities – Victim, Outlaw, Rebel, Hero – and allows a voice which can explore personal needs and vulnerabilities. 'The Wolf Woman' persona (over-turning Freud's *The Wolf Man*) also frees Mary from Miss X (the first Miss X, that is) who was always afraid of her sexuality. Rejecting an icon, an essentialised, archetypal 'lesbian identity', Mary accepts her erotic desires and celebrates that 'each of us is different, unknown, eXceptional' (p 189). 'Total identity is death!' (p 223): 'X' cannot always equal 'Y'.

Mocking Stephen's voice again at the end of *The Well*, 'We have asked for bread; will you give us a stone? Answer us: will you give us a stone?' (*The Well*, p 446), Mary Wolfe, about to sacrifice *her* 'Mary', finds great comfort and satisfaction in the stone. This is 'Petrus Borel', the name engraved into the stone paperweight which used to sit on Miss X's desk and now belongs to Mary. It is the 'Corner-stone' of the novel. Also, the 'Wolf stone', so called because 'Petrus Borel' was 'the name of a nineteenth-century writer called Champavert who raved against the Evils of Society and called himself "Le Lycanthrope": someone who imagines himself a wolf' (p 183). The Wolf Stone offers another source to assist Mary's understanding of identity. It is also the touchstone by which to imagine a 'New Rhetoric'. The stone helps her to formulate some kind of theory

> which, less concrete than a pebble, but in some ways more reliable, would suddenly bring the whole Novel into focus with a bang ... being able to *choose* my own identity perhaps for the very first time in my life. (pp 203–4)

The Wolf Woman is Mary's 'New Rhetoric', her personalised re-invention of the patriarchal stereotype which portrays the lesbian as predatory wolf: 'greedy, voracious, ravenous, rabid, rapacious, anthropophagic ... eXcessive' (p 92). She chooses identity/ies for herself and recognises the complexity of all identities. This allows her an historical and cultural specificity which challenges the universalist principles and exemplary status of earlier 'lesbian feminist' *Bildungsroman*. By reinventing her earlier reading experience, 'The Wolf Woman' discovers a space for herself within patriarchal language, literature and culture, and is able to say: 'For the wrong reasons, Baudelaire was right' (p 232). She *is* the wolf, but on her own terms. As 'The Wolf Woman' she goes out once more into 'The Wilderness', rummaging around in the 'interstices of society' where individuality can begin to take shape (Weeks, 1987, p 37). This isn't a return to the utopian mythology, but a re-working of that mythology in an effort to express the 'messiness' and diversity in individual lesbian lives. She is the 'lone wolf', at least for the moment.

I've accepted the challenge given to the Reader in this source-book of mythopoeic puns if indeed 'The power to draw analogies *is* what it's all about' (my emphasis, p 54). Perhaps I've been double-crossed all along. It feels satisfying to be the 'desirous reader' desired, to have a text rely on your capacity to be bamboozled (complacency shattered) in order to transmit its message about identity in flux. It's an elitist game that I've been playing, all these literary and mythical interconnections which assume the reader's prior knowledge. And, without an English translation to hand for the French passages, I've never quite managed to be the reader 'in the know'. Christine Crow could be savaged by some critics as 'politically incorrect', overstepping the invisible boundaries which keep lesbian fiction 'accessible'. I admire her experimentation and irony, even if I don't always understand it. She is prepared to confront assumptions of 'political correctness' which in their own way are oppressive, and 'pigeon-hole' lesbian writing. What is the 'Lesbian Feminist novel' of the 1990s? Isn't *Miss X or The Wolf Woman* one version? Not the ('PB') potboiler novel, but a touchstone novel, a source by which the 'desirous reader' can redefine herself and lesbian writing/culture again and again. It is an experimental *Bildungsroman* which challenges the origins and growth of both the intra- and extra-textual reader.

One other experimental *Bildungsroman* that has responded significantly to a changing society and a developing 'lesbian reader' is Jane DeLynn's *Don Juan in the Village*, a 'Feminist Book Fortnight' selection for 1991. *Don Juan's* contribution to (lesbian) feminism is to demonstrate that in any discussion and journey towards 'lesbian identity' there must be the challenge of individuality, the acknowledgment of diversity.[30] This novel shows that such developments in lesbian fiction are not limited only to the activities of a 'literary' elite. It is stories like these I want to chase in the libraries.

5   The Lesbian Thriller: Crimes, Clues and Contradictions

Paulina Palmer

'Something nice about a murder where all women are involved.'
(Mary Wings, 1988, p 172)

Introduction: genre and convention

An interesting feature of Barbara Wilson's *Murder in the Collective* (Women's Press, 1984) is the disagreements which intermittently erupt between Pam and Hadley, the lesbian couple who take it upon themselves to act as amateur sleuths. The two women argue about the role of the investigator and the contrary problems and attractions which it holds for the woman who identifies as a lesbian feminist. Pam expresses serious doubts about this role. As well as being uncertain if Hadley and she are capable of performing it successfully, she is worried about its moral implications. She urges Hadley: 'Let's look at our positions, I mean, are we detectives or what? We're not really qualified; we might really screw things up' (p 74).

The experience of interrogating suspects which the role of investigator involves serves to confirm Pam's doubts. Far from enjoying dominating her fellow workers in the Collective and invading their privacy, she finds behaving in this heavy manner repugnant and upsetting. When the suspect whom she is questioning suddenly bursts into tears, she admits to feeling 'a hypocrite'. 'How did these hard-boiled-egg detectives [in the traditional thriller] do it?', she wonders; she adds guiltily, 'I couldn't possibly get any information out of her without feeling like a heel' (p 144).

Hadley, however, suffers from no such doubts. She regards the role of investigator as valuable and argues that Pam and she, on account of the personal rapport they have with their co-workers in the Collective, are the right people to do the job. She asks Pam:

What's a detective except someone who wants to find out what happened? Don't you? I do. We have a stake in all this ... We're certainly more qualified than any old male detective they put on the case. Well, Pam, we know these people, don't we … (p 74)

These episodes from *Murder in the Collective* are relevant to the genre of the lesbian thriller as a whole. They epitomise and illustrate some of the contradictions which inform it. On the one hand, the format of the thriller holds obvious attractions for the lesbian writer. It provides her with an effective vehicle for combining a focus on lesbian romance with the discussion of feminist themes and issues.[1] These themes, as illustrated by the fiction of Barbara Wilson, Mary Wings and other writers, include acts of violence perpetrated by men, the injustices and social abuses which typify contemporary patriarchal society, and incidents of female victimisation and resistance. Some thrillers also contain an element of debate. As I shall indicate later in this chapter, they discuss topics of controversy among feminists such as women and violence, prostitution and transsexualism.

On the other hand, however, the format of the thriller confronts the lesbian writer with certain difficulties. The ideological attitudes associated with the genre constitute a hurdle. The approach to class and sex reflected in the detective fiction of Agatha Christie and Dorothy Sayers is, as critics point out, often elitist and puritanical (Kaplan, 1986, pp 18–19). The values endorsed by male writers of crime fiction such as Raymond Chandler and Ian Fleming conflict even more strongly with feminist attitudes (Anna Wilson, 1988, pp 1–2). The works of these writers, as well as being misogynistic and often racist, tend to perpetuate a cult of male arrogance and individualism. The moral contradictions which the thriller displays are cogently summed up by Rosalind Coward and Linda Semple(1989):

> In spite of the sympathetic, independent heroines and … the politically satisfying plots, the writers' acceptance of the individualist and machismo codes of violence are highly problematic. It is highly problematic for feminists to replace the tough gun-toting man with a female equivalent and include little or no criticism of the violence in the Gumshoe novels. (p 46)

There is yet another problem which confronts the writer of the lesbian thriller. In utilising the format as a vehicle for representing lesbian romantic attachments and sexual encounters, she seeks to combine two genres which can, in fact, be very different.[2] The two genres, as Anna Wilson (1991) points out, carry different expectations regarding characterisation and ideology. The protagonist of the romance (usually a woman) tends to display stereotypically 'feminine' affective attributes such as emotional sensitivity, a willingness to co-operate, and responsiveness to the feelings of others. The protagonist of the thriller, on the contrary, frequently a man, is portrayed as having typically 'masculine' instrumental attributes. These include powers of logic and deductive reasoning, along with ruthlessness and aggression. He is, moreover, generally represented as a loner. His methods of investigation are individualistic and he is intent on preserving his personal autonomy at all costs. Far from regarding romantic involvements and sexual encounters as the goal of life, as is the case with the protagonist of the romance, he sees them at worst as a threat to his selfhood and at best as a pleasurable, temporary distraction. It is interesting to note that, even in those thrillers where a romance narrative plays a key part, such as Dorothy Sayer's Lord Peter Wimsey novels, obstacles preventing the protagonist's consummation and enjoyment of love are introduced into the plot. As a consequence, s/he spends a considerable amount of time alone and is free to pursue her/his investigative activities unimpeded by the demands and interference of a partner.

Yet, while the characterisation of the protagonist of the thriller is certainly at odds with that of his romance counterpart, the contrary attributes which the two figures embody assist the writer of the lesbian thriller in creating the protagonist of her particular work. The figure of the lesbian, as constructed in contemporary culture, brings together attributes belonging to both. The woman who identifies as lesbian struggles to maintain her autonomy in the face of homophobic social pressures; like the protagonist of the thriller, she is often regarded by her heterosexual relatives and workmates as an individualist and a 'loner'. Simultaneously, however, she often seeks to become involved in the lesbian community and, like the protagonist of the romance, places value on love and sexual attachments. In fact, despite the role of loner assigned to her by the dominant heterosexual culture, she herself often envisages her life as a quest for involvement and love. The question which confronts the writer of the lesbian thriller is, how can she integrate these disparate attributes and achieve a balance between them? My aim in this chapter is to illustrate and discuss some of the strategies writers introduce to achieve this balance. I shall also discuss the current popularity of the genre as reflected in the number of writers who have contributed to it and in the place it is beginning to assume on feminist literary courses in colleges and universities.[3] As an initial step in exploring these topics, I propose to examine the different models of the thriller which lesbian writers employ and explore some of the different uses to which these are put.

The genre of the thriller comprises, in fact, two different subsections – *the detective novel* and *the crime novel*.[4] The key components of the detective novel, as its name implies, are the detective himself and 'the puzzle' (generally an act of deception) which he investigates and seeks to solve. The detective is often portrayed as a figure of exceptional intelligence. He pursues his investigation by interpreting clues and interrogating suspects. The detective novel tends to be conservative. It frequently has as its setting the enclosed, upper class location of a country house, academic college or luxury cruise. The firm note of closure on which the narrative generally concludes signals to the reader that the collapse of law and order has been averted and justice re-affirmed. Contributors to the mode include Christie, Sayers and Sir Arthur Conan Doyle.

The crime novel differs from the detective novel in a number of ways. The investigator, instead of being portrayed as a figure of unusual intelligence, often emerges as fallible and emotionally insecure (Stephen Knight, 1988, pp 80–2). The pleasure the reader takes in the narrative depends less on the intricacies of puzzle-solving than on the complexities of character and problems of a psychological nature. The ideological contradictions which the crime novel displays are of particular interest. While macho in attitude, it may introduce perceptions which are, from a social point of view, radical, since they pinpoint and expose injustices in the political and legal system. The urban setting which characterises the genre, exemplified by Chandler's image of the 'mean streets' of the American city (1964, p 198), gives the writer the opportunity to represent the sordid and violent aspects of contemporary life. Novels of this kind are often, to a degree, open-ended. The solving of the crime does not necessarily bring about a general re-affirmation of justice, since society is depicted as fundamentally corrupt. Writers noted for their contribution to crime include Chandler, Dashiell Hammett and, in the field of the spy thriller, John Le Carré.

In the lesbian thriller the two models described above do not always remain separate and distinct. Writers frequently combine elements from both in a single text, creating an interplay of conventions. This is the case with Wings's *She Came in a Flash* (Women's Press, 1988) and Iona McGregor's *Death Wore a Diadem* (Women's Press, 1989). The following analysis of the two novels illustrates the way the writer, while structuring her text primarily on one particular model, may enrich its design by introducing features from the other. It also gives an insight into the very different strategies writers employ to integrate themes of lesbian love and romance into the thriller format.

She Came in a Flash is chiefly indebted to the conventions of crime fiction. Like Wings's previously published novel *She Came Too Late* (Women's Press, 1986), to which it forms the sequel, it focuses on the adventures of the amateur sleuth, Emma Victor. Emma is articulate, fashion-conscious and exudes an air of glamour. She is also, as her name implies, eminently successful in her investigative activities – though not always so in the realm of love. On this occasion it is the disappearance and subsequent murder of her old school friend, Lana Flax, which prompts her to assume the role of investigator. Lana has recently become a member of the Vishnu Divine Inspiration Commune and, in exploring the mysterious circumstances of her death, Emma uncovers the nefarious practices in which the leaders of the Commune are involved. The crime and its investigation are neatly constructed but, as is often the case in crime fiction, they take second place to interests of a social and psychological kind. The novel's central theme, which gives it a polemical slant and a feminist interest, is the analysis of the attractions which the cult of New Age Therapy holds for women, along with an exposé of its phoney and dangerous aspects.

Wings's treatment of lesbian sex and romance in the novel also originates in the conventions of crime fiction. As is the case in Chandler's and Fleming's novels, the women with whom the sleuth becomes sexually involved can be divided neatly into the roles of 'villainess' and 'ally'. Bumper Lee, the ruthless member of the Vishnu Commune, is the former; she seduces Emma into a state of voluptuous passivity which makes her blind to danger. The disabled ballet dancer Roseanna, who works for the local women's community, is the latter; she encourages Emma in her investigations and, when necessary, provides her with a place of refuge. Emma's encounters with Bumper, it is interesting to note, are represented as overtly sexual, whilst her involvement with Roseanna is more on the plane of non-sexual woman bonding. Again, as in the works of Chandler and Fleming, the villainess is portrayed as an alluring vamp while the ally is relegated to the role of pal.

The relationships which Emma forms with both Roseanna and Bumper remain, on the whole, peripheral to the thriller storyline. This leaves her free to dominate the action and solve the murder-mystery relatively single-handedly.

However, although *She Came in a Flash* is indebted to the conventions of crime fiction in its general design, other features of the text reflect the influence of detective novel conventions. Wings centres the action on the luxurious, enclosed location of a Californian New Age Commune; she emphasises the yuppy affluence of the place and describes the delicious assortment of vegetarian food which the residents enjoy. This setting resembles the enclosed, elitist location frequently found in the detective novel. Wings also foregrounds themes of conflict and competition between a group of assertive, intelligent women. The confrontations in which Emma engages with 'the punk princess' Nebraska Storm (Wings, 1986, p 10) and the lawyer Willie Rossini recall episodes from the detective fiction of Sayers and P.D. James.

McGregor's *Death Wore a Diadem*, too, is informed by an interplay of different genres. While the text is structured chiefly like a detective novel, McGregor's decision to set the story in nineteenth century Edinburgh, combined with her lively description of constructs of femininity in the period, link it to the genre of historical fiction. The fact that she chooses as her focal location the Scottish Institute for the Education of the Daughters of Gentlefolk, a school catering for the education of aristocratic young girls, and makes a relationship between a pupil and teacher the central love interest, serves to connect the novel to yet another genre – one with pronounced lesbian connotations. This is *fiction of the gynaeceum*.[5]

The narrative, as befits its grounding in the detective novel, focuses on two puzzling events. A replica of a diadem belonging to the Empress Eugénie of France, who is due to pay a ceremonial visit to the Institute, mysteriously disappears from the building. Shortly afterwards Peggy Murdo, a housemaid at the Institute, is found murdered. A jewel from the diadem is discovered in a bag near her corpse, with the result that she is suspected of the theft. The person officially in charge of the crime investigation is James McLevy, ex-detective in the Edinburgh Police. His role, however, is quickly supplanted by Christabel MacKenzie, a pupil at the Institute. She decides to intervene in events and act as amateur sleuth. She is convinced of Peggy's innocence and, with the assistance of her lover Eleanor, a teacher, she succeeds in clearing Peggy's name. She also succeeds in tracking down Peggy's killer and solving the mystery of the diadem's disappearance.

Death Wore a Diadem re-works a number of motifs commonly found in works of detective fiction. The ability of the intelligent amateur to surpass in investigative skills the official representative of the police is one such. It appears in the novels of Conan Doyle and Christie. The plot structure of the novel reveals affinities with Wilkie Collins's *The Moonstone* (1868). As in Collins's novel, the apparent theft of a piece of jewelry turns out not to be an act of theft in the conventional sense. The explanation for its disappearance lies in the field of psychology rather than that of crime detection.

The treatment of lesbian relationships in *Death Wore a Diadem* differs markedly from Wings's *She Came in a Flash*. The romantic involvement between Christabel and Eleanor, the two central characters in the former, is rooted, as mentioned above, in the conventions of fiction of the gynaeceum. This genre, exemplified by Colette's *Claudine at School* (1900) and Dorothy Bussy's *Olivia* (1949), is one in which lesbian romance and sexual encounters traditionally play a significant part (Frith, 1989, pp 304–23). These themes assume similar prominence in *Death Wore a Diadem*. In contrast to Wings's *She Came in a Flash*, where lesbian sex is represented by Emma's brief but sizzlingly described romps with Bumper Lee, here it takes the form of a relationship which, while sexual, is also emotional and romantic. In fact, in order to highlight the importance of Christabel and Eleanor's relationship and to integrate it into the fabric of the thriller storyline, McGregor transforms the crime investigation into a co-operative enterprise. Although Christabel takes the lead in solving the mystery of the diadem's disappearance and in tracking down Peggy Murdo's killer, Eleanor assists her and makes her own distinctive contribution. The joint solving of the crime emphasises and reflects the closeness of their attachment.

McGregor also utilises Christabel and Eleanor's relationship to explore themes of class and social privilege in nineteenth century Scotland. The two women are portrayed as differing in social status. The fact that Christabel has connections with the aristocracy gives her access to certain privileges and freedoms which Eleanor, the daughter of a humble farmer, is denied. Eleanor's decision to give up teaching at the Institute and to train as a doctor also provides an opportunity for exploring women's efforts to challenge discrimination in the field of education. McGregor integrates these social and educational issues into the thriller narrative.

The investigator

The detectives and investigators like Conan Doyle's Sherlock Holmes or Christie's Miss Marple, whose adventures people the pages of the conventional thriller, pose problems for the writer of the lesbian thriller. The arrogant attitudes and ruthless methods of working which the investigator frequently adopts are at odds with feminist principles of co-operation and noncoercion. Her/his role of independent loner conflicts with the ideals of a feminist community. Moreover, the position of power and authority which many investigators, particularly the male ones, enjoy is highly inappropriate to the portrayal of the lesbian sleuth. The woman who identifies as lesbian, far from occupying a position of power and prestige in society, is likely to be a stigmatised and marginal figure; she is a member of an oppressed minority group. The role of investigator thus requires a degree of revision before it can become a suitable vehicle for the representation of lesbian themes and interests.

In re-modelling the figure of the investigator to conform more closely with feminist principles and allow for a focus on lesbian themes, writers of the lesbian thriller employ a variety of different strategies. On occasion they curb the attributes of self-sufficiency and power traditionally assigned to the sleuth, and simultaneously introduce an element of feminist camaraderie into the plot by transforming the crime-investigation into a co-operative enterprise. Alternatively, they may problematise the investigator's role by highlighting its contradictions and emphasising the risks and dangers which it involves. Another strategy which writers employ is to portray the sleuth as a naive figure, a target of humour and ridicule. They may even question and undermine the power traditionally assigned to the sleuth by linking her role to that of the victim of the crime. I intend to explore these strategies and discuss the effects to which they give rise.

McGregor's *Death Wore a Diadem* employs the first of the strategies described above; it transforms the crime-investigation into a co-operative enterprise. Another novel which takes a similar course is Barbara Wilson's *Murder in the Collective*. The narrative centres on a sudden outbreak of crime in two collective business organisations: the mixed Best Printing and the lesbian separatist B. Violet Typesetting. Pam, who works for the former, joins with Hadley, a member of the latter, and the two women investigate the crimes together.

The concept of a joint investigation, as well as introducing an element of feminist co-operation into the plot, also furthers the interests of lesbian romance. Romance is of key importance in *Murder in the Collective* since, as well as being a thriller, it is also a coming out novel. In the course of their investigative partnership Pam, who previously identified as heterosexual, falls in love with Hadley and the two embark on an affair. In the first half of the novel, episodes focusing on crime investigation interact smoothly with those treating love and romance. In the second half, however, the tension which exists between the genres of the thriller and the romance becomes apparent. The feat of solving the crimes in the collectives, which Pam and Hadley achieve together, ironically coincides with and is responsible for the break-up of their relationship. While interrogating suspects, Hadley happens to re-encounter Fran, an ex-lover. Fran is an alcoholic, and Hadley, deciding that she needs her help, breaks off the relationship with Pam and goes back to her. Pam thus returns to the position of 'loner', traditionally assigned to the figure of the investigator, which she occupied in the opening pages.

Another strategy which writers of the lesbian thriller employ to modify and adapt the conventional role of the investigator is to focus attention on its contradictions. They intersperse references to the power and prestige which the sleuth enjoys with others which highlight the dangerous and precarious aspects of the role. The fact that the sleuth in the lesbian thriller is a woman, does not have the protection of a man, and often operates in an urban environment, allows ample opportunity for the use of this device. It has the additional advantage of forging a link between the protagonist and the female reader, by assigning to the former emotions and perceptions with which the latter can easily identify. Wings makes effective use of this strategy in *She Came Too Late*. Having convinced the reader of Emma Victor's courage and quick-wittedness by portraying her engaging in some outrageously daring adventure, she suddenly punctures her 'superwoman' image and unexpectedly reduces her to the level of 'everywoman'. She reminds us that, like the rest of us, Emma experiences city life as dangerous and scary. In one particular episode Emma, who is escaping from the headquarters of the villain Stacy in the early hours, self-consciously draws the reader's attention to the fact that her sex makes her an obvious target: 'I could hardly be anonymous; a woman on the street at two a.m. in the morning' (p 174). In another, Emma takes precautions to protect herself from attack by inserting her ring of keys between her fingers and positioning them as a weapon of defence (p 9). In yet another, she gives us a detailed, step-by-step account of what she humorously calls 'The Women's Safety Game':

I saw a man on the other side of the street, passing under the glow of the streetlamp. I quickly stepped into the middle of the street. I walked past him, not looking down, but without looking straight ahead either. I walked by him. I let out a breath. The Woman's Safety Game is always trying to think with *their* minds, in case they're the enemy. Someone is less likely to attack you in the middle of the street, away from the cosy bushes, garden hedges and alleyways. So I walked along the middle of the street feeling like an ass, trying to think with the mind of a criminal who might just have walked past me. (p 171)

On first impression this somewhat banal and pedantic account of the precautions which a woman can take to avoid attack in an urban environment may appear superfluous and unnecessary, threatening to turn the novel into a safety manual for female pedestrians. However, it serves several useful purposes. As well as enabling the reader to identify with Emma, it gives her adventures a firm material and social base, lending them authenticity and conviction. And if the passage does have the effect of temporarily transforming the novel into a woman's safety manual, this may be to the good. One feature of lesbian thrillers, which no doubt helps to account for the popularity of the genre, is the practical, material details which they contain. In so doing, they conform both to thriller and to romance conventions. Chandler comments on the propensity of writers to introduce references to 'clothes by Vogue and decor by House Beautiful' (1964, p 190) into the thriller. The most famous exponent of this trend is Fleming who, in his James Bond novels gives detailed descriptions of sartorial fashion, drinks and haute cuisine. Following Fleming's example, Wings offers the reader detailed descriptions of fashion and cuisine. However, unlike him, she intersperses references to these topics with comments on matters of female safety and self-defence.

A more drastic strategy which writers of the lesbian thriller employ to undermine the investigator's pretensions to power and to problematise the attributes of arrogance and self-sufficiency which the role embodies, is to portray her as a naive persona and object of humorous ridicule. Barbara Wilson's *Sisters of the Road* (Women's Press, 1987) makes use of this device. Wilson cleverly develops and exaggerates the qualities of fallibility and insecurity which are features of the sleuth's character in certain works of American crime fiction (Knight, pp 80–8). At the start of the novel Pam Nilsen, again cast in the role of investigator, behaves in the arrogant, high-handed manner reminiscent of the male investigator in the traditional thriller. As the narrative progresses, however, her pretensions to authority and independence are punctured and deflated. A tension is established between the conventional manner in which Pam envisages the narrative unfolding, with herself dominating the investigation and her colleague Carole playing the subordinate role of side-kick, and the less glamorous and successful scenario which actually occurs. To Pam's astonishment and discomfort, Carole transcends the role of side-kick. Not only does she reject the pass Pam makes at her, but also she has the good sense, when Pam makes a blunder in interviewing an important suspect, to intervene to save the situation (pp 112–16). Pam, as a result, is reduced to a state of humiliation and embarrassment. As she shamefacedly admits, 'My high was failing me now and I felt a little foolish. In my mental script it had been Carole who was supposed to act the innocent kook, and me who was going to be cool and rational' (p 117). This deflation of Pam's pretensions to authority and self-sufficiency is significant in various ways. It reduces her from an omnipotent superwoman to a fallible human being with whom the reader can identify. It also holds up to scrutiny the attributes of arrogance and independence conventionally assigned to the sleuth, prompting the reader to question them.

In *Gaudí Afternoon* (Virago, 1991) Barbara Wilson develops this strategy further. The novel opens with Cassandra, the amateur sleuth, being commissioned by the mysterious Frankie Stevens to travel to Barcelona and track down the whereabouts of her errant husband. However, Frankie fails to divulge the full facts about her husband's identity, with the result that Cassandra makes a series of blunders. On arriving in Barcelona, she identifies the wrong person as the husband and finds herself embroiled in a complicated farce hinging on mistaken identity. She is reduced on several occasions to the butt of ridicule by both her fellow-characters and the reader.

Whereas Cassandra, the investigator in *Gaudí Afternoon*, is the target of laughter in a few particular episodes and has an element of humour in her composition, Sarah Dreher's eponymous sleuth Stoner McTavish (Women's Press, 1987) is portrayed in a consistently humorous manner. Described by a relative as 'a rough-and-tumble' tomboy (p 19), Stoner functions in the novel as a naive and lovable clown. She is a bundle of nerves and worries about every conceivable topic, including sex, death and her lesbian orientation. She is constructed, in fact, as a parodic antithesis to the self-confident, omniscient investigator who appears in the traditional thriller. Stoner is convinced that Gwen, the woman with whom she is in love, is in danger from her husband Bryan, and decides to keep a watch on the couple. Having followed them to Grand Teton National Park, where they are holidaying, she ignores Bryan's taunting description of her as a 'love-sick Bull dyke' (p 23) and succeeds in winning Gwen's trust. The portrayal of Stoner in the concluding episodes neatly combines the conventions of the thriller with those of the romance. The representation of her as a parodic version of the conventional male investigator is extended to encompass the romance stereotype of the knightly rescuer and champion. Riding a horse, which her lack of equestrian skill makes her ill-equipped to handle, she trots up in the nick of time and, buy a happy combination of luck and judgment, succeeds in rescuing Gwen, her damsel in distress, from the attack of the dastardly Bryan. Stoner's suspicions about him are correct: he was planning to murder Gwen.

One of the most inventive strategies which writers of the lesbian thriller employ to qualify and interrogate the attributes of power and authority traditionally assigned to the figure of the investigator, is to portray her not in the conventional role of dynamic agent who dominates the action but in the role of victim. This device gives rise to diverse effects. It is utilised by the British Rebecca O'Rourke, who introduces elements of pathos and vulnerability into the characterisation of the sleuth, and by the American Sarah Schulman who establishes a complex web of connections linking the investigator to the murder victim.

In *Jumping the Cracks* (Virago, 1987), O'Rourke develops the attributes of solitariness and personal insecurity manifested by certain investigators in American crime fiction such as Chandler's Marlowe (Knight, pp 80–2) to represent the feelings of loneliness, insecurity and alienation which the woman who identifies as lesbian frequently experiences in contemporary society. Living alone in London, where she survives on social security and occasional spells of casual work, the investigator Rats exemplifies the depressing aspects of lesbian urban existence. She is sullen and uncommunicative in her relations with employers and acquaintances, hiding her lesbianism under a defensive mask. Like the investigator in the American crime novel,she conceals attributes of intelligence and perception beneath a taciturn persona. Her isolated situation and precarious financial position make her an obvious target for victimisation – one which the villain Pershing is quick to exploit. He takes advantage of her friendless plight, threatening her with violent reprisal if she dares to intervene in his shady schemes. *Jumping the Cracks* is, however, a story of lesbian survival, not defeat. Rats epitomises, in fact, the contradictions of vulnerability and strength which are key features of the portrayal of the lesbian sleuth in both the British and the American thriller. Her negative attributes and air of pathos serve to highlight her positive qualities of tenacity and intelligence. These enable her to resist Pershing's attempts at intimidation and eventually to solve, single-handedly, the mystery of the corpse which she glimpsed dumped on the passenger seat of a parked car.

In order to emphasise Rats's courage and independence and to give her a free hand in solving the murder mystery, O'Rourke keeps the romance narrative which is a feature of the novel relatively separate from the thriller storyline. Rats's lover Helen, though initially helping her in the murder investigation, eventually loses faith in it. She dismisses Rats's efforts to discover the identities of the corpse and its killer as futile, and urges her to give up the enquiry. For much of the novel the two characters remain apart and have little contact. This enables Rats to maintain the role of independent loner which the figure of the sleuth traditionally occupies.

Schulman's *After Delores* (Sheba, 1990) develops the emphasis on the pathos and vulnerability of the sleuth, taking it to unprecedented extremes. Challenging the assumption, conventional to the majority of thrillers, that the positions of the investigator and the victim of the crime are poles apart, she creates a network of affinities and resemblances linking the two figures.

Nobody could differ more radically from the conventional blueprint of the investigator than the nameless narrator turned sleuth on whose subjectivity Schulman's novel focuses. A waitress in a New York cafe, whose depressive tendency to 'think about sad things' (p 9) is fast driving her to alcoholism, at the start of the novel she is preoccupied with matters very different from crime detection. She is consumed with feelings of rage and jealousy at her betrayal by her lover Delores who has jilted her for another woman. As this scenario suggests, the novel owes more to the conventions of the romance than the thriller. Indicative of this is the fact that the narrator assumes the role of sleuth by accident rather than by design; her investigative activities are motivated by passion, not reason. On hearing that her friend Marianne Walker, whom she nicknames Punkette, has been murdered, she transfers onto the circumstances of her death the anger and desire for vengeance that she feels towards Delores. The role of investigator, and the gun that symbolises it, confer on her a sense of power. They enable her temporarily to transcend the attacks of despair and paranoia to which she is prone. The following meditation illustrates the contradictions of her situation and the swings of emotion to which they give rise:

> Everybody's always pushing me around or walking out, or not showing up or somehow not coming through. And I'm the worthless piece of trash that's hurting like hell because of it.
>
> It was just then I jammed my hand into my jacket pocket and smashed my knuckles on a cold piece of metal. Then I remembered I had a gun in my possession. I could use it at any time I chose. I clutched it first and then tapped it slightly, running my forefinger along its chamber. I knew I didn't have to worry anymore, because next

time somebody went too far, I had the power to go further. I had a gun. Now everyone had to pay attention. (Schulman, 1990, pp 26–7)

There is another motive that prompts the narrator to adopt the role of sleuth and track down Punkette's killer. This is the ambiguous emotional response she feels toward her. She is sexually attracted to Punkette and, at the same time, identifies with her. She sees both Punkette and herself as victims of a gross injustice. They have both put their trust in love – and found it betrayed.

Schulman introduces a number of different devices to emphasise the identification between the two characters. The gun, which the narrator originally intended to use to revenge herself on Delores, becomes the weapon which she uses to revenge Punkette's murder. Fantasies of wreaking vengeance on Delores (smashing her face with a hammer, bashing it in) blur disturbingly with fantasies of shooting the killer of Punkette. Many of the experiences which the narrator undergoes in investigating the murder take the form of an uncanny repetition of Punkette's. Like Punkette, she encounters the exotic actress Charlotte and becomes for a time infatuated with her. And like Punkette, she becomes involved in an intricate triangular relationship with Charlotte and her lover Beatriz.

By establishing a sense of identification between the narrator and Punkette, Schulman achieves several different goals. She problematises the conventional role of investigator, demonstrating the inappropriateness of the attributes of authority, rationality and independence which s/he traditionally displays, particularly in relation to the position of the working class lesbian. The working class lesbian, Schulman suggests, in the respect that she is stigmatised, socially marginal and financially deprived, has more in common with the position and characterisation of the victim of the crime than with the investigator.

Schulman also perceptively delineates the specific features and complexities of lesbian love. Her portrayal of the narrator's ambiguous involvement with Punkette illustrates the fact that, as Judith Butler points out (*Inside/Out*, p 26), a frequent feature of lesbian relations, one that challenges a psychoanalytic assumption that identification and desire are mutually exclusive, is that the female subject feels attracted to another woman while simultaneously identifying with her. *After Delores* concentrates attention on and subtly explores the psychological processes of the coexistence of identification and desire.

Another striking achievement of the novel, one which no doubt accounts for its popularity with lesbian readers, is its vivid depiction of the anger and frustration experienced by the woman who identifies as lesbian in contemporary society. By combining the structures of the thriller with those of the romance, Schulman creates a powerful portrayal of lesbian passion and desperation.

Fiction of debate

In my book *Contemporary Women's Fiction: Narrative Practice and Feminist Theory* (1989) I draw attention to the advent in the 1980s of a new kind of feminist fiction to which I give the name 'fiction of debate' (pp 59–64). Fiction of debate, as the term implies, provides an arena for the discussion of controversial issues. Examples include Valerie Miner's *Blood Sisters* (1981), which discusses the contrary attitudes of Irish women towards the issue of national liberation, and Lisa Alther's *Other Women* (1984), which focuses on feminist therapy. I suggest that fiction of debate emerged in response to certain changes which occurred in contemporary feminism. The 1980s saw the gradual fragmentation of the Women's Movement into a variety of different and, on occasion, conflicting forms of feminism such as radical feminism, socialist feminism, lesbian feminism, feminism with a psychoanalytic slant and several other kinds. As the issues and questions confronting women have become increasingly complex and controversial, fiction of debate provides a forum for their discussion, popularising them and making them accessible to the reader. The lesbian thriller offers one format for 'fiction of debate', and a number of works of crime fiction, the majority written in the late 1980s and the 1990s, belong to this category. The tensions and contradictions which inform the lesbian thriller, illustrated above, encourage writers to utilise the genre for exploring issues of a controversial nature.

One topic of controversy among feminists, which emerged in the 1980s and is relevant to the lesbian thriller, is the question of 'female violence'. The debate about 'women and violence' has particular significance to women who identify as lesbian. Whereas in the 1970s lesbian relationships were generally assumed by feminists to be free from conflict and aggression (Elizabeth Wilson, 1983), in the 1980s this idealistic view began to be questioned. Although women were loathe to acknowledge the occurrence of acts of violence in the lesbian community, they found them increasingly difficult to ignore. They were forced to admit that lesbian relationships are as prone as their heterosexual counterparts to conflict and tension, albeit of a different kind (Lobel, 1986). Lesbian sadomasochism, with its acceptance of controlled acts of 'physical pain inflicted on one adult by another by mutual consent' (Farr, 1981, p 181) also challenges the notion that women are untainted by aggressive impulses and a desire to dominate. As a contributor to the Samois collection of essays *Coming to Power* trenchantly remarks, 'Power is not an invention of men' (Farr, 1981, pp 181–2).

It is understandable that questions relating to 'female violence' should receive discussion in the lesbian thriller. The contradictions embodied in the figure of the lesbian sleuth who, though intent on achieving justice, often employs ruthless methods to solve the crime, makes the thriller an appropriate vehicle for its treatment. Katherine V. Forrest's *Murder at the Nightwood Bar* (Pandora, 1987) illustrates this.

Murder at the Nightwood Bar hinges on the question when, if ever, is a woman justified in committing an act of violence? Forrest does not give a clear-cut answer but, by introducing episodes which focus on 'women and violence', prompts the reader to evaluate them and arrive at her own conclusion. The question is particularly pertinent to the investigator Kate Delafield. A member of the Los Angeles police, Kate exemplifies that most contradictory and controversial of figures – the lesbian cop. The conflict which she experiences between her professional life as a representative of a patriarchal law enforcement organisation and her personal life as the member of a stigmatised minority comes to a head when she is called upon to investigate a murder committed at the local lesbian bar. The women who frequent the bar are understandably suspicious of her. They regard her as a tool of patriarchy. Kate is also personally involved in an incident of violence. While interrogating a male suspect, she unwisely allows her 'rage as a lesbian woman' (p 109) to get the better of her self-control. She is so angered by his homophobic taunts that she loses her cool, attacks him and injures his nose (p 85). This violent outburst links her, in the reader's mind, to the figure of the murderer who, in this novel, is female. The debate about 'female violence' is also foregrounded in a conversation which Kate holds with Taylor, her second in command. Taylor, who regards women in a traditional light and stereotypes them as 'the gentle sex', expresses the opinion that the murderer must be male because no woman could commit an act of such brutality. Kate disagrees. 'We don't very often, but we're capable', she thinks, remembering her own act of aggression (p 157).

The question of 'women and violence' is central to other thrillers such as Barbara Wilson's *The Dog Collar Murders* (Virago, 1989). The novel hinges on the controversy between those feminists who hold men solely responsible for aggression and violence, dismissing women who perpetrate such acts as 'male identified', and those who believe that women also have aggressive instincts and are capable of engaging in abuses of power. The former point of view is represented by a group of anti-pornography activists led by Loie Marsh, the latter by Gracie London, a Civil Rights activist who is opposed to censorship. The novel also scrutinises the principles and practices of lesbian SM.

Loie and her companions condemn lesbian SM practices as a vicious and degrading abuse of power carried out by women who are 'male identified'. Nicky, a practitioner of SM, disagrees with their analysis. She defends SM practices on the grounds that they enable women to act out, in a controlled and safe manner, their violent fantasies and desire to dominate. She accuses Loie and her companions of hypocrisy since, in her opinion, they refuse to acknowledge their own aggressive tendencies. This theoretical debate about 'women and violence' is unexpectedly disrupted by an actual violent deed. Loie is found murdered. She has apparently been strangled with a dog collar, a symbol of the SM Movement. The crime investigation, led by Pam Nilsen, yields a varied assortment of suspects. They include feminists who are opposed to censorship, practitioners of SM, and Loie's former lover.

Lesbian SM also receives attention in other works of crime fiction. Wings and Schulman treat the topic in a less formal manner than Wilson. They concentrate not on lesbian SM *per se*, but on the part played by sadomasochistic syndromes in personal relationships. Wings's representation of the sexual encounters which take place between Emma Victor and her lover Frances Cohen in *She Came Too Late* alternates, as I illustrate in 'The Lesbian Feminist Thriller and Detective Novel' (Hobby and White, 1991), between images verging on the sado-masochistic, which portray the two women engaging in power struggles, and tender images of nurturance and love, reminiscent of the attachment between mother and infant.

In Schulman's *After Delores* the nameless narrator's involvement with her faithless lover is depicted as explicitly sadomasochistic in character. Her state of mind fluctuates alarmingly between a mood of servile dependence and brutal fantasies of smashing Delores's face and blowing her brains out. Her relationship with Charlotte, the glamorous actress who enjoys domination, is tinged with a strong element of masochism. The paradoxes which characterise this relationship are epitomised by the narrator's comment: 'I loved the feeling of pain that was taking over my arm. But, as soon as she [Charlotte] saw the pleasure in my face, she let go, and was sweet again' (p 183). The image of power and brutality which Charlotte projects is, in fact, the essence of her allure. The narrator masochistically observes:

> There was something so brutal in her smile. She was a very dangerous woman. She could really hurt me. And I realized that I wanted her fingers inside me right then. They were long and rough. (p 86)

The motive for the narrator's involvement in this kind of relationship is clarified by her remark: 'I feel close to people when I'm afraid of them' (p 157).

The emphasis which Schulman's *After Delores* places on sadomasochism is certainly disturbing – and is no doubt intended to be.[6] It represents a reaction against the idealised, somewhat asexual image of lesbian relationships, depicting them in terms of woman-bonding, which appeared in some works of fiction produced in the 1970s and early 1980s.[7] Certain writers working subsequently, such as Schulman and Jane DeLynn, go out of their way to foreground the sordid and harsh aspects of lesbian sex. Both these images of lesbianism are, of course, exaggerated and one-sided. In an essay written in the early 1980s, the critic Elizabeth Wilson accuses writers of failing to represent what she calls 'the dark side' of lesbian relationships and 'the ambiguities of passion, the excitement of danger' which it involves (1986, p 181). She should welcome this new trend in lesbian fiction!

Another topic of interest to feminists which is debated in the lesbian thriller is prostitution. As sociologists point out (Elizabeth Wilson, *What is to be Done about Violence against Women?*), the topic provokes conflicting responses in contemporary society. The image of the prostitute as a mercenary gold digger who exploits male sexual weakness contends with the image of her as the helpless victim of male exploitation. The view of her position as epitomising the contradictions of the sexual situation of women in general, conflicts with the view of her as deviant and fundamentally 'other'. The notion that it is economic reasons that prompt women to engage in prostitution conflicts with a psychological explanation of their motives. The representation of the prostitute's role as fixed and unchanging is at odds with the representation of it as a temporary shifting state (Elizabeth Wilson, 1983, pp 97–116).

Prostitution is a key theme of discussion in Barbara Wilson's *Sisters of the Road* (Women's Press, 1987). Her treatment of the theme is multi-faceted, juxtaposing and interweaving many of the contrary perspectives and points of view cited above. On this occasion Pam Nilsen employs her skills as sleuth in investigating a murder mystery centring on the death of Rosalie, a teenage prostitute. Pam gives protection to Trish, Rosalie's friend and co-worker. Through conversations with Trish and a number of other women, including a social worker and a feminist lawyer, she gains an education in the complexities of the topic.

When the novel opens, Pam's knowledge of prostitution is that of the average middle-class citizen. It is based, as she herself admits, on a confusing mixture of hearsay and myth. She makes the usual mistake of regarding prostitution as a unitary phenomenon and groups together all the women who ply the trade in the role of 'victim'. However, as she soon learns, the profession is marked by divisions and differences. A prostitute informs her that it is hierarchically structured and that 'the mistresses of wealthy men look down on the hotel call girls who look down on the women who work in massage parlors. Everybody looks down on the street hookers' (Barbara Wilson, 1987, p 148). The older, more experienced women resent the intrusion of young girls such as Rosalie and Trish who are new to the job and undercut prices.

Pam also discovers that, whereas certain prostitutes such as Trish and Rosalie, who are forced onto the streets by financial hardship and lack of parental care, merit the term 'victim', many other women do not, since they do the job from choice. They are efficient business women, very much in control of their own lives. Dawn, an acquaintance of Pam's, criticises the tendency among feminists to classify all members of the profession as 'victims'. She regards prostitutes as autonomous agents and is in favour of them improving their working conditions by forming unions. Dawn's views are endorsed by Janis, a feminist lawyer. Janis disagrees with the idea of legalising prostitution on the grounds that it would result in the women being financially exploited by the state. She is, however, in favour of its decriminalisation.

By interweaving these disparate perspectives and points of view into the narrative, Barbara Wilson gives the novel a dialogic element. She also de-mystifies the topic of prostitution by foregrounding the material base of the profession and exploring its mundane, economic aspects. It is, of course, not only Pam who gains information and understanding about the lives of prostitutes. The reader does too.

'Women and violence', lesbian sadomasochism, and prostitution are three of many topics which are discussed in the lesbian thriller. Other novels considered in this essay focus on different themes. Wings's *She Came in a Flash* centres on the debate about New Age therapy and meditation, while Barbara Wilson's *Gaudi Afternoon* discusses the controversial topic of transsexualism.

As illustrated above, the thriller format, despite the manifold contradictions and problems with which it confronts the writer, is an attractive vehicle for representing and discussing lesbian feminist themes and issues. In appropriating the conventions of the thriller and the roles associated with it, writers do not reproduce them unchanged. On the contrary, they subject them to critical scrutiny and make interesting modifications in their structures and value-schemes. As well as combining the conventions of crime fiction with those of the detective novel in innovatory ways, they introduce strategies to curb and qualify the independence and authority of the investigator. The changes which they introduce serve to make the attributes which the role embodies suitable to the portrayal of the woman who identifies as lesbian. Moreover, by centring the novel on controversial topics like 'women and violence' and prostitution, writers employ the thriller as a vehicle for disseminating information about and discussing feminist issues. It will be interesting to see the developments and shifts of perspective which take place in examples of the genre produced in the future.

Acknowledgment
For Cambridge Lesbian Line

6 The Worlds of Lesbian/Feminist Science Fiction

Sonya Andermahr

Introduction: women's movement fiction

In the last 20 years, second wave feminism has had a profound effect on the way women and men in the west think about the societies they live in. The women's liberation movement has addressed almost every aspect of western thought and experience, from workplace childcare to the sex of God, from interpersonal relations to saving the planet. This challenge has also given rise to a huge feminist literature which has both put forward and inspired the social, political and personal changes feminists have wanted to make. Some of this literature is specifically concerned with the imagination and exploration of alternative worlds to our own, with the fictional creation of societies in which there is no oppression on the basis of gender.

This chapter explores this body of work, lesbian/feminist science fiction (SF), and the uses which feminist and lesbian writers have made of SF genres and why these have proved popular and important vehicles for feminist ideas and concerns. It discusses the fictional treatment of the theoretical and political issues which have been central to feminism, such as reproductive and social technologies, male violence, motherhood and mothering, women's communities, gendered language systems, ecology and the peace movement. The politics of lesbian feminism and the stress on female community have been central to the development of the feminist SF genre as a whole and thus I have not distinguished rigidly between lesbian and non-lesbian works. As I will show, the values and preoccupations of lesbian feminism feature in both types of text, particularly in the utopia. While relating these representations to recent feminist critiques of the social order, this chapter also looks at the extent to which SF represents a means of articulating an alternative to the status quo, and at its capacity to form a collective vision of women's dreams and imaginings of a more woman-friendly world.

Gender and genre

Lesbian/feminist SF, like some of the radical SF of the 1960s and 1970s (such as Ernest Callenbach's *Ecotopia*, 1975, and Samuel Delany's

Babel–17, 1967), bears an oppositional relation both to dominant patriarchal cultural values and to the overt sexism of popular mainstream SF,
while employing many of the latter's conventions and devices, such as
parallel worlds, time travel and extrapolation. It also shares some of the
mainstream genre's thematic interests in confrontation with alien life
forms and the existence of multiple realities. Yet, whereas much
mainstream SF depressingly implies that women have no place in future
space other than as sex objects for men or as space adventurers' wives,
the lesbian/feminist genre makes women the central subjects of its
narrative quest, articulating a critique both of literary and social sexism
and of male domination.

Feminist SF can be divided into three main categories: space adventure,
in which either an earth woman travels in space (*Queen of the States*, 1986,
The Two of Them, 1986), or a space woman of the future travels to earth-
type societies (*The Watcher*, 1986); the utopia, in which sexual antagonism
has been erased (*The Wanderground*, 1979); and the dystopia, in which
male domination and female subordination have become absolute (*The
Handmaid's Tale*, 1986, *Benefits*, 1979). Although utopias and dystopias
are properly subgenres of SF, lesbian/feminist use of them has made
central to feminist SF practice. Moreover, these categories are not
watertight; feminist SF is characterised by hybridisation, and employs
conventions and strategies from a variety of SF and fantasy forms.
Marge Piercy's *Woman on the Edge of Time*, for instance, combines
utopian and dystopian narratives; *The Watcher* is a comic satire of the
SF genre; and Jody Scott's *I, Vampire* blends postmodernism and lesbian
vampirism with the SF stock-in-trade.

The utopia: blueprint of desire

The utopia represents the meeting place of political theory and imaginative or speculative fiction, the space where ideas about social policy
can be worked out and desire for another order can be expressed.
Thomas More's *Utopia* (1516), Samuel Butler's *Erehwon* (1872), and
William Morris's *News from Nowhere* (1890) are classics of the genre.
Before the 1970s women had produced utopian fictions; Sarah Scott,
for example, wrote about romantic friendship in an all-female household
in *A Description of Millenium Hall* (1762) and Charlotte Perkins Gilman
wrote the feminist utopia *Herland* (1915) which describes an egalitarian all-female society, but it was not until the emergence of second wave
feminism that the genre became one of the central forms of feminist
fictional writing.

Its popularity among lesbian and feminist writers, both within and outside the SF community, can be explained in terms of the opportunities it affords first, to work out and explore new social arrangements and relationships, secondly to critique and denaturalise by contrast the existing status-quo and, finally, to speak to the desires, both conscious and unconscious, of its authors and readers for something else, something the present lacks. The utopia's appeal is therefore three-fold: it possesses a theoretical/experimental aspect, a critical aspect, and an inspirational or envisioning aspect. Shulamith Firestone, writing in 1971 in her influential feminist manifesto *The Dialectic of Sex*, recognised the value and importance of utopian writing to political movements and lamented the absence of a feminist utopian tradition. Her book was itself the inspiration for Marge Piercy's feminist utopia *Woman on the Edge of Time* (1974), and throughout the 1970s and 1980s this kind of dynamic interaction has characterised the relationship between feminist theory, practice and fiction.

Feminist utopia: Green politics and the pastoral

The vast majority of feminist utopias share a commitment to ecologically viable and non-exploitative economic systems. They are mostly 'green' in both senses, depicting rural, subsistence economies founded on a holistic philosophy of nature/culture harmony. As Luciente in *Woman on the Edge of Time* says, 'We don't have big cities – they didn't work' (p 68). Generally, industrial capitalism has been superceded by environmentally-friendly economic systems in which production is based on need and co-operation rather than on profit and competition. The operation of feminist utopian systems is more or less worked out, in varying detail: Marge Piercy's Mattapoisett, for example, is represented very fully and realistically; Connie is shown its factories, homes, collective agriculture, meeting places, and her guide, Luciente, describes in detail the parthenogenetic process by which Mattapoisettians reproduce. *The Wanderground*, by contrast, is extremely vague about its systems of production and reproduction. It does not attempt to give any sort of utopian blueprint for a new society. Instead it privileges the emotional experience of utopian existence, and foregrounds the hillwomen's close, even symbiotic, relationship with the natural world of rivers, trees and caves. The Wanderground is a poetic, mythical world, rather than a tangible and realistic one. The environmentally-friendly societies of Piercy's Mattapoisett, Russ's Whileaway (*The Female Man*) and Sally Gearhart's Wanderground are clearly informed by contemporary environmental politics, such as the ecology movement and the women's peace movement, but their harmonious rural societies also hark back to the *pastoral*, historically one of the dominant myths in western art and literature. Part of the appeal of such societies is nostalgic; they signify a lost golden age before the advent of social conflict and contradiction.

The pastoral was a strong aspect of the socialist utopias of the nineteenth century and, in common with them, the majority of feminist utopias share a commitment to egalitarian, communitarian and democratic values. The *sine qua non* of the all-female utopia is, of course, the eradication of sexism and women's oppression; in a bisexual utopia such as Marge Piercy's Mattapoisett men have been feminised and become mothers themselves, so the basis for gender discrimination no longer exists. Democracy takes the form of communal decision-making and, although for practical reasons not everyone can be involved, attendance of the councils is open to all and varies according to peoples' interest and inclination. Likewise, in *The Wanderground*, whenever the community is threatened, as it is on the arrival of a man from the city, everyone participates in a 'Gatherstretch' to decide what to do. And, although differences of skill, and sometimes of status, exist in the feminist utopia, class stratification, racism, ageism and the privatised nuclear family have been eradicated in the majority. In Russ's Whileaway it is older women, because they do less physical labour, who are the central figures in the intellectual, cultural and philosophical life of the community. *The Wanderground* is a multicultural utopia which registers its commitment to anti-racism in its celebration of women and their bodies in all their racial differences.

However, there are exceptions to the egalitarian ethos characteristic of feminist utopia: Katherine V. Forrest's *Daughters of a Coral Dawn*, for example, operates a sort of autocratic oligarchy in its lesbian utopian community, Maternas. Decisions are taken initially by Mother, from whom the entire community is biologically descended, then by her daughters, and then by Megan, whom Mother appoints on the basis of her 'traditional' leadership qualities. Opposition to Megan's word is given short shrift and dissenters are shouted down. In the context of the women's liberation movement's commitment to non-hierarchical organisation and its rejection of the cults of leadership and personality, *Daughters* is an unsettling read, demonstrating perhaps just how entrenched, and even seductive, leadership cults are, even among groups of women.

Another novel which makes use of benign dictatorship is Camarin Grae's *Paz* (1984). In this novel the utopian heroine Drew possesses an extra-human 'zap' enabling her to erase the memories of those who enter the community. Although this is ostensibly a means of protecting the community from interlopers, her power is nevertheless a form of mind-control which does not sit easily either in a utopian or in a feminist context. As Bonnie Zimmerman has pointed out, Drew's 'zap' is a *deus ex machina*, or short-cut to utopia, which seeks to overcome the problem of how to get from the present to the desired utopian state (*The Safe Sea of Women*, p 155). The novel's authoritarianism is a product of the contradiction between utopian vision and the means of achieving it.

Utopias of state and process

As a result of this tension between their critical and visionary aspects, feminist utopias tend to fall into two categories: 'static' and 'in-process'. Static utopias comprise discrete, contained visions of another idyllic world, whereas the utopia of process is more consciously critical and interrogates the notion of utopia itself by insisting on the necessity of political action and struggle in order to effect change:

> Utopia is process. It is found in neither past arcadias nor future Elysiums. (E.H. Baruch, *Women in Search of Utopia*, p 207)

Because of the stress feminism places on social transformation, most feminist utopias belong to this second type, and recent feminist theorists such as Baruch have criticised static utopia for its apparent conservatism in failing to show how the 'might-be' of our dreams can be arrived at from the here and now. Nevertheless, static utopia, an example of which is Sally Miller Gearhart's *The Wanderground*, is an important part of the genre whose value lies precisely in its status as fantasy. Rather than being an escapist genre, fantasy, according to Rosemary Jackson, is a literature of subversion which, in its very difference, represents a negation of the status quo:

> The modern fantastic ... is a subversive literature. It exists alongside the 'real' ... as a muted presence, a silenced imaginary other ... [It] aims at dissolution of an order experienced as oppressive and insufficient. (*Fantasy*, p 180)

In feminist terms then, female fantasies of a seemingly impossible elsewhere represent an implicit critique of male dominated society and a desire for an apatriarchal, pro-woman space. Perhaps a key difference between the two forms is that static utopia often speaks to largely unconscious desires, whereas the utopia of process makes them into the manifest aims of conscious and political feminist will.

Utopia as dream fantasy

This idea helps to explain the popularity and accessibility of Gearhart's *The Wanderground* for both lesbian and non-lesbian readers. The novel does not attempt to offer a programmatic strategy for changing society; rather, it presents a romantic vision of a group of women living in harmony with each other and with their natural surroundings. It functions not as a blueprint for a better society, but as a myth of female community. Critical appraisal of the novel has stressed its mythic quality: Elizabeth A. Lynn, reviewing the novel, comments that 'We need such visions. Many women, reading them, will find their own dreams reflected' (back cover, Persephone edition). This suggests that the novel's 'vision' corresponds to a register of women's shared psychic experience, particularly around their feelings about relation to others and mothering. The novel's mythic realm allows women the freedom to express their love for one another and to rediscover lost forms of female bonding, which in reality have often been inhibited by the male monopolisation of female nurturance. The use of maternal and pre-oedipal archetypes allows the novel to address women's emotional needs in an appealing and unthreatening way, less available to approaches which stress struggle and change and which tend to reject myth as inimical to political praxis. Sarah Lefanu, in her book on feminist SF, *In the Chinks of the World Machine*, argues that

> In many ways the novel represents an imaginative recreation of an unthreatening childhood world, one that exists before the complexities and dangers of language and sexuality ... The Wanderground is a dream world, a world with its past named only through what it has rejected, a world without history or future, a world in which the questions 'now?' or 'by what process?' are irrelevant. (pp 67, 69)

Utopia as process

However, other feminist utopias make these questions their central enquiry. Marge Piercy's *Woman on the Edge of Time* cleverly combines two literary forms in order to articulate within the narrative the contrast between a dystopic present and an utopian future, rather than letting the utopia stand as its own critique of the status quo. As with many other utopias this text uses the device of a time-travelling protagonist yet, in this case, the protagonist is as different as possible from the traditional white, middle class, educated male; Connie is a working class, American Chicana woman from whose perspective the present is indeed dystopic. In this way the novel both demonstrates the social inequalities inherent in contemporary society and gives a voice to those most excluded from cultural self-expression.

Woman portrays Connie's daily struggle to survive in the face of racism, poverty and institutional oppression. At the start of the novel Connie's husband, Claude, has died of hepatitis as a result of a drug experimentation in prison; her daughter Angelina is taken into care; she herself is charged with child abuse, and is soon afterwards institutionalised in a lunatic asylum. In the meantime, Connie discovers that she is a 'catcher', a telepath who can first communicate with and then transport herself to an utopian future.

Connie is welcomed to the bisexual utopian society, Mattapoisett, by a guide called Luciente who shows her around the community and explains its social arrangements. The rest of the novel is concerned with Connie's experience in and comparison of the two worlds, intertwining and juxtaposing the two. Eventually Connie 'chooses' Mattapoisett as the best future for people like her and for her child; yet one of the strengths of the novel is that it does not make this choice easy: Connie oscillates between finding the utopia 'too good to be true' and primitive and disappointing – 'this podunk future' (p 72). She raises objections to many aspects of Mattapoisett social practices, most notably their refusal of the privileged female bond between mother and child which for her is the only precious aspect of life as a woman.

Like *Woman*, Suzy McKee Charnas's two SF novels *Walk to the End of the World* and *Motherlines* also interrogate the idea of utopia by foregrounding the process of change. But whereas Piercy combines dystopia and utopia in a single text, Charnas's examination is split across two open-ended texts. The first is a dystopian portrait of a patriarchal culture in disintegration and terminal decay, the second narrates the stories of the women who escape, the Free Fems, and of an utopian female community, the Riding Women. At the end of *Walk* the destruction of the misogynist Holdfast society makes possible the emergence of the female community, the Wild, which is the focus of the sequel novel. The two worlds exist simultaneously as in *Woman*, yet their linear separation into two novels highlights the necessity of overcoming one before the other can come fully into being. The two worlds and the two novels are bridged by the character Alldera whose movement in and between them produces simultaneously the sense of historical continuity and discontinuity.

Motherlines also incorporates this sense of process within its own narrative structure by juxtaposing the two female societies and using them to interrogate each other. The Riding women typify many aspects of lesbian/feminist utopianism, including egalitarianism, responsiveness to the natural world and collectivity; yet they do not share the perfection of Gearhart's hillwomen, nor even of Piercy's Mattapoisettians. They are more Amazonian than maternal, proud and powerful, but also aggressive, hostile, exclusive and resistant to change. These attributes are contrasted with the greater adaptability and passivity of the Free Fems. The novel suggests that a positive mixture of the two sets of attributes, openness to change and a strong independence, is the best combination for a sustainable feminist culture. As Sarah Lefanu comments,

> The question of what women and men are 'naturally' like does not arise; for once, in literature, women have been set free from societal constraints. It could, perhaps, only have happened in science fiction. (*Chinks*, p 164)

Deconstructing utopia

Joanna Russ's *The Female Man* represents the most thorough-going interrogation of the utopian genre. It uses the SF devices of time travel, parallel worlds, multiple realities and alternatives to the present in order to deconstruct the utopian myth, and then to reconstruct utopia to include political praxis and change. The novel presents four parallel worlds:

1. a 1940s world in which the Second World War never happened;
2. a contemporary world set in the 1960s (the novel was written in 1969);
3. a future dystopian world in which a genocidal sex war is underway; and
4. a lesbian utopian community, Whileaway.

The four worlds are shown to be linked, both through the characters of the four J's, Jeannine, Joanna, Jael and Janet, who inhabit them, and through praxis, or conscious political action. Like Gearhart's hillwomen, Janet is a dream figure, representing the 'not-yet' of fantasy, and registering the desire for lesbian universality. Yet, unlike *The Wanderground*, *The Female Man* incorporates a critical position towards this fantasy, stressing its fictional or constructed nature, demystifying it even as it insists on its necessity:

> Goodbye to Janet, whom we don't believe in ... but who is in secret our saviour from utter despair, who appears Heaven-high in our dreams with a mountain under each arm and the ocean in her pocket ... radiant as the day, the Might-be of our dreams, living as she does in a blessedness none of us will ever know, she is nonetheless Everywoman. (p 213)

The political separatist character Jael also serves to demystify Janet's utopian myth of the origins of Whileaway. Janet relates how her world came into being when a plague killed all the men. Like the 'Revolt of the Mother' in *The Wanderground*, the plague is a *deus ex machina* which avoids the problem of how utopia is to be reached by human agency:

> That 'plague' you talk of is a lie. I know ... It is I who gave you your 'plague', my dear ... I, I, I, I am the plague ... I and the war I fight have built your world for you. (p 211)

In other words, utopia is struggled for, it does not miraculously appear. People, motivated by utopian impulses, rather than by God or nature, are the only real agents of change. *The Female Man* refuses essentialism and metaphysical concepts of nature, seeking to represent history as a process of change initiated by political action. Utopia is not a static future, but a coming-into-being through radical action.

Worlds without men

Yet there is another important reason besides sexual essentialism and political separatism why so many female utopias exclude men, namely the difficulty of writing them in the terms of masculinity as it is presently constituted. In her introduction to *Daring to Dream*, Carol Kessler points out that of the 14 utopias by women published since 1970, half portray all-female societies (pp 9–10). Peter Fitting, in his article on single-sex worlds, explains this absence of men as a consequence of imagining a world in which women are no longer oppressed: for women, he argues, reaching 'full humanity' entails the abolition of male values, and if it is men who have largely constructed and embodied male values, then the simplest way of creating a female-friendly society is to exclude the male gender (p 103). For Suzy McKee Charnas, the author of *Motherlines*, this decision came through the writing process itself:

The decision to exclude men was not dispassionate and political. I tried to write them in ... [But] no matter what I wrote, men would not fit. Every scene they entered went dead. ('A Woman Appeared', p 105)

Utopias express what is wished for, although not always on a literal level. In excluding men, lesbian/feminist utopias are not necessarily advocating male genocide or writing blueprints for a post-male world; rather, they may be wishing for a time or place in which most of the power does not accrue to one sex, where gender is not organised hierarchically, or for a world free of sexual conflict and contradiction. Excluding men therefore becomes a means of achieving this end.

Charnas's remark suggests that lesbian/feminist SF is not simply a critique of the uncongenial nature of power relations for women in social reality, but that it also addresses the power relations of fiction itself in which both literary form and point of view have, quite literally, deadly consequences for women. Feminist SF at one and the same time releases writers and readers from the constraints of realism and centralises women's experience and perspective:

[I]nstead of having to twist 'reality' in order to create 'realistic' free female characters in today's unfree society, the SF writer can create societies that would produce those characters, not as exceptions of limited meaning and impact, but as healthy, solid norm ... SF lets women write their dreams as well as their nightmares. (*Khatru*, 3 & 4)

Charnas's views, echoed by Joanna Russ among others, lead to the fascinating implication that the precondition for women's representability as discursive subjects is a (literary) world without men.[1] Just as the male speaking subject has historically defined himself against female absence, so women's coming into speech depends on men's symbolic absence. And, as utopian texts suggest, this often also means redefining the female subject as lesbian.

Utopian sexuality in lesbian SF

Although lesbian/feminist SF displays an abundance and diversity of positive images of female relationships, portrayals of specifically sexual relations between women are almost absent from the canon. In the 1980s lesbian writers in particular have turned to romance and crime fiction in order to portray erotic relationships between women. Lesbian/feminist SF has tended to foreground nurturing maternal love rather than

(genital) sexual desire. One reason for this may be feminist writers' understandable desire not to reproduce the sexual objectification of women
common to male SF and fiction in general. Another reason is the
dichotomy characteristic of many types of feminist fiction between
autonomy and sexual desire (for men) where the latter is seen as an
obstacle to the former. Lesbian representation does not encounter this
problem because the fulfilment of lesbian sexual desire is not dependent
on male co-operation, so the similarity between lesbian and non-
lesbian feminist SF representations of sexuality must be explained in terms
of the particular model of sexuality employed in utopian feminist texts.
This model owes much to the lesbian feminist redefinition of female
sexuality as mutual caring, which became a dominant part of feminist
thinking in the late 1970s and early 1980s. Adrienne Rich's article
'Compulsory Heterosexuality and Lesbian Existence' (1981) is one of
the most influential articulators of this model. In it she argues that female
sexuality exists on a lesbian continuum encompassing caring, friendship,
mothering and sex. For women, there is no distinction between love
and sex; each partakes of the other with the result that all women's relationships, with mothers, sisters, friends, are eroticised.

This redefinition of female sexuality as an extension of sisterhood or
as pre-oedipal merger with the mother has dominated utopian representations of relationships between women in all-female environments.
This is not surprising given that this redefinition is itself essentially
utopian; Rich's lesbian continuum is a potent political and affective myth
of female relationality, occupying the same discursive terrain as Sally
Miller Gearhart's fantasy evocation of women's community. The
popularity of *The Wanderground* suggests that it accords with many
women's, both lesbian and heterosexual, feelings about relationship with
others and therefore that lesbian utopianism is capable of addressing non-
lesbian women. Yet in foregrounding female sexuality and, in particular,
lesbianism, as caring, this model tends to de-emphasise and even
marginalise specifically sexual relations between women, as the paucity
of erotic SF writing by lesbians testifies. Marge Piercy solves the
problem of utopian (hetero)sexuality by eliminating gender while
retaining men, making everyone bisexual, which allows her to incorporate sexual scenes such as that between Connie and (the male) Bee.
But in lesbian-feminist texts the blurring of the distinction between acts
of caring and acts of (genital) sex means that it is the former which is
emphasised to the virtual exclusion of the latter. Yet many lesbians have
argued it is precisely the sexualisation of relations between women which
men find so threatening and which patriarchy stigmatises, whereas

caring is the role which patriarchy assigns to women. For many lesbians it is their sexual desire for, rather than their identification with, other women which leads them to identify as lesbian. And it is this aspect of lesbian existence which is relatively absent from utopian representations.

Lesbian utopian romance

One novelist who has attempted a specifically sexual depiction of utopian lesbian relationships is Katherine V. Forrest whose novel *Daughters of a Coral Dawn* expresses a desire for something more than the mother's embrace. Forrest is an interesting writer in that she is not primarily a writer of science fiction or a feminist polemicist using the genre to carry feminist ideas. She is first and foremost a lesbian writer, writing in a variety of populist genres, including romance and the detective novel, both of which are traditionally 'sexy' genres, with the aim of introducing lesbian protagonists to a lesbian readership. Central to her project is the portrayal of sexual relations between women, both as a means of affirming lesbian sexuality and as erotic fantasy for lesbian readers.

Daughters is a sort of utopian space romance which combines an SF narrative of women founding a new matriarchal society on a distant planet with a 'girl-meets-girl' romance narrative. While *Daughters* uses many of the narrative devices and shares some of the thematics of feminist SF, it is idiosyncratic and atypical in its stress on lesbian sex, and even more so in its employment of dualistic gender roles. Bonnie Zimmerman, in her book on lesbian genre fiction, *The Safe Sea of Women*, draws attention to the novel's presentation of the relationship between the central couple as 'a parody of heterosexual marriage' (p 154). Despite its affinities with lesbian/feminist SF then, *Daughters* has less in common with women's movement fiction and owes more to the lesbian community's desire for erotic literature. This emphasis on sex and the novel's aforementioned anti-democratic character make the novel quirky and divergent on two fronts. It is possible that the two are linked and that the existence of power relations, disparities of age, status, attractiveness, make possible within the terms of traditional romance the eroticisation of women's relationships, adding a sexual frisson which is less prominent in the relationships between Gearhart's interchangeable hillwomen for example. *Daughters* unashamedly exploits the power of sex appeal and personality cult as the basis of both its social system and its sexual images:

Mother waved a hand … '[T]ry to keep one thing in mind at all times. Even in a group such as this, all aspects of leadership psychology apply. Leadership imagery, for instance. Black and white are power colours – so dress all the time as you are now. Power attracts, Megan. Irresistibly. My gifted children are no more immune to the charisma of the leader than anyone else … especially such a leader as you. Many women will soon want to occupy your bed … I'm sure they do anyway', she added, coolly surveying me. (p 33)

Dystopian visions

If the utopia concerns women's dreams and hopes for a better world, the dystopia addresses their nightmares and fears of a worse world. Like the utopia, the feminist dystopia takes dissatisfaction with contemporary society as its starting point, but rather than offering a favourable alternative, it presents a 'worst case' vision of how the present could deteriorate into a situation where male domination and female subordination are total. As such, feminist dystopia acts as a warning against complacency and political non-involvement.

Because they are rooted in the present, dystopias tend to use a realistic mode, rather than the mythic mode characteristic of utopia. The world of Zoë Fairbairns's *Benefits*, for example, is identifiably that of 1970s Britain with its crumbling inner city tower blocks and urban decay. Whereas the utopia situates itself in a rural landscape, the dystopian experience is predominantly an urban one, located in the city. The urban settings of feminist dystopias allow feminist writers to register women's fears of city life and their typical experience of the urban landscape as dangerous and threatening. The feminist dystopian city also has affinities with other twentieth century conceptions of the city, notably with 'the mean streets' of Raymond Chandler's crime fiction, and with Fritz Lang's conception of the city as malevolent machine in *Metropolis*. It underscores the metropolitan concentration of power in centralised authoritarian systems which is a crucial determinant of women's oppression in *Benefits*.

Benefits engages with one of the major feminist debates of the 1970s around the issue of housework. At the time, the Wages For Housework campaign argued that housework would only be recognised as work if it was integrated into the capitalist system and paid for. Other feminists argued that this would only consolidate women's inferior status in the home. *Benefits* presents both sides of the debate, and through extrapolation, asks the question: 'What would actually happen to you, me and the woman next door if a British government introduced a wage for mothers?' ('On Writing *Benefits*', pp. 255–8). It shows convincingly that the 'pay off' is that women who can't or won't become mothers, and sexual dissidents such as lesbians are marginalised and criminalised, rounded up into re-education centres and in some cases murdered as enemies of the state.

Margaret Atwood's *The Handmaid's Tale* takes this idea of institutionalised and forcible motherhood to its ultimate conclusion. In Gilead the reduction of women to their biological function is absolute: young, fertile women are forced to become handmaids; they have no other function than to conceive and bear children for the elite class. Infertile, deviant or rebellious women are shipped off to a radioactive wasteland where they face certain death or end up in a city brothel like Offred's lesbian friend. The novel shows how the system uses the capacity for reproduction to divide women; the elite but sterile wives and the enslaved but fertile handmaids are encouraged to hate and fear each other, making solidarity virtually impossible. Like *Benefits*, *The Handmaid's Tale* engages with contemporary feminist politics, specifically with the 1980s debate about surrogate motherhood. Where *Benefits* asked what life would be like for women given paid maternity, *Handmaid* asks what it would be like if surrogacy came under the institutionalised control of a patriarchal elite. Both novels register deep suspicion of the wisdom of handing over to the state the means to control women's reproductive power.

The politics of motherhood

The basis of female oppression

The question of reproduction and motherhood is a central issue of most lesbian/feminist science fiction. If dystopias examine the different ways in which women lose control over their own bodies, utopias seek to elaborate situations in which women might regain it. Although there are marked differences in approach, the feminist treatment of reproduction and motherhood tends to fall into two types: the celebration of maternity and the critique of the ideology of mothering.

Woman on the Edge of Time is an example of the second approach. Significantly, Connie's decision to consent to the utopian alternative turns on the question of motherhood. On the one hand it is her maternal love for her daughter and her desire to give Angelina a future which leads her to give her consent, on the other, Mattapoisett denies the value of the exclusive mother–child bond in whose name Connie acts. For Connie, the Mattapoisettian deconstruction and transformation of motherhood is the most problematic and unattractive aspect of its utopia. For Mattapoisettians only technological extra-uterine reproduction will bring about sexual equality:

> It was part of women's long revolution. When we were breaking all the old hierarchies. Finally there was that one thing we had to give up too, the only power we ever had, in return for more power for everyone. The original production: the power to give birth. Cause as long as we were biologically enchained, we'd never be equal. And males would never be humanized to be loving and tender. (p 105)

Eventually, after observing the quality of adult–child relationships and the caringness of both female and male 'mothers', Connie accepts the necessity for women to relinquish their reproductive powers. Piercy's novel dates from 1974 when feminists felt more enthusiasm for the possibilities of reproductive technology; like contraception it appeared to offer women more freedom. *Woman* presents in fictional form the argument forwarded by Shulamith Firestone in *The Dialectic of Sex* which locates the basis of women's oppression in biological reproduction. Many feminists have since raised objections to this theory, arguing that it is the *social* and *political* organisation of reproduction which oppresses women, rather than women's reproductive capacity *per se*. Like Connie, many feminist readers are uncomfortable with this aspect of the novel yet, in my opinion, the power and subtlety of Piercy's portrayal of artificial conception and collective childcare does much to dispel these misgivings.

A model for human relationships

As well as redefining motherhood as a social rather than a biological experience, *Woman* also proposes it as a model for all human relationships; on Mattapoisett all relationships, be they between friends, parents or lovers, are characterised by mutual caring and nurturance. This is a characteristic of many lesbian/feminist utopias, but perhaps its most thoroughgoing and committed expression is found in Sally Gearhart's *The Wanderground*. Gearhart's utopian community Whileaway is an all-female society whose inhabitants have escaped from a genocidal sex war. The women have rejected what they see as masculine values, including exploitative and unequal interpersonal relations. However, the basis for this change is not so much a rejection of biology as it is in *Woman*, but an embrace of it: whereas in *Woman* mothering could be practised by all regardless of gender, in *The Wanderground* femaleness is the prerequisite for maternity and indeed any positive relationship. The novel is a celebration of maternalism and, significantly, the whole community depends for its well-being on Mother, both the earth itself and its spiritual aspect. In fact, the Wanderground owes its existence not so much to the women who live there as to the 'Revolt of the Mother': 'The earth finally said "no"' (p 158). The section entitled 'The Deep Cella' demonstrates the differences between *The Wanderground*'s and *Woman*'s treatment of motherhood. It describes the hillwomen's conception ceremony in terms of one of the character's feelings and physical experience of the journey to the womb-like caves:

> Fora reached out in her mind to touch each one ... [She] was lost in the splendid drama that passed before her eyes, that moved within her body .... She visited entirely within herself, inside ... (p 46)

This almost mystical rendering of the experience is in marked contrast to Piercy's much more matter of fact and scientific depiction.

The Wanderground is much more pessimistic than *Woman* about men's capacity to change; it also has a much more rigid and conservative concept of sexuality, suggesting that masculinity and femininity are innate rather than acquired behaviours. This is not true of all lesbian and/or women-only utopias. Joanna Russ's *The Female Man*, for instance, whose very title suggests sexual mutability, focuses on linguistic rather than biological definitions of woman.

Gendered language systems

The exploration of language as a system which both constitutes and perpetuates women's subordination to men is a central focus of the lesbian/feminist SF canon, and the equation of masculinity and femininity with particular linguistic modes has become commonplace in feminist literary practice. For example, in *The Wanderground* the encounter between the hillwomen and the gentles (a group of men who have relinquished male values) is conveyed in a different linguistic register to that used by the women amongst themselves. In this encounter thoughts do not travel back and forth harmoniously; instead, words are exchanged combatively. Meaning lies not in the saying as it does in woman-centred language, but in what is said. The text makes clear that this shift is a result of 'the cock-centred energy' of the city and that, in this context, it is more appropriate to speak of a 'woman-fucker' than an 'enfoldment',

the hillwomen's term for erotic experience. In *Woman on the Edge of Time*
Marge Piercy elaborates a woman-centred language system which
privileges the present continuous tense and verbalises nouns, making states
dynamic rather than passive propositions. Mattapoisettians make no
linguistic distinction between men and women, using the pronoun 'per'
to refer to both. These systems share an assumption that verbs, especially
perfect tense or transitive ones, are somehow masculine, and nouns and
states of being are somehow feminine. In privileging the latter, female
experience is validated.

These linguistic experiments attempt to undermine what French
feminists, Wittig among them, have called phallogocentrism. Hélène
Cixous has demonstrated the ways in which patriarchal binary thought
works to subordinate the 'feminine' through an equation with the
'negative' pole: activity/passivity; sun/moon; culture/nature;
father/mother; head/emotions; intelligible/sensitive; logos/pathos (T.
Moi, *Sexual/Textual Politics*, p 104).[2] Yet, there is a danger that rather
than subverting these constructs, feminist utopias reinforce them by
uncritically celebrating the 'feminine' pole. *The Wanderground*, for
instance, utilises these equations as if they were metaphysical rather than
socially constructed categories and its whole philosophical and political
system is based on the very binary oppositions identified by Cixous.

Much feminist SF also makes use of the SF concepts of telepathy and
ESP, suggesting that these pre-linguistic systems of communication are
particularly female or feminine. Connie in *Woman* is a natural 'catcher'
or telepath; Gearhart's hillwomen can communicate without speaking
and even enter into the consciousnesses of other animate and inanimate
things; and Magdalen in *Queen of the States* undergoes an out-of-body
experience to communicate with alien life forms. Such fantasies register
women's historical exclusion from the Symbolic Order, the realm of
language use and cultural expression, and the desire for another mode
of communication which is not constructed by and for men's use.
They also register a desire for a pre-linguistic realm before the emergence
of sexual difference and antagonism. Moreover, the equation of
femininity and non-verbal forms of communication implies the existence
of a female nature outside language. As Sarah LeFanu writes:

> The implication here of a residue of truth, lying underneath the prob-
> lematics of language, is the corollary of the notion of an essential
> femaleness. Language is seen as a barrier between thought and thing;
> remove it and thoughts become material. Womanness exists inde-
> pendently of, and before, the construct of language. (p 68)

Yet this idea undermines the feminist belief that language is a prime site of feminist struggle and that women must have access to it if they are to enjoy full social and political freedoms. If women can better and indeed fully express themselves in non-verbal forms, then linguistic struggle becomes unnecessary and redundant.

Suzette Haden Elgin's *Native Tongue* takes as its starting point this idea that language is a site of struggle and a tool of women's oppression. The novel explores the relationship between language, gender and power, and represents an attempt to construct a female language system from scratch as the basis of a feminist politics. It depicts a dystopian future world in which men's domination is absolute and women are barred from all forms of power. Earth society is composed of non-linguist citizens and 13 dynasties of linguists, known as the Lines, who hold immense power as a result of their unique abilities to communicate with alien species on other planets. However, the women of the Lines, despite having equal language abilities with the men, are, if anything, even more enslaved than their non-linguist sisters. Owing to the demand for linguist babies, these women are part linguisticians, doing invaluable government work, and part breeding machines. They live crowded into collective houses under the jurisdiction of a ruling patriarch, and are forced to work from babyhood as linguists, and to bear at least eight children from the Line before being sent to the Barren House, the destination of infertile, and hence, redundant women. Despite their pivotal importance, the women have absolutely no status, and are reviled by the general population as well as held in contempt by their own men. Male ideology reinforces their productive and reproductive enslavement through its conceptualisation of woman as thing-for-man, as emotional, irrational and untrustworthy.

Yet, despite the novel's promising premis, and Elgin's own credentials as an academic linguist, in my view *Native Tongue* fails adequately to address the relationship between language, ideology and political consciousness. The novel's exploration of language is almost wholly confined to an empirical elaboration of a female-centred vocabulary, without demonstrating how such a lexicon arises out of a situation of oppression or struggle. Apart from their busy invention of new feminine words, the linguist women are barely visible as subjects of their own discourse owing, I would suggest, to the novel's positivist theory of language. It contrasts radically with Monique Wittig's *The Lesbian Body* (1986) which enacts in the body of the text the construction of woman as a desirous, speaking subject. It was originally published in French, and became popular with English speaking readers in translation. *The Lesbian*

Body essentially stands outside the Anglo-American tradition in its linguistic 'foreignness' and in its stress on the 'amazon' virtues of strength, physicality, violence and militancy, rather than the 'maternal' virtues of empathy and nurturance. The novel undertakes a remarkable dismemberment of the lesbian body into its anatomical parts in order to deconstruct the representation of woman in patriarchal discourse. For Wittig, the affirmation of the lesbian as subject starts with the body and with the body's inscription in language:

> To recite one's own body, to recite the body of the other, is to recite the word of which the book is made up. The fascination for writing the never previously written and the fascination for the unattained body proceed from the same desire. (Author's note, p 10)

Joanna Russ's *The Female Man* shares Wittig's deconstructive emphasis on language as a signifying practice rather than as a mimetic object which mirrors female experience. The novel eschews both realism and the mythopoeic mode in order to interrogate the terms of fictional representation. Whereas *The Wanderground* celebrates women's ostensible closeness to nature, *The Female Man* shows how this ideological construction of woman as nature has excluded women from the category 'human':

> You can't write woman and human any more than you can write matter and anti-matter. (p 151)

For Russ, as for Wittig, utopia is not a static object but a radical literary practice, a way of writing. Whereas *Native Tongue* seeks to invent a discrete woman-centred lexicon as object, *The Female Man* suggests that utopian writing is an activity rather than a product. It is interventionist, disruptive and self critical, or self reflexive, that is conscious of itself and of its own history and myths. *The Female Man* addresses the (lesbian/feminist) reader directly, inviting her to participate in the text's utopian project. It represents a cultural intervention in the politics and history of both gender and writing, consciously placing itself in a tradition of feminist literary and political practice:

> Go little book, bob a curtsey at the shrines of Friedan, Millet, Greer, Firestone … do not complain when at last you become quaint and old-fashioned … when you are no longer understood … Do not reach up and punch the readers' noses.
>   Rejoice little book!
>   For on that day we will be free. (p 213)

Conclusion

The uses to which lesbian and feminist writers have put the SF genre are varied and reflect the different strands in feminist theoretical and political thought. While fantasy utopias such as *The Wanderground* express the cultural feminist stress on natural femaleness and mothering, critical utopias such as *The Female Man* demonstrate the unnaturalness of all gender constructs. Nevertheless, despite these different emphases, the lesbian/feminist SF genre as a whole is united in its location of women as the central protagonists of the quest narrative, as active, speaking subjects in their own right and in its prioritisation of female community and relationships between women. Lesbian/feminist SF allows writers and readers to imagine worlds of possibility and adventure in which women are freed from the constraints of contemporary sexist society and are no longer 'the second sex'. Perhaps the narrator of Joanna Russ's *The Female Man* best sums up the basis of lesbian/feminist SF, its capacity to liberate woman-as-subject:

Remember, I don't want to be a 'feminine' version or a diluted version or a special version or a subsidiary version or an ancillary version, or an adapted version of the heroes I admire. I want to be the heroes themselves. (p 206)

7 Lesbian Cinema, Women's Cinema

Penny Florence

Queer women's pictures

Is lesbian cinema about women or about being gay? As soon as the question is put, I want to pull it apart. Why is it 'about' either? Why is it useful to create such distinctions? What is meant by 'cinema' in this context? There are no answers. Yet I still want to explore the questions, because my understanding of cinema is inseparable from a sense of crucial intersections; cinema crosses broad political and social issues with sexuality and signs in a uniquely powerful blend of realities.

What follows, then, is a preliminary attempt to define lesbian cinema. As part of my inquiry I shall try to outline a division that has developed in film theory, one with which feminist film criticism is closely bound up. The reason why this complex and sometimes difficult ground has to be explored before we can move forward is closely linked with the politicised role sexuality has to some degree in everyone's life, but most especially in lesbians' lives. The tendency is for criticism to divide its arguments at exactly this juncture between sexuality and socio-political matters, and it is becoming urgent that the currents are brought together. The language of the psychoanalytic criticism through which sexuality in film has most fruitfully been discussed fails when it comes to some forms of political engagement. It is also underdeveloped with regard to women's sexuality and, partly as a consequence, close to silence and structural incapacity with regard to lesbians.

These differences in approach cloud many of the crucial issues. It is not easy to describe them without oversimplification, but the one tends to be more descriptive and to be structured primarily on the extra-textual – historical, experiential, political – while the other tends to be more technical and/or formal and to underpin its arguments through an analysis of how the film is made and the ways it positions the spectator. Both may well be informed by theoretical understanding, and clearly there are moments of convergence, and this is only a very rough indication of approaches that partly, but not wholly, reflect the split within feminism between those whose well-founded distrust of masculine theorising has led to seeking new epistemologies, and those who, while sharing the same distrust, challenge patriarchal theories from the standpoint of informed dissent. I would aim to bring the strengths of each approach together; the division is a derivative of the false dichotomy between abstract thought and other 'inner experience' that limits masculinist theory and contributes to women's alienation from it.

There are signs that this is changing, though it would be premature to argue that a framework adequate to the task of describing Lesbian Cinema has been developed. Among such signs are the growth of what is known as 'queer theory' and feminist work on the body.[1] Lola Young points another way in her article 'Representation and British "Racial Problem" Films' when she explores 'race' from, in her words, 'a conceptual framework that is able to assess critically the effect of the collision of two discourses – that of "race" and that of female sexuality. The question of sexuality is central to a consideration of "race": its representational presence or constructed absence is an essential component ...' (Young, 1991, p 41)[2]

This is highly relevant to film criticism in general, and to lesbian cinema in particular, because cinema is the form of signifying practice, and film is the medium, that has the potential to create fictions that can cross another false boundary, that between 'inner' and 'external' experience, in highly specific and potent ways. The visual phantasmagoria of cinema, even if it cannot approach the totality of lived experience, invents forms that mesh with it on multiple levels (the most obvious being verbal and visual) and therefore offers an entry into otherwise unrepresentable meanings. What Young says of 'race' illustrates her point about the collision between sociopolitics and female sexuality; we need 'to rethink difference and to recognise the composite nature of the reality of those relationships. Textual reality is only a fraction of reality; the whole is unknowable and, possibly, unspeakable' (p 50).

In a society which denies our collective and social reality films seem to offer the seductive possibility of imaging ourselves. Lack of understanding of the processes involved leaves lesbians and other underrepresented people vulnerable to manipulation. This said, I also believe that many of us who are marginalised are highly sophisticated as audiences and perform complex manoeuvres when watching films that make it possible to gain pleasure against the grain of the representational and narrative structures.

But for now, for a brief moment, dim the lights, raise the curtain and dream.

A dream of moving pictures

Have you ever woken up with your lover to discover you have dreamed the same dream? If a dream is the fulfilment of a wish, have you dreamt in this way because your desires are fundamentally in accord? Is the satisfaction of the movies closely linked to that of dreams, and are their ways of producing and structuring meanings sufficiently closely allied to allow the watching dreamer to come to know and understand through dreams and films in comparable ways? And what might this say about the importance of the movies in the domain of socialised identities and culture as opposed to the private, as forms of dream dreamed together in the common dark? Perhaps cinema is inseparable from the erotic and from desire, in which case it is a vital cultural space for lesbians in the construction of meanings and the understanding of subjectivities. Perhaps cinema as a public cultural form has particular collective importance for the variety of cultural identities designated 'minority' in a way that differs from videos or TV seen in private. If so, cinema may be significant in developing a more sophisticated sense of what 'group identity' might be, one that both breaks down the way of conceptualising 'groups' which tends to fixity, exclusion or hierarchisation, and fosters a freer and potentially more subversive understanding of multiple and mobile collectivities. Perhaps the oracular dream-film is the one which crosses the border between the individual and the collective, between ontology and, if not, phylogeny which is the term Freud uses as the opposite of ontology,[3] then some other way of conceptualising the collective? When Freud tried to adjust his meanings to account for the lesbian elements of Dora's dreams and desires, was it some meaning related to this shift in his conceptualisation of the collective 'Man' he could not allow himself to divine; that her desires were beyond him, yet must affect him, and that she was not alone? Did he fear that her desire, by disrupting his masculinist notion of phylogeny and of desire, would annihilate his?[4]

On varying and complex levels these are questions that reflect not only on the whole issue of lesbian cinema as a category, but also on different ways of talking about it. As yet there is no substantial body of writing about lesbian cinema, no shared sense of what is meant by it. This essay has as one of its aims a move towards a lesbian definition of the oracular, liminal space that is, at its best, the cinema, the place where we can figure as part of each others' dreams; or so we can at least imagine.

Lesbian cinema

What, then, is lesbian cinema? Does it exist, and if so, where? I would suggest as a preliminary formulation that it exists as a complex of inter-connections between lesbian filmmakers, lesbian representations, lesbian readings and lesbian 'spectatorship',[5] and that it traverses other defini-tions and categorisations within cinema. Or again, perhaps the value of the question resides as much in the issues it raises as in any answers that might be produced, because its drive is at the present historical con-juncture inherently transgressive.

What strategies do lesbians, especially Black and Asian lesbians, adopt in order to deal with the dearth of representations that even approxi-mate to our sociosexual realities and phantasies? More radically, how far and in what senses does this dearth matter? How central is feminism to any understanding of lesbian cinema?

Clearly it is not going to be possible to deal with all these questions in this essay. Nevertheless I want to raise them to give an indication of the breadth and complexity of the issues, first of all for lesbians, but also for all female subjects and, ultimately, male subjects, gay and straight. The reason I am writing first, but not exclusively, for lesbians is partly because otherwise self-definition runs the risk of self-marginalisation, but it is also because any refiguring of sexuality, desire and the subject has implications for all subjects.

Some basic concepts

Since the 1970s, when groundbreaking work was done in film criticism, especially by feminists, certain key concepts have come to seem indis-pensible, although, unfortunately, they do not always mean exactly the same. This is not the place to try and elaborate them, but I shall very briefly mention those which are the most important from the lesbian point of view and urge the reader to discover for herself whether she wishes to get to grips with the kinds of thinking behind them. The gaze (or look), spectatorship, address, the subject (subjectivity), desire, pleasure: even listing them like this gives an indication that what is at stake is a pattern of seeing, who makes what visible and for whom. The subject, when applied to the spectator or to representations of individuals viewed as part of cultural formations rather than as a 'character', is a term deriving from psychoanalysis, usually related in some way to Jacques Lacan.[6] An initial working definition could be: 'the mature individual who has a place in language and culture.' It is thus a cultural definition and is linked indissolubly to a system of language and representation in which seeing is a crucial element.

A major problem with this kind of theory is that it is constructed according to heterosexual male experience, based on various derivations from the oedipus complex,[7] Freudian ideas around the boy child's identification with his father and desire for his mother, and the girl's supposed realisation of her castration. Of crucial importance to thinking about film is the fact that this fundamental psychic moment involves seeing or the gaze. Women's status as subjects within both the original theory and its derivatives is highly problematic, and lesbians hardly get a look in.[8] A further difficulty arises because the crucial activator in the process of significance is desire, and desire, according to the Lacanian thinking that has so far been the most influential, and despite asseverations that it is secondary, is always characterised as male. In Lacan's delightedly masculinist version, desire's elusive darting along indefinable pathways looks distinctly like a would-be escapist ricochet into dead ends from a lesbian point of view.

Why are these difficult and often blocking theories relevant to lesbians? One way of answering this question was indicated by Sue Clayton when she said that 'The structuring of cinema codes in relation to male desire is a topic that needs to be fully explored within its context of linguistic theory and psychoanalysis' (Clayton, 1983, p 91).[9] Clayton is discussing Laura Mulvey's pioneering article, 'Visual Pleasure and Narrative Cinema', which has become a landmark within a major strand of feminist and other progressive film criticisms. Clayton's observation is relevant to lesbians because it is the structuring role allowed to male desire that is used to justify assertions such as Mulvey's that 'woman is tied to her place as a bearer, not a maker, of meaning' (p 7). Mulvey has, of course, developed her position since 1975,[10] and much has been said about the issues, but the debates have become locked into too restricted a range of issues, with too ready an acceptance of theoretical dicta, especially around desire and the gaze. Theorising lesbian desire seems to be ensnared in inappropriate structures of masculinity and heterosexuality, and, to borrow a phrase from Gayatri Spivak in another, related context, 'we must change a morphology to a storyline' (Spivak, 1990, p 220). This is where recent feminist and epistemology and queer theories, together with the new representations with which they are interlinked, may well have a key role to play in shifting the premises of intractable logical difficulties. Mulvey's intention was originally 'to make way for a total negation of the ease and plenitude of the narrative fiction film' (Mulvey, 1975, p 8). As will be evident in what follows, I find this too totalising and prescriptive. While it signals the importance of interrogating certain dominant forms of pleasure and, while it was an extremely important approach which cleared the way for new understandings, it fails to take account of the subversive ways women have always found to become makers as well as bearers – of meanings and much else.

What, then, has lesbian desire in the movies to do with 'male desire'? One approach to understanding the question is through the most common lesbian stereotypes, those of the masculine-identified woman and the child-woman.[11] In *The Killing of Sister George* (1968), the two main lesbian characters are – yes! – Childie and George and they are to an extent symptomatic of a principal limitation that mainstream cinema has had in figuring lesbian desire. Male directors have been unable to conceive of desire that is not based on their own or that is not immature. In *The Killing of Sister George* there is even a nun-joke scene, admittedly quite funny almost because of its predictability, in which George, pissed out of her head, takes a taxi which is already occupied by two nuns. 'Well, hello, girls!', she leers, in truly macho style, while the nuns cower in the back, as vulnerable and ignorant as Childie. Lesbian desire in this account is some version of immaturity, denial or mimicry, all of which imply absence. It doesn't really exist, but is rather a symptom of maladjustment; thus it remains arrested or copies the male.[12] It is a deviation that has to be punished; George loses her job (this is the 'killing', the axing of her role in a proto-soap) and is emotionally destroyed. The similarity between these stereotypical lesbian images as either child or man and Freud's interpretation of Dora's desire as a kind of return to infantile (auto)eroticism through masculine identification is undeniable and, what is more, it is through representations (Dora's dream and the painting of the Madonna) that Freud made his judgments. Even if the lesbian who really wants to be a man exists, she is only *one* lesbian psycho-social identity among many.[13]

What an understanding of lesbian cinema will require, however, is not necessarily that we throw these constructions out. Rather it is that we read them for what they say about male desire and its limitations, contrasting them where necessary with our own, and not fearing them when they coincide. The details of how stereotypes play a part in making cinematic meaning will be complex, and not always straightforwardly negative or cancelling as regards lesbians, as witnessed by the woman in *We've been Framed*, who responded quite differently to *The Killing of Sister George* when she saw it at a women only screening.[14]

It will already be apparent that the ways in which received theories and structures limit both representations of women and readings of them has not been left unchallenged by lesbians and feminists,[15] and that there is still a long way to go. This is especially so where lesbians are concerned, and where the elaboration of structures fully capable of elucidating plural subjectivities is involved. At the level of theory, it is still hotly contested whether it is possible to adjust the frameworks to rectify inadequacies;[16] in practice, much excellent work has been done appropriating the terms, even if the same double-binds recur around the disavowal of sexual difference and the difficulties this leads to when seeking to understand how the image of 'woman' functions within cinema.

Lesbian cinema, women's cinema

How far do the debates around the definition of women's cinema[17] help to refine any initial answer to the question of what lesbian cinema might be? What might be the relationship between lesbian cinema and women's cinema and, to turn the question round to the spectator, what might the differences be in the way a lesbian spectator is positioned within women's cinema and the way she is positioned in other broad categories: gay, mainstream, 'alternative', all problematic, as I shall argue, in ways sometimes similar and sometimes widely different?

There is a fundamental reason why it is not straightforward to recognise and articulate the differences between women's cinema and lesbian cinema. It is that both require the construction of a fully realised female subject. This means that it is necessary for women to be represented as both the subject and object of desire.[18] This inscribes the lesbian relationship into the representational structure at its basis. It also makes use of psychoanalytic broadening of the concept of desire to incorporate its operation as a signifying function as well as an element of individual sexuality.

I am not saying that there are no differences between lesbian cinema and women's cinema, but rather that they mainly arise at a secondary level, for example, that of events within the narrative or of the representations of varying kinds of community, rather than that of the narrative structure or the articulation of the symbolic. This matters because it makes an important point about homosexuality, while at the same time showing how the alignment of lesbian cinema with women's cinema rather than with gay cinema foregrounds different issues for lesbians. The point about homosexuality is that it is an indispensable element of all desire, including the heterosexual. On these fundamental levels at least, the absence of lesbian meanings has been a crucial node in the dynamic that has limited women's culture in the past, and it intersects with that which has necessitated the dissembling or disguise of male homosexual meanings. Gay male films do not come up against the same problems as lesbian films because male desire has an established and pivotal role in signification. Desire between men is thus articulable. *Looking for Langston* can explore a territory that is already, if imperfectly, mapped; desperation is not imposed on his seeking. But on the other hand, to acknowledge fully same-sex desire in men is to admit it in women, and therefore to acknowledge the authentic possibility of lesbian subjecthood.

The common theoretical double bind, that lesbian desire is impossible (one which elicits laughter from other perspectives!),[19] functions to mask for heterosexist thinkers the unacceptable fact that if lesbian desire is indispensable to women's desire, then heterosexual desire is inseparable from homosexual desire: inseparable, not identical, and not collapsible, the one into the other.

Two criticisms, two cinemas?

I come now to a more detailed consideration of the division I referred to at the beginning. It serves here as one way of furthering the conceptualisation of lesbian cinema by setting it in the context of the separation between 'mainstream' and 'alternative' that has tended to characterise feminist criticism and ideas of women's cinema, as well as practices and actual histories within film-making. It is an opposition around which important arguments have been explored. It also has a base in historical fact, which has been vital for the growth of women's cinema and lesbian cinema. While I shall argue that it is time to rethink any such conceptualisation, I do not underestimate its value hitherto.

The alternative or 'Independent' movement has its immediate roots in the social and political upheavals of the 1960s, though it extends back to the lower budget avant-garde tradition of non-studio produced films, such as those by Maya Deren. In its more recent guise, this tradition has included the women's film and video workshops, such as Leeds Animation Workshop, Sheffield Film Co-op, Witch (Women's Independent Cinema House) and Red Flannel. The same movement was also the crucible for the new Black British cinema, with collectives such as Black Audio, Sankofa and Albany Video. Isaac Julien's recent documentary *Television, Memory, Race 1968–92* points out that Black workshops were rather more successful than white ones in producing films that both break silence over and contextualise gay and lesbian experience, *Passion of Remembrance*, for example. The British Independent movement overall, however, has not produced a great deal of lesbian work, and now that what remains of its base has shifted towards community video, it seems unlikely to do so on a large scale.[20]

There were once powerful reasons for seeing cinema in terms of 'mainstream' and 'alternative' even though, especially from a lesbian viewpoint, the broad tendencies in film-making practice do not exactly correspond to those within criticism (one set of practices giving rise to a certain kind of criticism) but rather overlap according to other general currents with their origins outside cinematic production and, to some extent, exhibition. The position is no longer clear, however, as is signalled by de Lauretis, although she does not go so far as to question the basic utility of the division, but rather to suggest important modifications:

> ... does the notion of alternative cultural forms have anything to do with hegemony and class or racial struggle, as it did in the parlance of the 60s and 70s, or does it loosely refer, in a perspective of postmodern pluralistic democracy, to those sectors of the social field that are allowed some cultural expression in the margins of what is called the mainstream? (de Lauretis, 1990, p 10)

Her discussion traverses notions such as Third Cinema and 'subaltern media' in the course of defining her own notion of 'guerrilla cinema'

> ... posing the question of desire and its representation from within the context of actual practices of both lesbianism and cinema ... self-conscious, self-critical, feminist intervention amidst the various representational strategies, both feminist and anti-feminist, that aim to expropriate and delegitimate lesbianism as irreducible sociosexual difference, or to recontain it in acceptable, legitimate forms ... (de Lauretis, 1990, pp 24, 25)

The terms of this debate were set up about 15 years ago, and they are closely linked with the kind of theorising that followed Laura Mulvey's article, mentioned above (Mulvey, 1975). The practices (lesbian, feminist, and cinematic) from which they are inseparable are no longer so clear, and while this has entailed losses, it need not be read as the appropriation of the alternative by the mainstream, or not only. Rather it can be seen as the kind of breakdown of oppositional structures that is consistent with a feminist dispersal of binary thinking, and from a lesbian viewpoint there are powerful reasons for ceasing to prioritise one over the other. There is no inherently 'good' or 'bad' cinematic practice, and continuing to argue in these terms has contributed to aspects of what has appeared to be an impasse in certain areas, repeated returns to the same issues and controversies.

Mulvey outlined how the camera and editing process are used in complicity with the male protagonist in many films, as if the relationship between the (usually male) director's way of seeing and the camera, together with the male's directional look in the film, sets up a complex of gazes available to the male spectator. Women's place in the web of controlling looks is that of the object, the one who is looked at. Often she is to be controlled, since she is a threat to the satisfactory resolution of the plot.

Presumably if she is lesbian (lesbian desire was not under discussion), this would be all the more so. The processes referred to above range from the complex and subtle to the basic, as in the film in which the earliest lesbian character appears, *Pandora's Box* (1929). The film is edited to show the lesbian Countess Geschwitz dancing with the bride, cutting to the man's conspiratorial glances around the small group of people with whom he is standing. He then cuts in on the dance, isolating the lesbian, whose point of view is not shown.

While a full understanding of what the totality of small camera and editing moves like this builds up to mean for lesbian subjectivity is very difficult to imagine in critical modes that are not informed by psychoanalytic and structural understanding, such readings require careful handling if they are to avoid the blockage-points. The meanings of 'desire' and 'the gaze' are evidently only partially accessible without psychoanalytic readings, so that even though some feminist film criticism raises important issues without them, they cannot be precise about cinema or about the ways individuals mesh with social identities (and the crucial feminist insights around 'the personal' or 'autobiographical') without in some sense passing through psychoanalytic thinking for the very reasons I floated at the beginning: cinema is inseparable from subjectivities and desire, and psychoanalysis is the language through which they have so far been articulated.

A limitation in the way these ideas have been applied has sometimes meant that the gaze is taken to be unitary, and the spectator assumed to be 'fixed' by it.[21] As a simplified example, attention could be paid to how the gaze has changed over time in relation to lesbians, for example comparing a scene similar to the one in *Pandora's Box* with one that occurs in *Sammy and Rosie get Laid* (1987), where the lesbian kisses a woman watched by an older man. But this scene does not set up the same controlling looks; the reaction shot is as much about how the man is disturbed by what he sees and the anxiety he experiences as a result as it is about his controlling look. The lesbian meets his gaze challengingly and kisses the woman again. Furthermore, the characters are British Asians, so that the complexity of social codes of meaning for the false neutrality of the 'mainstream' audience (white, straight, male) are raised in a way that is relatively unfamiliar in the movies; what does it mean for a British Asian lesbian to kiss a woman in front of an older Asian man in this way, and how does it relate to the same action by a white British lesbian? This is not an argument for *Sammy and Rosie get Laid* as a progressive film for lesbians; the point is that looks are ambiguous and their subjectivities and address are more complex than is sometimes allowed. Furthermore, politics is located also at the moment of spectatorship, not only in the modes of production, exhibition and theorisation, with which it forms a force-field.[22]

Lesbian spectatorship

A politics of spectatorship is an issue relevant to lesbians particularly because the lesbian gaze is more ambiguous in relation to what is being called male desire and the male gaze than the straight woman's (and I do not say that her gaze is unitary by any means).[23] Heterosexuality is at issue here as much as gender or anatomical fe/maleness. Nor is the lesbian spectator who places herself in the position of the male character opposite a woman trapped into merely undergoing an unconscious and manipulated identification with the male.[24] That identification can be the means of access to the woman, female desire across the male, the assumption of aspects of his role, not a deep desire for merging with his subjectivity.[25] The lesbian does not have to choose between female and male, because she refuses the heterosexual patterning according to which these alternatives dominate. Her desire is therefore potentially both mobile and transgressive. Identification with the 'masculine' position need not necessarily signify 'wanting to be a man'; it can also be seen as one known means of access to the female body.[26]

Identification is clearly important on another level, as is evidenced by most of the lesbians' personal testimonies in *We've been Framed*. Many were looking for role models, especially if they were just realising their sexuality. One woman 'identified' with Vivian in *Desert Hearts*; another was using gay male images 'to create my own identity' in the absence of gay female movies; for this woman, the problem was heterosexuality before gender. Another woman found herself 'writing myself in as a man' opposite her favourite actresses. Clearly it will result in distortion to switch from identification at this level and the meanings of identification in psychoanalytic terms; nevertheless, it is also distorting to leave it out of the account. What is needed is a way of making the connections, not least because psychic structures themselves are mobile and relived, not laid down once and for all.

Being part of an all female audience is a further element relevant to lesbian spectatorship, as mentioned earlier in relation to *The Killing of Sister George*. The Asian woman in *We've been Framed* who described her response to an Indian film *Razia Sultan* (1983) made the same point, when she gave her account of an unusual version of what is a set piece in mainstream Indian films, the lover singing to a woman. This time, the lover–singer is a woman, though the scene is interspersed with dissolves to a man on horseback. The interviewee described how she enjoyed the scene, despite the man on horseback, especially when she watched the film as part of a women-only screening. Although the direct address of the film is to straight men, the spectator was able to subvert the structuring gaze, her pleasure being increased by the knowledge of the heterosexual tradition (man singing to woman) and by being part of a female audience. Re-encoding the film's address according to a shared code of lesbian spectatorship, this woman was able to see two Asian women as desiring subjects. This is a genuine intervention into the codes of both Asian and Western cinema, one which overrides the unsubtle attempt at recuperation within the film. The interviewee was adjusting the look of the film to her own gaze in response to a perceived need of her multiple subjectivity as an Asian lesbian in Britain. The same is true of the Black woman in the programme who found in Whoopi Goldberg's screen presence in *Ghosts* (1990) an image of Black lesbianhood otherwise unavailable to her. Too often the assumed identity of the camera with the spectator's gaze does not take sufficient account of this form of resistance and appropriation.

The capacity of the audience to disturb the codes and meanings set up by the text is determined at least in part by the existence of some other version of the overall set of practices that make up 'cinema', and I do not say that the spectator can make any scene or film mean what she likes. Our ability to shift meaning in this way on any deep level of the imaginary or the symbolic derives from transgressive, contextual meanings through which the complex mesh of varying trajectories are made to intersect and hold the signifier for that cinematic moment; hence the crucial role of the 'alternative', not as opposition, but as part of the process of breaking down the dominant. Its function and value is not a straightforward challenge to the mainstream but rather the creation and development of new forms and meanings addressed to a particular audience (lesbians in this case) which are then made to engage with the dominant forms and meanings *at the level of the spectator*. (I assume this is part of the reason for de Lauretis's choice of the term 'guerrilla', emphasising as it does a collectivity of separate individuals or cells rather than a mass movement.) Since the meanings are not locked up in the can with the celluloid, the lesbian cineaste with her own culture may understand, say, the kiss between Thelma and Louise as expressive of lesbian desire, where her straight sister sees it as women's desire, any potential contradiction being suspended in the mesh of practices that is cinema. Restricted and partially 'secret' information and understandings are an important element within sub-cultures, where readings are inflected with social and contextual meanings. The role of gossip about movie stars such as Dietrich and Garbo is an example which allows their performances/characters to be read in specific ways (Weiss 1991). Such meanings re-circulate in *Meeting of Two Queens* (1988) in which clips are used to construct a fantasy romance between the two legendary stars. Playing on the 'leakage' between social and textual, the film re-positions the spectator and the actress within its system of meanings and against what is the usual grain. An analogous shift is effected in relation to the writer in Kwietnowski's *Brief Encounters*, which revisits homosexual writer Noel Coward's straight play, to construct its quite different narrative involving two men in a railway station.

This is why the fact that few representations of lesbians which merit serious attention ever make it to the screens of the dominant industry does not mean that our cinema is limited. It is of course a lamentable and artificial state of affairs, maintained partly through censorship; there is a long list of 'de-lesbianised' movies.[27] I have outlined some of the ways lesbians experience pleasure within dominant narrative cinema, but the possibility should also be borne in mind that recognition is not the only way for the subject-spectator to interact with representation. Representations of lesbians are not the *sine qua non* of lesbian cinema, though of course I do not wish to belittle their importance; against all this discussion of identifications on various levels I would set the resistance of the image itself and its capacity to conjure spaces that can be recuperated by nobody.[28]

Lesbian sexual desire

So far the notion of desire I have explored has been in the expanded psychoanalytic sense. But what of the explicit portrayal of sexual desire with which it may intersect, but with which it is not simply identified? The question creates almost inevitably (at present) a potentially explosive conjunction of feminism with pornography, which some feminists regard as among the worst symptoms of patriarchy, and others as potentially liberating for women's sexuality. It is very difficult to discuss sexuality even in its expanded sense without raising the issue of pornography, arguably impossible when it comes to film.

Is a specifically lesbian porn possible outside the structures of male porn? Are direct representations of lesbian sexuality inevitably enmeshed in oppressive, controlling or objectifying ways of looking? How do lesbians deal with issues around the position of women who work in the pornographic film industry?

Male pornography not infrequently uses lesbian scenes. This is an instance where the gaze is always unequivocally male, and the scene usually acts as foreplay introducing a heterosexual encounter. The independent film *Sigmund Freud's Dora* challenges just this structure, making visible through a series of formal devices and through an interweaving with Freud's case history the ways in which these films follow the same patterning as what is taken to be the classic Freudian and oedipal construction of the development of female sexuality; the mature female 'must' transfer her attachment away from her mother and on to her father. In this way, her diverse and multiple feelings for her mother are only a prelude to the main, simplified, event, the love of men and of their authority, as represented in the father and his laws.

Lesbian porn seems to present some of the same problems, and some new ones. What I have to say is extremely provisional since I have not made a study of it, and should be read as a personal response. What I have seen is the programme at the London Film Festival in 1991,[29] and much of the material seems to manifest the same structural patterning as the dominant. This may well be partly why women's arousal is often described as invisible and unrepresentable, since pornography focuses on genital arousal and penetration with the penis as the token of visibility.[30]

For me, part of the difficulty with pornography rests in its isolation of sex from other areas of experience, and not infrequently, in its fragmentation of the body into erogenous zones, which is perhaps connected with the former. The lesbian pornography films I have seen show little awareness of the ways in which the camera can be used to deconstruct the conventions of ways of looking that have been oppressive to women and that have failed to show anything like the broad range of sexualities and sensual experience. I would argue in favour of cinematic structures which aim to bring film closer to representing lesbian desire/s and which could be used to reconstruct the cinematic experience as regards explicit sex between women.

While not taking up a position in favour of censorship, I do not want to see a lesbian pornographic cinema that aims straightforwardly to produce for a female pornographic market along the pattern of the male, as portrayed in *Perils or pleasure? Feminist produced pornography* (USA 1989).[31] While sexuality, lesbian pleasure and so forth are clearly at issue, so is money and its part in the construction of male sex-power. This contextualised reading does not seem separable from the critical analysis of pornography, and women film-makers have sought to address its complex and far-reaching implications. Chantal Ackerman, for example, uses a variety of what might be called anti-cinematic devices in her films – static long takes in wide shot, real time – which allow the spectator to ask whose gaze is being represented by the camera. *Je Tu Il Elle* (Belgium 1974) is in three parts, starting with Julie (played by Ackerman) alone, moving to Julie on the road where she masturbates a lorry driver, and ending with her seducing a woman friend in a long lovemaking sequence. Among the issues Ackerman raises is voyeurism; how far her film is pornographic, or whether its refusal of the conventions of pornography prohibits its being seen in this way. The following is an extract from an interview with Ackerman by Angela Martin:

AM What impressed me was the lesbian love-making scene, but as much, the scene with the lorry driver, because it's even more rare to have male sexuality talked about in a film.[32] What kind of feedback have you had?

CA It's strange – from some women who have problems about their own lesbianism. They say it's not like that – you know, it wasn't charming or nice-looking. That was one point – like it wasn't shown in a very aesthetic way, which for me makes it strong.

AM Presumably that would precisely be a complaint about other films (that is, pornographic films)?

CA Well, you know, they have problems with their own image, which is very understandable. I can't stand myself in the movie. I'm not a model and I know what it's like, it's hard. It's hard for people to talk about it too, they talk *around* the movie. And critics don't write in their own name ... it's as if their writing comes from somewhere else. (Martin, 1974)

Ackerman's oblique reply points up potential areas for consideration: the specific ways women's subjectivity and spectatorship are inflected by our own self images in interaction with the disembodying effect of perfected mainstream images on the one hand, and of the fragmented erogenous zones of pornography on the other; and the need for critical honesty and self examination when it comes to discussing difficult material, more personal and risky strategies.

Another of Ackerman's films, *Jeanne Dielman, 23 Quai de Commerce, 1080 Bruxelles* (1975), relocates prostitution in the respectable home of Jeanne Dielman. The name of the street in the title is typical of her understated irony. Jeanne's routine life is irreproachable in bourgeois terms, except that it is financed by her clients whose visits are as regular as her daily menus. One day, however, she unexpectedly has an orgasm. Her control has been disturbed and she kills the man. The portrayal of Jeanne through long takes of the details of her mundane regime which are indistinguishable from her sexual activity denies the possibility of voyeurism.

But one problem with such anti-cinematic strategies is that they can also deny pleasure. (This way, according to Mulvey, was an aim of radical feminist cinema.) They may result in the denial of all desire, including the female. Such alienating results have been attributed to Lizzie Borden's films, including *Working Girls* (see de Lauretis, 1990, p 14). This film is also about prostitution, portrayed through deliberately anti-erotic camera and editing techniques.[33] It is possible to ask, though, whether it is 'really' a denial of female desire that results, since what is being refused is one particular construction of pleasure, not some pure essence of pleasure-in-itself. This would locate the spectator's pleasure outside; and even if the 'outside' is not shown, it is implied. To relocate desire and its satisfaction is arguably to undermine masculinist constructions of desire. Narratives that enact anaesthetized female desire may furthermore give rise to an experience of the threat of annihilation which is resisted, and it is worth exploring spectator resistance as well as pleasure, especially since the *un*pleasure of resistance can be projected onto those who defy norms.

Implicit in these arguments is the point that cinema is inseparable from the erotic and from desire. Since this makes it a vital cultural space for lesbians in the construction of our meanings and the understanding of our subjectivities, the issue of pornography assumes some importance.

Discussion of cinematic lesbian pornography reflects the polemics of the pornography debates overall, and they are too vast to deal with here. My own position is complex; I have serious doubts about pornography as it exists at present, with my reservations about it stemming mainly from its inability so far to go convincingly beyond the constructions imposed by current modes of articulation. This is not to say that the erotic should always be discreetly veiled, or that the explicit is necessarily oppressive. I also find it useful to keep sight, for instance, of the difference between feminist interrogation of problematic areas and sociopolitical taboos.[34] Furthermore I do not see that a need for 'the thrill of the forbidden' is specifically helpful in expressing lesbian desire (Smyth, 1990, p 154), since sexual pleasure is to some degree forbidden in many different heterosexual contexts and cultures, and since certain kinds of legitimation also have radical potential. Romanticising the forbidden may be a useless political strategy, and positively dangerous in the era of AIDS.

Parveen Adams's discussion of lesbian sadomasochism[35] as having genuinely separated sex from gender (Brennan, 1989) opens on to possibilities for theorising lesbian desire that could be of importance in theorising lesbian pornography. My own disagreement with her hinges on her acceptance of a necessary relation to the phallus and the absence of any adequate analysis of power and the attribution of value; but there is no space here to do more than signal the arguments on either side. Suffice it to say that my assessment of lesbian pornography, as conservative rather than as radically progressive cinematic practice, is based on structural reasons analogous to those through which I would critique Adam's position. As Butler does (Butler, 1990, p 57), I question the reasoning that claims that 'the phallic' can only be defined according to the phallus as privileged signifier; the notion that lesbians can only theorise the representation of sexuality in film (or anywhere else) in relation to 'Laws', Lacanian or otherwise, appears to serve the interests of paternalist power too neatly. It is to remain within hierarchised systems of thought which are bound to become blocked because they attempt to fix and polarise psychic structures and events which are mobile and multiple.

For Teresa de Lauretis the controversial *She Must Be Seeing Things* (1987) is able to 'reclaim the function of voyeurism by rearticulating it in lesbian terms' (de Lauretis, 1990, p 23). For me, a crucial element in this is to be found in director Sheila McLaughlin's remark, 'I wanted to undermine the idea of women as narcissistic extensions of each other because I don't think it's true. That's not why women are together' (de Lauretis, 1990, p 23, and see Butler, 1987). The two protagonists, Agatha and Jo, are very different; Agatha is Brazilian and a successful lawyer, Jo is a blonde North American. 'Race' is an important element among many 'differences', but not the dominant. The stereotypes of the male-identified and childlike lesbian are played with and used to challenge the idea of the phallic power that produces them. McLaughlin describes a scene which is part of the process like this:

> ... when Jo does her dance in her little baby doll outfit, the camera starts off with a very 'male' point of view, as she does this traditional sex-strip dance. But it's undermined by the music she puts on. The image-sound tension makes it into a very weird thing that she's doing, and she makes it absolutely ridiculous. Agatha laughs at it, and when Jo puts her stockings on, there's a hole in one of them and her foot goes through it. (Butler, 1987, p 24)

The psychoanalytic structures I have been referring to throughout this account are explicitly at play in the film (and play is an important element), and the narrative resolution is brought about when the two women are viewing Jo's film in which a version of the woman's oedipal situation is rewritten:

> ... instead of the woman killing her mother in order to take her place, to be with the father, the man is killed and the woman runs away with the woman ... it becomes a sort of happy ending. (Butler, 1987, p 26)

The question of address is highly relevant to thinking about this film. McLaughlin thinks it is impossible for cinema to be non-voyeuristic, and so she chooses to explore whether 'the voyeuristic gaze can be anything but male ... What I wanted to do in the film was to make a voyeuristic female and constantly put her in the position of taking on the look' (p 27).

Nevertheless the question of whether the audience's relation to the film is intrinsically voyeuristic is worth exploring. De Lauretis's formulation offers the potentiality of a film that would '*address the spectator as female*' by which she means a multiple social subject: '... such a film's textual space would extend towards this spectator "in its erotic and critical dimensions, addressing, speaking-to, making room but not ... cajoling, soliciting, seducing"' (de Lauretis, 1990, p 14).

She Must Be Seeing Things may be used to introduce the final part of what I want to say here about lesbian cinema concerning form and whether innovative structures are necessarily more conducive to producing the new meanings essential for the development of lesbian cinema than classical narrative or other popular or mainstream structures. De Lauretis contrasts *She Must Be Seeing Things* with 'romance or fairy-tale formulas', including *Desert Hearts*.[36] While I have some sympathy with elements of her argument in this respect (especially as regards *Liana* and *I've Heard the Mermaids Singing*) I would not wish to imply that it is a necessary principle that formal innovation is necessary to semantic innovation.[37]

The issue has elements in common with literary debates about 'écriture des femmes', and the French film-maker Agnes Varda indeed names her (anti)cinematic practice 'cinécriture' (p 286). Susan Hayward has argued for Varda's work as 'femme-filmécriture' in relation to *Sans toit ni loi* in 'Beyond the gaze and into *femme-filmécriture*'.

> The film is a series of gazes, of one-way exchanges from different specular positions. Each contributor fixes their gaze not on Mona but on their perception of Mona as a figure of their desire. As such, each portrait offered up to the spectator is revealing of the relator and not of the related. The effect is to empty the mirror of ascribed meanings. Male discourses (whether uttered by women or men) cannot produce her identity. (Hayward and Vincendeau, 1990, p 286)

In the end, Mona (who is a corpse at the beginning of the film), 'leaves no trace' (p 286). It is a kind of refusal of identity which I find difficult to reconcile with my sense of lesbian or women's desire as going beyond male emptiness; its strategy seems rather to be towards a decon-structive narrative about masculinist desire.

The other side of this question of whether avant-garde form is nec-essarily progressive is clearly whether established or popular form is necessarily retrograde. I would not want to overstate the case for *Desert Hearts*, but its romanticism can belie its achievement in some respects, and it was knowingly constructed for a lesbian audience at a particular time. Its popularity suggests it found it.

Very few films, indeed, take up the position of *Desert Hearts*, whose primary address is to lesbians, but to lesbians as a knowing part of the mainstream audience. It is for this reason that it is indispensable when talking about lesbians and films. I have many reservations about the film itself, but its situation on the edge of the mainstream is an interesting one.[38] As will be clear so far, the position of the lesbian movie-goer and film critic is often either that of eavesdropper on multiple cultural events enacted across her or in the position of performer of complex subjective manoeuvres which allow her to change, more or less radically, this position. Much of the pleasure of watching *Desert Hearts* may well derive from its simplicity in this respect. It draws on popular genres, but is unambiguously lesbian in storyline. Whether the same is true of its structural narrative meanings is less clear, since it remains an open question whether the relationship between Cay and Vivien will survive transposition into the world outside the transitional space and time of the period of waiting for Vivien's divorce.

Firmly situated as it is in the mainstream, perhaps *Thelma and Louise*, ostensibly a straight film, may serve to illustrate the point that a romance formula can work within the context of lesbian cinema, and indeed with 'guerrilla cinema'. The reviewer who said that *Thelma and Louise* would do more for women than all the writings of Andrea Dworkin, despite his crassness, has almost touched on a point.[39] What he didn't allow was the intricate processes through which activists like Dworkin or experimental film-makers – the culturally marginalised – contribute to bringing to public consciousness the issues underlying *Thelma and Louise*. The film was more widely reviewed by mainstream film writers than almost any other film which raises feminist issues and arguments. Yet a virtual silence was maintained over what relation it might bear to lesbianism.[40]

The commonest interpretation of the narrative was as one of revenge, even 'the perfect fantasy of revenge',[41] and on the surface it is easy to see why. Yet revenge is the motivating force behind none of the structural events and only one minor comic scene (where Thelma and Louise humiliate and frighten a tanker driver, ultimately blowing up his vehicle by mistake), which could be removed without affecting the narrative structure at all. Reading the film in terms of revenge, however, keeps the story within the dominant terms of reference; as a form in English drama, it is tragic, and its resolution is that the defeat of the 'hero' effects, or makes possible, the return to morality and order. Events turn on the machinations of the 'hero' and (usually) his story is meaningless without reference to the prevailing power structures. The catharsis, or the emotional satisfaction, comes from the inevitable and justified defeat of the vengeful.

None of this is applicable to *Thelma and Louise*. It is carefully constructed to be liberally fair to the good guys, but they are irrelevant to what becomes the women's quest for freedom. The narrative turns on the women's resistance to an act of sexual violence which produces an outcome more violent than would be conceivable otherwise; the characterisation of both main protagonists is consistent, almost scrupulous,[42] far from stereotyped, and neither of the women is violent. Louise finds Thelma about to be raped, pulls out the gun she is looking after for Louise, who can barely stand to touch it, uses it to stop the rape, and not until the would-be rapist attacks her with verbal violence does she shoot him. It later emerges that Louise herself is a rape survivor; her one violent act is thus a partial consequence of male violence against her, the other part being male violence against her friend. The women's subsequent transgressive acts are all motivated by provocation and/or necessity if they are to achieve their goal, which is Mexico, an 'elsewhere' beyond the laws they have broken and the identities they have left behind. As Louise says near the end, they have 'crossed over', something she realises very early on in the film. Thelma has much further to go, but through a series of choices also comes to the same realisation, concisely symbolised through parallel shots of her use of the wing mirror of the car that is the material means of their movement beyond: at the beginning she looks at herself, posing. At the end, she looks at the landscape ahead and behind, realising that, for the first time in her life, she is fully awake. The final decision, to drive into unknown immensity (in the case over the edge of a precipice into the Grand Canyon), recapitulates what they have been doing all along. Before it happens, they share an unerotic kiss. Then they drive over, hands joined in triumphal salute. Crucially, the final frame is a freeze of the car in flight; it does not land, there is no twisted metal or broken bodies. It cuts quickly to repeat optimistic moments from earlier in the film. The effect is exhilarating and the narrative resolution affirms the women's true freedom with each other. They have lived, and it was only possible by breaking patriarchal laws enforced by violence.

Leaving aside its symbolic truth about lesbians' contemporary position, and its potential as an allegory of many formerly straight-identified women's realisation of their lesbianism, the question I want to stay with is that of how the narrative can be read as moving towards lesbian desire. Teresa de Lauretis, as we have to an extent seen, finds that *She Must be Seeing Things* is almost unique in that it poses in its formal structure the question of representative possibility itself; 'how to represent a female, lesbian desire that is neither masculine, a usurpation of male heterosexual desire, nor a feminine, narcissistic identification with the other woman' (p 24). By making visible the 'cultural imaginary' of the dominant cinema and the relations of desire within the fantasy, the film is seen to pose 'the question of desire and its representation from within the context of actual practices of both lesbianism and cinema' (pp 24–5).

Clearly this is a different project from *Thelma and Louise*, and an extremely important one. Yet there is a level on which using popular form[43] inflected with a clear feminist articulation of the transgressive possibilities of women's desire is a complementary strategy for the 'guerrilla cinema' for which de Lauretis powerfully argues. The film is situated within the realities of contemporary western women's experience and moves from a situation in which autonomous friendship between women is impossible (Thelma has to get her infantile husband's permission to go away – not doing so is her first transgressive act) to one in which a return to men is impossible.[44] The trajectory of the narrative does not follow that of heterosexual, masculine usurpation or feminine narcissism, and the women are both portrayed as subjects and objects of desire. If that desire is not containable within recognisable forms of male desire, but rather reaches beyond them, perhaps that is the point.

Acknowledgment

Thanks to Lizzie Thynne for her comments on the first draft of this chapter and for sharing her knowledge of film with me.

8   Lesbians and Popular Music: Does It Matter Who Is Singing?

Barbara Bradby

Authorship, identity and everyday life

Much recent lesbian writing both about subjective identity and about the question of 'authorship' has been preoccupied with what it means to 'be', or to write as, a lesbian, and, combining these, whether it matters if the author of a text 'is' lesbian. Judith Butler (1991), for instance, writes interestingly of what it feels like to go to a conference 'as' a lesbian, and the element of performance involved even for someone who from late adolescence has always recognised herself as lesbian. Sally Munt (1992) poses a series of questions about the relationship of personal experience, and the personal text, to a lesbian criticism which arises in part out of post-structuralist theory, and which therefore recognises neither 'the author', nor, in any simple sense, 'the subject', lesbian or otherwise. Her piece suggests that one should neither prohibit, nor insist on, the validity or primacy of personal experience, but should rather see it as an historical construction:

> A less essentialising version of experience would recognise its construction in ideological practices, allowing for the expression, perhaps, of essentialist moments as an expedient political trajectory. (Munt, 1992, p xvi)

These debates echo those around the notions of 'woman' and 'women's writing' of the previous decade. Toril Moi's influential *Sexual/Textual Politics*, for instance, was similarly open to the 'schizophrenic' solution that insisted on the death of the white, male author, and simultaneously asserted the 'political' importance of female, Black, lesbian, and all other 'marginal' authors (1985). She based her feminist textual politics in the notion that such marginal authors and critics could expose the fallacy of liberal humanist versions of 'the author', which linked the text to the subject as the expression of an inner being. For feminist critics to attempt to fix the woman's text as the expression of any inner female essence, even if revised to include 'anger' (Gilbert and Gubar, 1984), was simply to fall into the practices

148

of the dominant ideologies. Against such arguments, literary critics like Nancy Miller have turned again to the personal narrative, in a way that exposes the contradiction involved in accepting both post-structuralism's rigorous deconstruction of 'essences' and the need to value and write women's experience (Miller, 1990, 1991).

In the area of popular music, it seems that everyday listening practices raise similar puzzles around the performer of a song as are raised around the author of a text. There is a similar illusion of the 'presence' of the singer through her/his voice, which speaks apparently to us even as we listen to what we know is a recording (Bloomfield, 1993).[1] Women as singers of popular music are in a peculiarly ambiguous position, since 'rock' criticism has continually used traditional models of authorship to *discredit* female performers in the search for male authority figures such as 'the producer' (Greig, 1989; Bradby, 1990). Madonna's rise to critical acclaim (which is not the same as her rise to fame) could be charted through the appearance in criticism of the words 'in control', an authorial myth of herself as her own producer which she has to carry to ever greater heights.[2]

One of the impasses in these ongoing debates seems to have been the failure to see any level of social investigation *between* the literary or cultural text and autobiography; or put another way, the failure to see 'consciousness' and 'experience' as themselves socially generated in interaction. The project implied by Munt, of research into how 'essentialist' ideologies were part of the social process that was the early women's movement, remains largely to be carried out. Instead, she herself seems to see personal experience, or 'feeling', as opposed to intellectual reasoning:

> Myself, in the main I agree with Fuss that 'lesbian' is a historical construction of comparatively recent date, and that there is no eternal lesbian essence outside the frame of cultural change and historical determination.[3] However, this strictly intellectual definition wouldn't stop me *feeling*, and sometimes behaving, as though the total opposite were true. (Munt, 1992, p xviii)

In the continuation of this passage, however, she produces a more *sociological* explanation for her 'feeling':

> We need our dream of a lesbian nation, even as we recognise its fictionality – rather as we need our Madonna myth: an image of lesbian sexuality which we have projected as authentic, as the 'real' Madonna. The pleasure derived from this reading, that of an apparently knowing

reinscription, is of her belonging to us, and as readers/consumers our oppositional sexual desire is affirmed, ironically, by an apparently paradigmatic heterosexuality. It is a fantasy which effectively cements a common identity (but trivialises contradiction). (Munt, 1992, p xviii)

Munt here recognises the *social* nature of lesbian myth-making, a process which I shall argue is prior to individual 'feelings'. She does not go one step further and see this process as actually worth social investigation. It was evident, for instance, in the research I did for this paper, that the 'Madonna-myth' meant different things for different lesbians, and that aspects of Madonna-as-lesbian could be used by lesbians in ways that were oppressive to other lesbians.[4] And there is also presumably a history of how and when this Madonna-myth arose, in which media stories about Madonna's lesbian affair would have been important, as well as the release and 'banning' of the video for 'Justify My Love' in 1990.[5]

The process that Munt is pointing to (in what is, for her, only an aside about Madonna) is one which involves an interplay between personal identity and the identity of a performer, a process which is socially mediated through the everyday practices of the lesbian 'community'. This approach has much in common with Richard Dyer's approach to authorship in the lesbian/gay film text, when he confronts the same paradox of needing to 'believe in' notions of 'the author' and of 'the homosexual' which he knows rationally are only historical constructs (1991). Dyer produces what is effectively a sociological reason for his continued 'belief' in lesbian/gay authorship:

What is significant is the authors' material social position in relation to discourse, the access to discourses they have on account of who they are. For my purposes, what was important was their access to filmic and lesbian/gay sub-cultural discourses. In other words, because they were lesbian or gay, they could produce lesbian/gay representations that could themselves be considered lesbian/gay, not because all lesbians or gay men inevitably express themselves on film in a certain way, but because they had access to, and an inwardness with, lesbian/gay sign systems that would have been like foreign languages to straight filmmakers. (Dyer, 1991, p 188)

Such a grounding, he argues, takes one away from purely 'textual' readings and a concentration on a limited number of 'lesbian/gay' texts, but neither does one have to take refuge in the other extreme of 'camp', where anything can be appropriated as gay/lesbian according to the context (Dyer, 1991, pp 188–9).

Dyer's emphasis is, however, still on the film *texts*. The sociology of particular authors, their position within particular societies and their relations with the other 'authors' within the team that produces a film, are important for what they tell us about *the meaning of the film*, albeit as a representation of lesbian or gay lives. Valuable as this approach to authorship and identity is, it does, like other textual approaches, obscure the meanings which actual audiences take from such films. If what we are ultimately interested in is lesbian and gay people, then we need to reverse the questions that are being asked, and see how film, or other cultural products, are given meaning by people in social life, treated as a process rather than a text.

More broadly, Munt's notion of 'a fantasy which effectively cements a common identity' can serve as a starting-point for looking at the role that popular music has been made to play in establishing and reproducing this lesbian community. In other words, instead of trying to use textual methods of investigation to determine whether a song has a lesbian meaning or not, I shall be using sociological methods to see what importance the identity of the performer has in the everyday processes of lesbian interaction. Reversing the terms of Dyer's approach, the question becomes *why and how the question of authorship matters in the lives of those who live the particular culture*. This approach seems to me to return the focus of investigation onto lesbian lives, but without taking refuge in a 'personal' experience, which ironically ends up 'speaking for' and excluding other voices and experiences.

This was part of a broader research question of what is the meaning of popular music in lesbians' lives, in the context of a local setting in Dublin. In this research the question of 'authorship' emerges as the everyday question of 'Is she/isn't she a dyke?', which underlies not only talk about pop music, but perhaps also any display of competence as a member of the culture. In other words, part of the shared sign system of the lesbian world *is* a knowledge of who is a lesbian, whether as 'out' or 'closeted', in the world of pop performers. But this knowledge should not be thought of as simply fixed for all time: rather, meanings are negotiated in conversation, and in the relationship between conversation and texts, both written and musical (Smith, 1987). Conversation is a process, and meanings may be worked and reworked, in response to new information that becomes available, or as new theoretical perspectives on feminism and lesbianism work their way through into everyday life, or simply when what was a sort of collective fantasy about someone loses its originality and fades. This everyday knowledge, then, includes a range of options between the lesbian and the straight, such as 'she might be', 'she deserves to be', 'she isn't but she looks like one'; and it is across this range that everyday conversations choose, discriminate, and rationalise such choices. My argument will be that such meanings are not simply inherent in musical or song texts, but that they are produced socially in interaction, and in turn embodied in material practices such as the exchange of cassette tapes, DJs' promotion of certain musics, dancing at discos.[6]

When I started on this research, it was with the expectation that I would find a straightforward dichotomy between 'lesbian music', deriving from the 'women's music' movement in the United States in the 1970s and 1980s, and lesbian *appropriations* of mainstream popular music. The former had, as far as I knew, never been particularly well-known in Ireland, while the latter, from my (very intermittent) acquaintance with lesbian bars and discos in the first half of the 1980s, I found interesting, but often disturbing. I had vague memories of being 'turned off' by the playing of male rock classics in lesbian contexts, songs which I had myself at that time rejected because of the way they objectify women. At the time I was more interested in reclaiming once-popular female performers, briefly in making up tapes for feminist discos, and more long term, as a topic of academic research.

Returning to the scene, or rather, a different scene, after several years of late motherhood, and in the context of research rather than feminist politics or pleasure-seeking, I found this dichotomy much less straightforward than I expected. The American 'lesbian music' did figure in women's lives largely as history, and was ridiculed by some, but at the same time, the personal history in which it figured was often the crucial period of 'coming out'. On the other hand, the process of 'appropriation' of the mainstream tended to be overridden by two different processes. One was the process of differentiation among lesbians along complex lines of class and 'politicisation', which I feel reflects less social class origins than class mobility. The other was the generalised, but fluid process of claiming mainstream musicians *as* lesbian. It was here that as an outsider to the culture I found the most immediate difficulties in my lack of knowledge of shared assumptions. But precisely in the encounter between myself as outsider and the insiders I talked with, these assumptions, and the reasoning and emotions underpinning them, had to be spelled out, and so became more 'visible' on the surface of conversation than might otherwise be the case.[7]

The fieldwork on which this chapter draws has been limited in scope. It was carried out in May–June 1992, and is based mainly on in-depth unstructured interviews with five lesbian women, and one self-defined bisexual woman in Dublin; three of these are or have been DJs, the other three being friends of mine who were prepared to be 'interviewed' about how popular music figured in their lives as lesbians. Two of the DJs made me up tapes of some favourite tracks, in one case, or of records that were played a lot in the club in another. Several women taped other material for me, or lent me tapes. I also have notes on music played in the two discos at present operating on Friday and Saturday nights respectively in Dublin, and on some conversations about music and 'singing along' to songs in these clubs. I make no claim to have covered all aspects of lesbian music in Dublin: a serious omission is the lesbian band Zrazy, who happened to be touring England while I was doing this work, and are shortly to release their first single.

The interviews are not intended to be representative. The age-range, in particular, is limited, all the women being in their thirties or early forties. All are Irish, though one is resident in the United States and was back for the summer vacation from her university job. Four of them have at least one third-level degree, and of the two who do not, one is starting a degree course next year, and the other is working teaching drama and other courses for women. I have given the women I talked with pseudonyms, apart from Joni, who wanted her real name to be used. (The name of one of the pubs where a weekly disco is held has also been changed, since the DJ working there thought this was preferable.)

I have transcribed the interviews literally, i.e. indicating spoken repetition, interruptions, overlap, and some tone variation. Such 'real' speech is difficult to read, but I prefer to work with it rather than with an edited version, which turns the raw material of everyday life into something more like the text of a play, and which introduces the biases of the editor. I see these transcripts as part of an (always incomplete) ethnographic project through which the researcher tries to describe a culture from the point of view of its members. Within this approach, I see the detailed analysis of interview conversations as important. My analyses are interpretive, and to that extent subjective, and make no claim to a rigorous method. They draw eclectically on insights from qualitative methods in sociology, in particular the notions that conversation is a collaborative social process, and that it is important to describe not only what people are saying, but also what they are 'doing' with what they say. Notes on transcript conventions are given at the end of the chapter.

The next section looks at what the people that spoke to me had to say about the 'women's music' genre, that is, music produced by lesbians for a lesbian audience, mainly emanating from the United States. Listening to such music, reading record sleeves, etc, one is left in no doubt that this is 'lesbian music', whereas with almost any other of the performers who are popular among lesbians, there is no such certainty. Most, but not all, of the women I interviewed, distinguished this music from that of performers on mainstream record labels, even where these performers are 'known' to be lesbian. I deal later with what people said about these practices of 'knowing' (which overlap with those of 'fantasising') a performer to be lesbian. Also, I will look more briefly at processes of 'appropriation', that is where there is no supposition that the performer 'is' lesbian, and yet the song can be heard as a song for lesbians and used as such. Finally I will draw some conclusions in relation to the questions raised in this introduction.

'Women's music' and lesbian identity

The origins of 'women's music' in the United States in the 1970s were closely bound up with the politics of protest song and of the women's liberation movement (Lont, 1985), but it quite soon developed, as did part of the women's movement, into a specifically lesbian form, so that its very title assumes the identity of 'woman' with 'lesbian' (Clark, 1982). Lesbian feminism was manifested not just in the songs themselves, but also in the social relations of producing and distributing the songs (Lont, 1985). Record labels such as Olivia and Redwood in the United States were organised along non-hierarchical principles, outside of the commercial circuits of the mainstream record industry, and distribution was through women's bookshops and other alternative outlets, such as the Women's Revolutions Per Minute organisation in Britain (Lont, 1985, Steward and Garratt, 1984, p 71). One DJ I interviewed had got a few records from WRPM, but on the whole, 'women's music' has never been easy to access in Ireland.

If we look first of all at how such music was received in lesbian discos, Joni recounts a negative experience as DJ of the longest-running disco:

Extract 1 (interview with Joni Crone, 25/5/92, transcript p 1)

1 B Anyway so (.) em one of the one of the central questions that, the you know has eme-, emerged in talking to people is how important is it that a woman, *is* a dyke, when you hear her sing (.) to, whether it becomes lesbian music, whether it becomes popular, lesbian music?

2 J I think it's far less important, em it's not important in fact at all I'd say, and and the kind of evidence for that if you like is my own experience in trying to introduce dyke music, music *on* Olivia records written by and for dykes about, you know, dyke lifestyles and em, using the words lesbian, dyke, whatever, and em, even without using the words, lesbian love songs written, to lesbians and for lesbians, and, you know, it's much harder to popularise that or to even make it familiar to people than, the top twenty, music that people are familiar with and identify with

Paradoxically, then, lesbians can 'identify' more with chart music than with 'lesbian' music. It would seem that the identity of the performer is not actually important to the reception of music by lesbians. The positive identification with chart music is elaborated in the following extract, where Joni also points to an opposition between 'lesbian' and 'feminist' identity:

Extract 2 (interview with Joni Crone, 25/5/92, transcript p 1)

1 J I mean I'm thinking more recently of Michael Jackson, for instance, the the whole album 'Bad' is very popular, in lesbian discos and the videos and all the rest, I mean we didn't show any videos, but to me all the videos are highly pornographic, explicitly pornographic, you know, and a lot of S and M stuff, leather stuff, it seemed to be very whoorish the images of the women so that didn't seem to have any effect on the majority of, lesbians who wanted to dance to this music.

2 B ((talks about song she can't remember title of))

3 J And there's I he did one with Paul McCartney as well, My Girl or something,[8] and you know they're kind of, arguing over, yeah? I mean I used to make a distinction myself as DJ, I just took my own feminist consciousness, but I was forever ((laughing)) appalled huh huh huh, at the kind of lack of discrimination

It was 'lesbians' who wanted to dance to this music, displaying 'lack of discrimination', while 'feminist' consciousness would have rejected it. Joni goes on to argue that the political importance of the disco lies in its social function as a meeting place, the function of the music being to make that environment 'familiar' for lesbians, a term first raised in the opening exchange of the interview (extract 1 above), and which is repeated several times.

The contrast between 'feminists' and 'lesbians' is also overlaid with class meanings:

Extract 3 (interview with Joni Crone, 25/5/92, transcript p 6)

1 B   And your life must have been absolutely fascinating, em, you
        know, watching that community grow and everything that's
        happened since, but at the same time, there's a repressed history
        there

2 J   Yeh, and I think the kind of exciting part of the disco was
        seeing women from so many different walks of life, like I think
        it did start out more as a (.) em, a feminist, maybe middle-class
        mixture of highly politicised women, and then it changed to being
        more kind of working-class and women into, what we'd now
        call bar dykes, heavy drinking and darts playing and pool playing
        and stuff, and then it changed again into more sort of//

3 B   /Where can you play darts and pool?/

4 J   Used to be able to in P.J.'s and also in Tailors' Hall, so seeing the
        way that it's grown, you know, and the mixture of classes (.)

In turn 2 here, Joni deconstructs my suggestion of 'community' in turn 1, and brings me firmly back to the class differences within lesbian culture. I unfortunately interrupt her before she finishes her analysis. Her notion of a 'mixture of classes' at turn 4 perhaps produces some reconciliation with my notion of 'community'.

Earlier on, Joni has said that she did play 'more folk music' in the late 1970s, and mentions 'Peggy Seeger and "I wanna be an engineer" and stuff'. It seems that this was 'political' music for a 'politicised' audience, and that as the bar became more working-class and more 'lesbian' in orientation, it became more difficult to play music that denoted 'politics', including the Olivia Records music that Joni talked about. The process that Joni is pointing to, which is one that happened over time, seems to be one of internal differentiation among lesbians, in which different kinds of music ('political' lesbian music versus 'chart' music) became symbolic markers of difference. Joni describes this difference in class terms, yet class cannot necessarily be taken as a determinate external factor. For instance, Joni herself saw her own class origins as 'definitely working class', immediately qualifying this by saying that her mother reared her with 'more middle-class values': but Joni's alignment in the bar is with the 'maybe middle-class' feminists, rather than with the 'more kind of working-class' bar dykes. This could imply that certain kinds of lesbian behaviour (more 'feminist' or more 'bar' oriented) come to have 'class' connotations, rather than economic class simply determining behaviour.[9] Such a process of differentiation would help to explain why it was that the music that was most overtly committed to the expression of open lesbian desire was actually rejected by those whom Joni called 'lesbians'.

How then do the consumers of this 'women's music' see it now? In extract 4, I am talking to Cliona, a friend of mine who sees herself as bisexual, and who has lived in a lesbian partnership for about seven years now. Just prior to this, I have mentioned the fact that Cliona has to leave soon, and we are initially here trying to identify music that she could tape for me:

Extract 4 (interview with Cliona, 12/6/92, transcript p 3)

1 B um (.) Who's the other person you said that, you listened to a lot (?)
2 C Cris Williamson?
3 B Oh yeh, have you got a ta- have you got a record of hers
4 C (?) yes, I have, yes, yes (.) and a woman called Ferron, have you come across her?
5 B Who?
6 C Ferron, F-e-r-r-o-n// {American again},// again passed// {on to} me// by, other women, and there's somebody else ((whispers a rhythm, as if irritated not to be able to remember a name)) de-de-di-dah
7 B /{Heard the name yeah}/ /no/ /{yeah}/ /yeah/
8 B (.) Have you heard of Phranc at all, with a p-h
9 C No(.) Phranc?
10 B Yeah, Phranc with a p-h, she's an American woman, again coming out of that scene, erm, Holly Near do you listen to at all?
11 C ((non-committal tone)) Yes, yeah
12 B Um, and would these be things that you listen to a *lot* at home

13 C   No ((laughs slightly))

14 B   ((laughs slightly)) No

15 C   They were, at one stage, maybe, at the coming-out stage, people
        would have given me those tapes and I would have listened avidly
        to them and, now I just listen to music, full stop, and

16 B   Yeah

17 C   Emm, Tracy Chapman I would listen quite a lot to, probably
        would be, of them all would be, emm, *funny* things get adopted,
        d'you know that Le Mystère des Voix Bulgaires, did you hear
        those//(?) those women, they were taken on (and) big by by a
        certain *kind* of lesbian, by sort of, could be more, political sort
        of, amm, and there was somebody else, somebody very unusual
        like that, that we had discovered ourselves, and then discovered
        that a lot of other women that we knew were listening to them
        as well (.) but I suppose simply that they w- it was an all-women
        group maybe and amm and the music was *wonderful*

18 B   /*Oh yes*!, they were incredible yeah/

We seem here to be operating with different definitions of 'women's
music'. My own definition is really a 'marketing' one, which distinguishes
the 'women's music' of the alternative lesbian music scene, from
mainstream music sung by women performers who *appeal* to lesbians,
(and who may even 'be' lesbian, but who are not 'out' to their heterosexual audience). For instance, Tracy Chapman, who is on the
'major' US label, Elektra Records, would be for me a 'mainstream'
musician, while Cris Williamson, who is on Olivia Records, would be
a 'lesbian' artist. Cliona does not, on one level, acknowledge this distinction. She has already talked extensively about how she 'knows' that
Tracy Chapman is lesbian, and talked about Cris Williamson in a very
similar way. It seems that what is most important for her is the network
of exchange with other women which popular music provides.
Exchanging tapes is a practice that creates a friendship network, and
through listening to other women's tapes, one learns about other
women, and becomes part of a network of shared cultural knowledge.
Tapes given and lent in this way of course come with less written information than would records bought in shops. This may facilitate Cliona's
construction of a social 'map' of lesbian music which grows out of her
local friendship networks, rather than out of any marketing categories.
In a sense she recognises women's music, not 'women's music'.

Of course, on another level, Cliona does make a distinction which
coincides with my categories, even if it has a different rationale. Tracy

Chapman is someone that she would 'listen quite a lot to', whereas the other three she does not. Even here Cliona talks of Chapman as the one 'of them all' that she would listen to, implying that 'they' do all belong to the same category. But it is interesting that she does not identify Chapman as 'American', whereas she does signal this for Cris Williamson and Ferron, and I do the same for Phranc, and by implication for Holly Near. This suggests that Cliona hears Chapman's music as more 'global' than the other performers, for whom their 'American-ness' has become a *localising* characteristic (Frith, 1991).

But Cliona has one clear personal association for this American women's music, and it is with the period of 'coming out'. Despite the slight laughter that this music evokes for her now, it obviously was important for her in the past, and a bit later in the interview she says that she still gets it out again from time to time, and would 'scream out the lyrics going along in a car', or would put it on when 'in a holiday mood with a lot of housework to do'. Perhaps this indicates some residual loyalty, both to the music, and to the life-stage with which she associates it.

Some similar points emerge in an interview I arranged with two women I knew from the university context. Amanda was back from the United States, where she teaches gay/lesbian studies in a university, and Mairead completed a Master's in Women's Studies in Dublin last year. I had talked to both of them independently about the project I was doing, and had introduced them briefly in one of the lesbian weekly discos a couple of weeks before, but otherwise they did not know each other. Extract 5 shows how important a certain 'expert' knowledge of music, in this case 'women's music', is to being accepted as one of the lesbian community:

Extract 5 (Interview with Amanda and Mairead, 21/5/92, tape 1, transcript p 5)

1 B Yeah (.) And what about um all this ehm what I associated with
      lesbian music in the seventies, or early eighties// Holly Near, er,
2 A /Holly Near/ aaagggh, yell Holly Near,/// Oh, OHH
3 M /I don't know Holly Near/. Oh
4 B Cris Williamson,// Meg Christian?
5 M /Oh, Cris Williamson, yeah/
6 A Yeah

Amanda's exaggerated display of emotion when I mention seventies lesbian music and she chips in with Holly Near's name (turn 2), indicates both that this is something she is very familiar with, *and* that it is something she doesn't like. 'Yell Holly Near' presumably evokes ironically the mass adulation that Holly might receive among a certain group of lesbians from whom Amanda's irony distances her. All this displays a lot of insider knowledge very economically, but also demands a lot from her audience, and it is difficult for Mairead to remain uninvolved. Perhaps the disapproval evident in Amanda's 'aaagggh' in turn 2 gives Mairead a basis for admitting that she has never heard of Holly Near (turn 3). Nevertheless it is a risky strategy that immediately excludes her from the group of insiders, and could warrant a putdown. Luckily she recognises the next name I mention (this all happens quite fast, and my turn 4 is only the continuation of turn 1). At turn 5, she repeats the name 'Cris Williamson' after me in a tone that indicates both recognition of the singer, and a location of the musical genre we are talking about. She has shown that she does share insider knowledge and so is back in the group again, and her inclusion is acknowledged by Amanda (turn 6).

In the immediate continuation of this conversation (extract 6), Amanda makes it clear that there is a difference between the Irish and the American context in relation to such music, which in a sense excuses Mairead's never having come across it. She then goes on to set this music up as a joke, an object of humour (extract 6, turn 2):

Extract 6 (Interview with Amanda and Mairead, 21/5/92, tape 1, transcript p 5)

1 B does that mean anything to you, do you, do you listen to it at all

2 A It certainly didn't when I was *here*, then when I went to the States, you know, a lot of my friends are all into that, an um, you know, I have the one Cris Williamson that I play almost for, like, *hu*mour's sake, more than anything else, you know, filling up and spilling it over, that one, and I always, end up, falling around the place *laugh*ing, (did) Holly Near make, no they really just, the music doesn't interest me.

3 B {What sort of music would you categorise it as}

4 M {You see that's just, yeah}

5 A ((laughing)) Women's music ((laughter)) // she says, WHHAMM, and women's music festivals, I mean you know,

and Alex Dobkin, there's a whole, there's a whole group of women and you know, sometimes I stop myself, because now it's really become a thing to dump on all those women (.) you know, a lot of, like I heard this (sort of) lesbian comedian (.) in Atlanta recently, and she just went *off* on Holly Near, and (.) it was, it was very, it was very funny and very sharp, and then afterwards it left a bad taste in your mouth, I mean (.) why does one need to rip Holly Near to pieces, I mean after all, she's not exactly a cultural icon, // you know

6   M   ((laughing)) /yeah, you get, yes, yeah, yeah/ /right/

My question at turn 3 only increases the joke for Amanda. Throughout the interview she presents herself as *not* an expert on popular music (though clearly an 'expert' lesbian), and therefore unable to fulfil the role of pop quiz contestant that my questions sometimes imply. Her 'silly' answer at turn 5, 'women's music' (that is, a restatement of the obvious, when I might have expected an answer such as 'folk' or 'protest'), nevertheless succeeds in economically making a point about what 'we' have now rejected in separatist politics. Mairead (interruption at turn 6) joins in appreciating this point. Amanda immediately continues by reflecting on what she has just said, referring to herself in the third person ('she says') and to the destructive purport of what she has just said ('WHHAMM'). Then after another set of references to the American women's music scene, she says 'sometimes I stop myself' (as she already just has), and proceeds to distance herself from those who make fun of this scene.

However, clearly the joke had been *made* before this ironic distancing process, so that it is necessary for Amanda to justify her dislike of this music. She semi-jokingly introduces the notion of 'sophistication': 'it's not sophisticated for us cool, clean dykes of the 1990s'. Then she continues with a more political analysis, in terms of the alignment between 'radical feminists' and the 'anti-pornography movement' in the United States. Such feminists, she argues, see sexuality as needing to be contained, and women as morally superior beings; 'women's music' goes with these beliefs. This opinion is certainly not unique. Steward and Garrett in writing about American 'women's music' describe it as 'often fairly safe, folksy-sounding music' (1985, p 71). This comes back to the question of musical style which was also raised by Joni in trying to explain the paradox of lesbians not liking 'lesbian music'.[10]

Another possible resolution of the paradox lies in what one might call the 'life-cycle' of lesbianism. 'Coming out' is a stage in a life which is usually *recalled*, and the person who is recalling tends to see this stage as a transitional one out of naivete and misrecognition of self, into a more sophisticated present self. Amanda, elsewhere in the interview, described her coming out in very much these terms, and also talked of the importance of Joan Armatrading's music to her in this transitional period. Both she and Cliona seemed to have a residual *loyalty* to this music that accompanied, and often illuminated this stage in their lives, even though both the music and, in Amanda's case, the life-stage itself, were now a source of some humour.

Appropriating the mainstream (the girl is mine?)

That is a difficult area to write about, partly because 'appropriation' is an analytical term, and those whose practices might be analysed as 'appropriation' don't call it this; and partly because where some might see 'appropriation', other lesbians see simply political incorrectness. What am I to make, for instance, of one DJ telling me that in the other club (there are two) they used to play a lot of 'male stuff' including Van Halen and Status Quo, music she describes as 'sexist'? This echoes my own past unease with hearing male rock in the same lesbian bar. But my present experience of this bar, 'P.J. Murphy's', and an interview with Patricia who does DJ there, when we went through her record collection, doesn't actually confirm this. There is much more 'chart' music played than in the other bar, but it seems to me quite carefully selected. And so *much* pop music is open to appropriation. I was struck by two women singing along to Cliff Richard's 'It's so funny, how we don't talk any more', making eye contact across a table as they did. Later Patricia explained to me that this was a new 'dance' version of his hit, and that was why she had played it. But this was irrelevant to the use the women were making of it. I was also struck by the amount of conversation there was about popular music in this bar. A woman sat down beside me and started up a conversation about Shakespear's Sister's video for their song 'Stay', which was number one in the charts during those weeks. When I said something about the old theme of division among women, a sharp retort came back about my 'feminist analysis', and inability to see the joke. 'I mean, this was two women arguing over a *corpse*, ferchrissake.'

'P.J.'s' has an uneasy status within the lesbian community. Mairead, who admitted to never having been there, referred to it as a 'meat-market', and Amanda, who would have gone there 10 years ago, but not now, talked about all the 'fights' which used to happen there. Even

Joni, long time DJ there, seems to have felt pressurised by her audience there. In extract 2 above, Joni gave a concrete example of a song whose use she disapproved of, the Michael Jackson/Paul McCartney collaboration, 'The Girl is Mine', a hit single in 1982, and on the Michael Jackson *Thriller* album. What seems to me objectionable about this song from a feminist point of view is not its tug-of-war love triangle, but the way in which it establishes a 'buddy' relationship between the two male singers: the musical message seems to me to be that no woman is important enough to come between two men. But if two *women* were to sing this song, or even to imagine themselves in its principal parts, the meaning changes, since the relationship of friendly rivalry over 'the girl' is set up between two women. If women were able to say to each other that romantic involvement should not destroy friendships, it would surely have a very different meaning from men saying this in a heterosexual context.[11]

Finally I turn to a case where Mairead is talking about her own practice of 'appropriation' and how this is disallowed by other lesbians. The context is that of a slight misunderstanding with Amanda about what she means by 'political correctness':

Extract 7 (Interview with Amanda and Mairead, 21/5/92, tape 1, transcript p 6)

1 M Yeah, the the the the whole P.C. thing bothers me, because I think there's something inherently very oppressive within it, and it really bothers me,// {so if you listen}

2 A /{Well I still don't know}/ what you're even talking about, what, what, in what sense d'you mean P.C.

3 M Well, I mean, OK//(?)

4 A /(?) does that mean women's music/

5 M Yeah, yeah sure, I mean I have made tapes, I have a *wide* variety of musical collection of everything you can imagine,// right? Barbara knows that, I'm just into anything, if it sounds good, I listen to it, basically, now, if it's, it it's *really* sexist, I just don't want to hear it, (.) but I also have like, Bonnie Raitt (.) brought out an album and I just *love* it. Nick of Time, rhythm n blues, and it's just really good stuff, and, when I have taped for my (.) you know, feminist friends, or separatists, se- ((almost a small laugh)) or whatever, they're certainly in that area, I've had to *re-move* the *songs* from the album when I'm *ta*ping, 'n' they don't want to *hear* songs about (.) *Bonnie*'s heterosexual re*la*tionships,

and the things that are they (.) just don't want to hear it, and that
irri*tates* me, because to me it's just reversing the same thing as
you remove anything about *les*bian relationships I mean just I just
(.) in *prin*ciple I can't agree with it and it just annoys me// and
I find it oppressive because I c- I ca- I'm not *then* able to say well
look I really like this song, I can relate to it, I can *make* the
necessary transfers, I can make the

6   A   /Yeah/ /yeah/

Mairead here talks about the practice of tape exchange which we have
already encountered. She seems to be looking for understanding of her
difference from her lesbian (feminist, separatist) friends, as it manifests
itself in these day to day practices of listening and exchanging tapes. In
the preceding turns, Amanda has criticised lesbian separatism that she
has encountered in the United States, which gives Mairead the cue to
tell her own story. But importantly for the argument of this section,
Mairead states clearly that she can 'make the necessary transfers', that
is, from the heterosexual to the lesbian context, which seems to amount
to what I have called 'appropriation'.

A whole new pearly gate scenario: the fantasy of the performer's identity

In a recent article on lesbian popular music that appeared in the British
periodical *Trouble & Strife*, the practice of collective fantasising about the
sexual identity of pop singers came in for some condemnation (Ainley
and Cooper, 1992). The authors mention a list of musicians that
includes Madonna, Tracy Chapman, Anita Baker, Sinead O'Connor,
Nina Simone, Dusty Springfield and k.d.lang.

> Superficially these artists appear to be in control – not just in the song
> but artistically and emotionally too; the sorry truth is that most of them
> are just vehicles for male producers, writers and musicians. This is par-
> ticularly true of dance music where women's voices are used
> interchangeably, Soul II Soul and Bomb the Bass being two prime
> examples. Are we so easily bought off by images of strong women
> usually conceived by male image makers?
>   The answer is a resounding yes. Some of this is wish fulfilment: the
> hope that these artists may actually be lesbians directs our musical taste.
> That old adage 'any woman can' has become 'any woman performer
> might be'. (Ainley and Cooper, 1992, p 11)

To explore these criticisms at length would involve making distinctions between the performers cited, and would involve getting behind the fetishisation of the singer as 'star' in popular music, and looking more concretely at the division of labour in the recording of a song (Hennion, 1982).[12] This article is more concerned with description than with criticism of lesbians' practices, and here I found this element of 'wish fulfilment' or of fantasy to be an important component part of some collective practices around popular music.

However distinctions have to be made between the way fantasy works in different situations and for different people. Cliona, for instance, has a strong belief in something like *intuition*:

Extract 8 (Interview with Cliona, 12/6/92, transcript p 1)

1   B   It is quite interesting this, because the more you look at all these people who are thought to be possible (.) or who are even thought to have come out at some stage, the less you find that any of them have

2   C   Yes I know and there's every possibility that Tracy Chapman, but there's something about her songs are very assertive and very amm political and I suppose tha- a lot of them, I suppose there's a lot of social commentary in a lot of them as well,// so all that would, at least a feminist, and there's something about herself and her voice and the way she sings them, and I just feel, h- heh heh, only a woman who loves women could sing like that, there's something in it, it's very hard to define it, but there's something that, listen, listen to it and you might hear

3   B   /Oh sure there's all that/

4   B   Well it's very helpful to hear someone say that, yeah I mean, em (.) and you're obviously someone who's you know on the political side of things and you're somebody who's thought things through a lot, em

5   C   And not just me but a *lot* of other women, and I suppose most of our friends would be politically, aware as well, would have, and the first time I *heard* her, I had she had, she had that sort of effect on me, awh, in the gut, and Kate sort of the same, *and* what's that other woman (.)

6   B   k.d.lang?

7   C   about two years ago, I had gone to bed and Kate came upstairs and, said, you've *got* to *hear* this woman, singing she said, I can bet you *any money* she's a lesbian, she said, it said nothing about

her, she just sang one song, but I just *know* she is, and, forgot all about her and didn't hear anything about her until about a year ago when (suddenly stories) burst into headlines in music papers and somebody gave us a loan of a tape and said listen to this, you'll love it, amm

Perhaps Dyer's theory of the 'inwardness' of lesbian/gay sign-systems can explain this intuitive feeling that a singer is lesbian that precedes any more public knowledge about their identity.

Joni, on the other hand, was aware of the process of collective construction that goes into the circulation of what she calls 'rumours'. She was also well aware of the appeal of these fantasies to her lesbian audience, and made deliberate play on it. Like the tape exchanges, 'rumours' are exchanged along local and international networks, in this case the Irish–American one:

Extract 9 (Interview with Joni Crone, 25/5/92, transcript p 8)

1 B Did you always play music by female singers, or em do you play men at all, a few men

2 J Oh I played yeah, a huge mixture, but I would tend to, to play more female yeah, I would try to play, deliberately more female singers, and obviously anybody l- em like rumours about Donna Summer or Tina Turner whatever, or if there was even a rumour about them, ((laughing)) I'd play them huh huh huh huh

3 B Where do these rumours come from?

4 J Em (.) oh I dunno, they come on the scene, or sometimes people are you know travelling, there's this lesbian and gay migration goes on all the time, y'know, people travel back and forth, am, and, rumours would spread, and then we did have a friend who was, who was living in Los Angeles so she was talking about, this is more recently now, am, Tina Turner, and Whitney Houston, am Kelly McGuinness and (this) Jodie Foster, so this would be between em film stars and then singers, y'know so

((digression on 'outing'))

5 B But I mean um, back to Whitney Houston and Tina Turner for instance, in in their cases it's nothing's been written about them, it's they've been seen in a gay bar somewhere, is it, or

6 J Yeah, well in a, Tina and Whitney I think it's more as I say we've, more from the horse's mouth, kind of thing, like I used to do lesbian news which would be saying, just what was happening

on the lesbian scene or any kind of international stuff that you'd hear or whatever, announce it, or any concerts that'd be coming up, and then we'd just in jokes and things about people and y'know and of course, Have you heard the latest, you know, Tina's having an affair with Whitney, just for fun you know

7 B   Were they supposed to be together

8 J   Just using them as an example, So, you know, and then I'd play them, like there was never any rumour about Annie Lennox and Aretha Franklin but I mean I'd play it and say Of course, you know, we know what's going on there, or something like this, you know, for fun

9 B   When you did lesbian news, you mean as a DJ

10 J   Yeah just have a little break, and say, this is the lesbian news, make announcements and stuff

In this passage, Joni does make a distinction between rumours, coming 'from the horse's mouth', and things that are said 'just for fun'. In the latter case, there is no attempt at creating an illusion: everybody understands that this *is* a joke. And yet, there is clearly a value in surrounding the music itself with this kind of fantasy, allowing the possibilities in it to be realised by listeners.

This latter practice seems to suggest that the actual identity of the performer is not what is important, but the ability to create fantasies around that identity. Mairead brings this out again, emphasising the pleasurable 'fun' of this practice:

Extract 10 (Interview with Amanda and Mairead, 21/5/92, tape 2, transcript p 7)

1 M   One of the things I love in conversation about everybody fantasising about who they would love to be a dyke (.) //that's that's really// fun you know, you know, you know, I wonder is she, I'd love her to be, who cares, let's pretend she is regardless of ((laughing, A joining in)) whether she is or not

An example of this shared fantasising in process occurs very near the beginning of my interview with Amanda and Mairead:

Extract 11 (Interview with Amanda and Mairead, 21/5/92, tape 1, transcript p 1)

1 B   When did you start to listen to k.d.lang? or?

2 M A few months ago, really, when I started mixing with women that were listening to her, and I started seeing what *they* were

3 B Yes (.) So how important is the fact that she is a declared dyke, or (.) the rumour says that she is ((slight laugh))

4 M [Yeah, (.) yeah (.) yeah, yeah she is (.)] ((low, sexy voice)) I know her personally

5 A {Yeah I think it's (.) clear she is, isn't it?}

6 All ((uproarious laughter))

7 A LUCKY YOU! ((laughter continues))

8 M ((laughing)) I don't want to share that right now. Let's not talk about the war

At turn 3, here, by using the term 'rumour', I insinuate some doubt about whether k.d.lang is 'a declared dyke'. Both Amanda and Mairead (simultaneous turns 4 and 5), interpret this as a doubt about whether k.d. is lesbian, and affirm this strongly. Mairead reinforces this claim with a joke fantasy of personal knowledge of the star (turn 4). We all collapse in laughter, Amanda's 'lucky you' (turn 7) reinforcing the sexual insinuation of Mairead's joke statement. The shared joke affirms the dominance of the insider knowledge of the lesbian world over the outsider status of academic knowledge, for instance, based on what k.d.lang has (not) said in interviews.[13] But this example does make it clear that even where there is this certain knowledge that the star is lesbian, the element of fantasy increases the pleasure of sharing that knowledge.

Finally, I turn to a memorable passage where Amanda talks in a semi-fact, semi-fantasy way about an American women's percussion band:

Extract 12 (Interview with Amanda and Mairead, 21/5/92, tape 2, transcript p 12)

1 A Well that's the other thing like um gay and lesbian pride marches and on the big gay and lesbian rights march in in Washington, there's a there's a women's band in, it would have to be California wouldn't it? there's like a hundred and fifty women ((starts to laugh slightly)) all doing percussion.//

2 B /Yeah, yeah?/

3 A It's fucking amazing,// ((normal voice)) oh it's like if I ever, y'know, wanted to believe in heaven this would be like, you know//, it would be a ((starting to laugh)) whole, a whole new way of having a pearly gate scenario, you ((laughing loud)) knoow, ((normal voice)) yeh, you'd get beaten in, ((laughter)) hhhhh // huh huh hhhhhh oh it's massive, it was absolutely brilliant.

4 M /Oh that'd be *brilliant*/ /(('amazed' tone)) percussion/ /Ooh I
       love it/
5 B What sort of instruments, when you say percussion (.) anything
       and everything you mean
6 A {Things that BANG ha ha ha ha}
7 M {Anything that makes a noise, *rhythm*}
8 A Yeah
9 M ((semi-whispered for emphasis)) A hundred and *fifty* (.) that
       must be incre- that'd alter, that'd alter your cs-*beta* waves or
       whatever the hell goes on in your head (.) that will alter your
       consciousness

Again, partly what is interesting in this interchange is what Mairead
makes of it as *fantasy*. It's not even clear from Amanda's telling whether
she has actually been there, or only heard about this women's band, but
very quickly the two women are *both talking* as if they have seen this
band (I remain in the role of detached outsider). For instance, at turn
7 Mairead answers my question, which is intended as a factual one to
clarify what Amanda meant by 'percussion' in relation to this band. By
so doing, she once again uses musical knowledge, even this *fantasy* musical
knowledge, to align herself with Amanda as a lesbian insider.

Clearly, this example shows that the actual identity of the performer
is important. It is different from the other examples we have looked at
in that there are no voices involved, so that there is a reliance on visual
signals for the gendered meaning. (One is reminded of 'orange' and
'green' marching bands in the Northern Ireland context.) But the
element of fantasising in what starts out as a witness account means that
even here the desire for identity is not simple. The processes of 'rumour'
exchange, of fantasising, or of elaborating on sexual identities, emerge
from this section as themselves part of the everyday practices which go
into negotiating lesbian 'identity' with other lesbians. The processes
themselves are fluid, both with respect to the imagining of identities for
public performers, and with respect to the definition of self in relation
to these performers. The last two examples have shown these processes
in motion, as it were, demonstrating the way in which individual
identities are shaped in social interaction.

Conclusion: does it matter who is singing?

What this research seems to show is that it does matter to lesbians 'who
is singing', but not in any one, straightforward way. Not only Joni in

her emphatic answer at extract 1, but other women too were adamant that they would not listen to music 'just because' the performer was lesbian. Yet the various forms of myth-making, fantasising and rumour circulation that we encountered above do seem to show that, *especially at an imaginary level*, the identity of the performer is indeed important. It is not that this identity is necessarily evidence of some continuing 'liberal humanist' ideology of the author in everyday listening practices. Rather, it seems more to point to certain *functions* of the way we use (the fiction of) the author, along the lines that Foucault pointed to theoretically in his article 'What is an Author?'. In seeing 'the "author" as a function of discourse', Foucault argued that 'the function of an author is to characterize the existence, circulation, and operation of certain discourses within a society' (1977, p 124). In this sense, the invention of the mythic or fantasy identity of the popular performer is what serves as the social basis for the circulation of certain discourses in popular music as lesbian discourses. In the specific situation of the lesbian culture, the need to categorise people's identities as a means to 'cementing a common identity', is a generalised function, even if categories themselves are in a continual state of flux. The case of authors/performers in the public sphere then becomes a particular case of this more general practice.

On the other hand, the section on 'appropriation' in this chapter looked at some ways in which music that is clearly understood as mainstream and heterosexual can be enjoyed and used in a lesbian context.[14] Difficult as such processes are to research, they are the ones that point most clearly to an operational 'death of the author' in practice in everyday life. Yet in two of the cases I encountered in the interviews, allowing the author's identity to 'die' was a source of some conflict and accusations of 'political incorrectness' (Joni's disapproval of the use of 'The Girl is Mine', and Mairead's friends' refusal to listen to Bonnie Raitt songs that she enjoyed through 'transfers'). There is a sense in which 'who is singing?' becomes an accusatory question for an identity-based lesbian feminism here.

As Ainley and Cooper remarked in their article, one common thread in lesbians' use of popular music is the 'lusting after images of independent women performers' (1992, p 15). This is abundantly clear, but still needs to deal with the fact that, as they themselves say at the beginning of the article, one is left with a repertoire of women performers that would probably not differ much from any heterosexual feminist's record collection. This would suggest that the difference of lesbian from 'straight' feminist use of music has to do with fantasy. What this chapter has tried to show about the fantasy level of the relationship of lesbians to the performer, is that such fantasy is a collectively shaped and shared part of lesbian experience. While these are fantasies and myths *about* identity, they do also, of course, continually challenge the everyday assumption of heterosexual identity. It is in this sense that the audience practices which have been looked at in this chapter can be seen as radical, and as an important component in the ongoing process of constructing lesbian identities in everyday life.

Transcription conventions:

(.) indicates a pause

, where ungrammatical, indicates a short pause

(word) indicates that the word or words in brackets are uncertain

(?) indicates that something is said but it is not distinguishable

// indicates interruption of the current turn by the following one

/words/ indicates that these are the words that interrupt the previous turn; where there are several interruptions, these are listed in order

{words} indicates that these words are overlapped by similarly bracketted words in an adjacent turn

((words)) indicates that these are descriptions of tone, laughter, etc. added by the transcriber

word in italics indicates spoken emphasis

WORD in upper case indicates speech which is loud in volume

Notes

Introduction

(1) Quotations from 'Annotations' by J.P. Hollerith in *Beautiful Barbarians: Lesbian Feminist Poetry*, ed. L. Mohin (London: Onlywomen Press, 1986), p 123.

Chapter 2: Mid Twentieth Century Lesbian Romance: Reception and Redress

(1) Barbara Grier maintains this in the documentary *Before Stonewall*.
(2) This series, comprising five novels (*Odd Girl Out, I am a Woman, Women in the Shadows, Journey to a Woman* and *Beebo Brinker*) was republished in 1986 by Naiad Press, the lesbian press set up by Barbara Grier in 1973.
(3) An on-the-spot account of setting up the Daughters of Bilitis can be read in Del Martin and Phyllis Lyon's *Lesbian Woman*.
(4) References to the conditions out of which Matachine arose can be found in Andrea Weiss and Greta Schiller's *Before Stonewall*.

Chapter 3: History with a Difference: Telling Lesbian *Her* stories

(1) Another book of lists that should be mentioned here is Lynne Yamaguchi Fletcher and Adrien Saks's *Lavender Lists* (Boston: Alyson Publications, 1990).
(2) For women's visibility in a previous feminist political campaign see R. Strachey's *The Cause* or Jane Marcus's *Suffrage and the Pankhursts*.
(3) This conflict surfaces right at the end of *Rubyfruit Jungle* where Molly, depressed at not being able to get a job to suit her abilities, states: 'My bitterness was reflected in the news, full of stories about people my own age raging down the streets in protest. But somehow I knew my rage wasn't their rage and they'd have run me out of their movement for being a lesbian anyway. I read somewhere too that women's groups were starting but they'd trash me just the same.' (p 246)
(4) This stance ignores all independent women, spinsters, celibate women, lesbian women who for whatever reason are not engaged in an immediate lesbian relationship and replicates a misogyny detailed, for instance, in Sheila Jeffreys's *The Spinster and Her Enemies*.
(5) Ann Allen Shockley's 'The Mistress and the Slave Girl' offers a narrative in which similar power structures govern the central lesbian relationship.

(6) To return to a point made at the beginning of this chapter: it is significant that the one female co-editor of *Hidden from History*, Martha Vicinus, is a professor of women's studies.

(7) And it wouldn't be to her discredit if she grew hopeful at a title like 'Women's History behind the Dykes: Reflections on the Situation in the Netherlands' in *Writing Women's History*, although the essay is not about what the title might suggest.

Chapter 4: Lesbian Bibliomythography

(1) I am following the model for the *Bildungsroman* proposed by Buckley (1974). For a further exploration of the *Bildungsroman* see Hirsch (1979). Studies specifically examining women's relationship to the *Bildungsroman* are Abel, Hirsch and Langland (1983), Labovitz (1986) and Felski (1986 and 1989).

(2) The existence of oral history archives such as the Hall Carpenter Archives Lesbian Oral History Group (1989) and of collections like the Adelman anthology (1986) helps us to create our own stories, and allows us to share the stories of others' lives.

(3) Adrienne Rich makes a similar point (1975 {1971}, p 93): 'My own luck was to be born white and middle-class into a house full of books.'

(4) I was inspired when I read Catharine R. Stimpson's (1990) essay. Stimpson reclaims the pleasure of reading, arguing that any texts can belong to a paracanon if it is loved. No distinctions are to be made between 'high' and 'low' art; the only criterion is passionate feeling for the text.

(5) I use the term 'text' rather than 'book' to show that the text needn't be in written form. It may be a particular 'reading' or interpretation of ancient or modern cultures, a myth inherited through oral tradition, a homophobic insult or attitude, etc.

(6) I enjoyed Patricia Duncker's (1992) examination of this point. See the chapter 'On Autobiography' (pp 55–88). Duncker calls this book her 'autobiography of reading', (p 210).

(7) In the introduction to her extensive 'myth of origins' (1984, p xii), Judy Grahn writes: 'My methods for gathering information can be called eclectic. I used dictionaries and history, anthropology and sociology, poetry and the occult.' The reader may be interested to know that a new revised edition of this book is now available.

(8) In introducing the personal/autobiographical into criticism I am keen to follow Nancy K. Miller's suggestion that it is important to acknowledge the context of your occasional writing. See Miller's (1991) discussion of a mode of writing she calls narrative criticism. This 'siting' of the text is also important because of the significance of this episode in my development coming out story.

(9) I mention the following journeys: Alison Hennegan (1988); Judy Grahn (1984); Lee Lynch (1990); Maureen Brady (1990); and Audre Lorde (1984).

(10) Thanks to Sally Munt for this pun. I have taken it from a review on the back cover of Zimmerman (1992).

(11) Of course this isn't yet true. Lesbian 'culture' is very much centred in the large cities, and many women are unable, for social and economic reasons, to move to these 'centres' (and/or would not wish to). Also, not everyone reads, and even those women who do sometimes find that books aren't always enough. As long as oppressive legislation exists, eg, Section 28 (previously Clause 28) of the Local Government Act 1988, we remain only too aware that the progress which has been made so far can easily be taken from us. Section 28 prohibits local authorities from 'promoting' homosexuality, or producing any material which promotes homosexuality. Although hard to define, this has dangerous implications for the censorship of lesbian and gay lives and literature in schools, colleges and libraries. Section 28 also suggests the inferiority of lesbian and gay relationships by labelling lesbians and gay men, and their children, a 'pretend family relationship'. For the lesbian and gay response to 'The Clause', see Kaufmann and Lincoln (1991).

(12) Alison Hennegan became editor of The Women's Press Bookclub in 1984. In a recent conversation with a woman who works at The Women's Press (she prefers to remain anonymous), I learnt that an attempt to change the design of fiction covers, removing the distinctive stripe, proved unpopular with suppliers and readers. This stripe has now been restored, although it now changes colour according to the main colour of the book cover. I'm glad the stripe remains, but I'm sad to see the black and white go. It was, in some ways, a friend.

(13) Diana Fuss (1989) provides an interesting discussion of essentialism and lesbian and gay politics.

(14) In *The Conversations with Cow*, Suniti Namjoshi explores Asian myth and identity and her own relationship to 'lesbianisms' through a series of comical transformations and a central character who is a Brahmin lesbian cow.

(15) This description of a 'dyke' (a word now synonymous with 'lesbian') as a powerful woman-oriented woman brings to mind Adrienne Rich's 'lesbian continuum'. Here Rich states (1985 {1980}, p 51): 'I mean the term ... to include a range ... of woman-identified experience, not simply the fact that a woman has had or consciously desired genital experience with another woman ... [Expanding] it to embrace ... bonding against male tyranny, the giving and receiving of practical and political support ... marriage resistance ...' I don't agree with Rich's 'lesbian continuum' for it seems to deny the sexual and erotic side of being a lesbian, to make what is a powerful identification for some women (myself included) virtually meaningless, and to deny the quite separate oppression which these women face. I prefer Stimpson's more 'literal' description (1988, p 97): 'She is a woman who finds other women erotically attractive and gratifying ... Lesbianism represents a commitment of skin, blood, breast and bone.'

Having said this, however, I still think we have to be aware of how definitions of 'the lesbian' change through time and within different cultures.

(16) Quoted by Zimmerman (1992, p 23). The quotation is taken from an interview by Claudia Tate with Audre Lorde in Tate (1983, pp 100–16). The actual quotation appears on p 115.

(17) Hirsch (1979, p 300) has suggested that the novel of development is 'the most salient genre for the literature of social outsiders, primarily women or minority groups'.

(18) A detailed definition of the *Bildungsroman* genre can be found in Buckley (1974, pp 17–18).

(19) See Patricia Duncker's description of her brief field research into sales of *The Well of Loneliness* (1992, pp 167–8): 'The first thing that the young women read ...'

(20) See Vera Brittain's account (1968). The trial is also documented in Dickson (1975).

(21) I prefer to use the word 'hero' to refer to female protagonists instead of the more conventional 'heroine'. The word 'heroine' implies to me a diminutive sort of 'hero', and I think oppressively gendered language needs to be challenged.

(22) Coming out is often perceived or represented as a 'coming home' by previously isolated lesbians. Examples from tape-recorded interviews with lesbians are given in Ponsé (1978, p 131).

(23) As a white, western woman I do. I will suggest later that Sappho may have less significance for women with other cultural backgrounds.

(24) See Monique Wittig's essay 'Paradigm' (1979); and her two essays 'One is Not Born a Woman' (1988a) and 'The Straight Mind' (1988b). See also Jan Hokenson (1988).

(25) Printed on the back cover of *Rubyfruit Jungle*.

(26) This is Elizabeth Wilson's word (1988, pp 31–6). She warns of the dangers of demanding women to be heroes, in life as well as in fiction: 'To demand of women that they be wonderful on our behalf is to see them as abstractions, not as women, and is to deny them ... the right to try new identities, new ways of living and new forms of relationship – and to *fail* ... all writing must question the meaning of experience and cannot rest content with a preconceived "right answer".'

(27) See Yvonne M. Klein's essay (1990). She writes that the lesbian novels of the 1970s have a 'hollow ring' in relation to political circumstances in the 1980s and that the notion of a 'Lesbian Nation' is 'all but dead' (p 330). She describes autobiographical fiction of the 1980s: 'Rather than projecting forward a vision of a new community of living Amazons, they reach back to reinvent a mythic history of female power out of the shards and scraps of their childhood and their culture' (p 331). *Zami* is one such text.

(28) In desiring to tell her own story, Mary is relying upon the 'talking cure', another name for psychoanalysis. However, the process of writing may be a form of 'therapy' for Mary, but by placing herself in the hands of a reader, not an analyst, Mary shows a willingness to deconstruct the 'authority' of

the analyst and to break free from psychoanalytic definitions. A plurality of readers are the listeners and interpreters who, ironically, may have no knowledge of psychoanalysis, and/or are free to reject 'psychoanalytic' readings.

(29) 'Both/and' suggests an end to the dichotomised universe and an end to a system of polarised opposites which support hierarchical structures. It provides a remedy for 'heroisation'. DuPlessis writes (1986, p 276): 'A both/and vision born of shifts, contraries, negations, contradictions, linked to personal vulnerability and need ... A both/and vision that embraces movement, situational ... Structurally, such a writing might say different things, not settle on one, which is final. This is not a condition of "not choosing" since choice exists always in what to represent and in the rhythms of presentation.'

(30) I find it interesting that *Don Juan* should have been a 'Feminist Book Fortnight' selection. This itself shows a shift in the parameters of 'political correctness', for this novel offers a highly individualistic account which does not attempt to engage the reader with an exemplary character as many 'feminist' confessional narratives have, nor does it give a very optimistic picture of women-initiated activities. Not having to fulfil heroic expectations, the protagonist ('Don Juan') is allowed 'to have greater vulnerability, to be more graphically sexual' (Brady, pp 56–7). She can tell the stories of self-doubt and inconsistency which lesbians have at certain times feared to tell, but which are a vital part of our growth.

Chapter 5: The Lesbian Thriller: Crimes, Clues and Contradictions

(1) See Sally Munt's 'The Inverstigators ...' in Susannah Radstone, ed *Sweet Dreams*, pp 91–119; and Paulina Palmer, 'The Lesbian Feminist Thriller and Detective Novel' in E. Hobby and C. White, eds *What Lesbians Do in Books*, pp 9–27.

(2) For a discussion of the romance see Jean Radford, ed *The Progress of Romance*; and Janice A. Radway, *Reading the Romance*.

(3) Certain courses in literature and Women's Studies at the University of Warwick refer to the lesbian thriller. It is also a popular topic for graduate dissertations.

(4) See Julian Symons, *Bloody Murder*, pp 162–4; and Gerry Palmer, *Thrillers*, pp 40–52.

(5) For references to fiction of the gynaeceum see Elaine Marks and George Stambolian, *Homosexualities and French Literature*, pp 353–77; and Gill Frith, *The Intimacy Which is Knowledge* (PhD dissertation, University of Warwick, 1989), pp 304–35.

(6) Tania Modeleski gives a cogent analysis and critique of SM in *Feminism without Women*, pp 135–63.

(7) See Elizabeth Wilson, 'I'll Climb the Stairway to Heaven', pp 191–5; and Paulina Palmer, 'Contemporary Lesbian Feminist Fiction', pp 51–6.

Chapter 6: The Worlds of Lesbian/Feminist Science Fiction

(1) According to Sarah Lefanu, in 1975 Charnas took part (with Joanna Russ, Ursula LeGuin and others) in a written symposium on women and SF, later published as the double issue of *Khatru 3 & 4 (In the Chinks of the World Machine*, p 105).

(2) My account of Cixous's ideas is based on Toril Moi's analysis of her work in *Sexual/Textual Politics*, pp 102–26.

Chapter 7: Lesbian Cinema, Women's Cinema

(1) See, for example, D. Fuss (1991), J. Butler (1990) and E. Grosz (1989).

(2) The films Young analyses include *Sapphire* (1959), *Flame in the Streets* (1961) and *A Taste of Honey* (1961). Recent lesbian videos shown at the 6th London Lesbian and Gay Film Festival included *Among Good Christian Peoples* (1991) and *Rootless Cosmopolitans* (1990), the former about 'Growing up Black and Gay', the latter about Jewishness and identity. *Ann Trister* is an excellent Canadian film about a Jewish lesbian artist. Vron Ware elaborates how the invisibility of 'race' and 'whiteness' among whites is part of the historical construction of 'race' as referring to 'non-whites' and a 'problem' for whites (Ware, 1992).

(3) Freud uses these terms in opposition. Ontology pertains to the development of the individual being, phylogeny to the 'tribe' or race. It is one of the difficulties of using Freud that the usage of such terms shifts; the latter term especially has changed in its connoted meanings sufficiently to have lost some of its resonance and precision for many contemporary readers.

(4) Freud's incomplete analysis of Dora (1901/05) has been much discussed in psychoanalytic literature. Freud wrote two papers directly involving lesbianism (Freud 1901/05; Freud 1920), both of which are most interesting for their internal struggle with unsatisfactory arguments and conclusions. See especially Rose (1978) who is led to compare the two papers but not in order to classify Dora 'as homosexual in any simple sense, but precisely because in this case Freud was led to an acknowledgement of the homosexual factor in all feminine sexuality' (p 33). Forrester (1990) reads the case as involving 'a mode of analysis in which Freud found himself feminised' (p 61).

(5) Issues of spectatorship are taken up below. See also J. Stacey in C. Gledhill (1991).

(6) Both M. Bowie (1991) and E. Grosz (1990) offer exceptionally clear, gender-aware introductions to this difficult thinker. Grosz contextualises Lacan in relation to feminism through a discussion of J. Kristeva and L. Irigaray. Bowie does so more generally, but his chapter 'The meaning of the Phallus' refers to Melanie Klein's divergences from Lacan and finds that 'Women in general – and not just the lesbians who serve as their advance guard – set out in quest of something that they, unlike men, already have' (p 149).

(7) See especially E. Grosz (1990), p 68 *et seq*. She summarises four major changes brought about for the child through the oedipus complex, two of which are around sex and gender, and two around the social. This is an indication of why it is so important for criticism to resolve the split in its approach to the sex-social nexus. See also Butler (1990), pp 58–65. For a critical analysis of oedipal narratives in relation to women in film, see de Lauretis (1984), esp. chapter 5.

(8) M. Bowie points out of Lacan: '... in the thick of his masculinising theoretical exposition he works out a view of desire that not only discards all distinctions of gender but makes them unthinkable ... (The) embedding of alternative views inside each other is a sign that Lacan's psychoanalysis ... has struck again upon an issue that it cannot resolve.' (Bowie, 1991, p 131)

(9) Her article is, among other things, a good illustration of how the issues around women's cinema appeared in the early 1980s, since it takes the form of an account of four courses she taught, the syllabi, rationale and student response.

(10) Mulvey (1989, 1991). Her film, *Riddles of the Sphinx*, co-directed with Peter Wollen (1976/7), was another landmark. She returns to further her analysis of the Oedipus story as suggesting 'a movement from an earlier "maternal" stage to a later "paternal" or "patriarchal" order.' (Mulvey, 1991, p 27)

(11) *We've been Framed*, shown at the 1992 London Lesbian and Gay Film Festival and on Channel 4's *Out* series, is a witty examination of how lesbians have been portrayed in Hollywood. It includes in its list of negative lesbian stereotypes that of murderer, psychopath, vampire and child-woman. Clips to illustrate this were taken from: *Pandora's Box* (1929), *The Lair of the White Worm* (1988), *The Bitter Tears of Petra von Kant* (1972), *The Killing of Sister George* (1968), *Olivia* (1950), *The Loudest Whisper* (1961), *The Fox* (1967), *Dracula's Daughter* (1936), *Blood and Roses* (1960), *Caged* (1950), *The Nun* (1966), *Another Way* (1982), *Personal Best* (1982), *Basic Instinct* (in production 1991). Further movies with a lesbian theme (listed in Mellen, 1973, now dated but with a chapter on 'Lesbianism in the Movies') are *I, A Woman Part III* (1970), *The Silence* (1963), *Persona* (1966), *The Conformist* (1970), *The Cousins* (1958), *Les Biches* (1968), *Ann and Eve* (1970), *Therese and Isabel* (1968), *The Lickerish Quartet* (1970), *Rachel, Rachel* (1968), *Her, She and Him* (1970), *Doctor's Wives* (1970), *Flesh* (1968), *Trash* (1970), *The Children's Hour* (1962).

(12) J. Butler puts the arguments against the false assumption of priority or originality within heterosexual frameworks – that the gay or queer is somehow a copy of the straight – and proposes instead a 'performative' model in which gender identities do not exist outside their constitutive actions (eg, Butler, 1990, pp 24–5).

(13) D. Hamer (1990) provides a more ambivalent view. One problem for me is that she elides the equation of lesbianism and masculinity with the usurpation of 'the sexual and social privileges associated with masculinity': the second is that she accepts as one of two 'competing narratives' analyst Joyce McDougall's view 'that homosexual women see themselves as separate

from all other women' (p 141), a view which cannot account for many lesbian-feminists' construction of women-centredness. Hamer includes a quotation from McDougall citing lesbians ('homosexual women') as castrated men in our deeper fantasies. 'To be a woman meant to be nothing, to have nothing, to create nothing. Activity was the privilege of the male ...' (Quoted in Hamer, 1990, p 142). This may well be a fear we have to get through, but lesbians' rejection of the category 'woman' has no necessary or deep connection with an identification with the category 'man'. Wittig's description of lesbians as escapees from the category 'woman' offers another perspective. (Wittig, in S. Hoagland and J. Penelope, 1988, pp 431–47)

(14) See note 11.

(15) Some of the most far-reaching work is by, or derives from, L. Irigaray. See M. Whitford (1991) for her outstanding critical assessment.

(16) For an excellent sense of the breadth of feminist psychoanalysis debates see T. Brennan (1989). On the complexities of gender in psychoanalytic accounts of homosexuality see J. Butler (1990).

(17) T. de Lauretis, in her brief survey of the use of the term 'women's cinema', points to 'not just a set of films or practices of cinema, but also a number of film-critical discourses and broadly cast networks of cinema-related practices that are directly connected with the history of feminism ...' (de Lauretis, 1990, p 7). Her detailed and thorough essay, though ostensibly about women's cinema, also poses important questions about lesbianism; my essay is indebted to it.

(18) Defining the effects of the feminist project of inventing new images and forms of community, de Lauretis writes of 'the construction of conceptual, representational and erotic spaces where women could address themselves to women and, in assuming the position of subject – of speaking, thinking and desiring subject – women could then concurrently identify and recognise in women *the subjects and the objects* of a female desire' (1990, p 15). She is writing here about women's cinema in general, not specifically lesbian cinema.

(19) Again, desire here has several meanings which are not confined to sexual desire, but rather may be seen as meshing with it. Lesbians' understanding of desire can be used as a point of departure from which to scrutinise the inadequacy of some theoretical frameworks which seek to deny it; at these points it is the mechanisms of masculinist and/or heterosexist disavowal that require scrutiny.

(20) C. Sheldon's comic short *17 Rooms, or What Lesbians Do in Bed* and Sandra Lahire's work are exceptions, but they are not typical of the workshops in either their practice or their films. There is an essay by Lahire entitled 'Lesbians in Media Education' in Robinson (1987), pp 274–83. H. Wistrech, director of *Het Up*, is a former member of Witch. There is little that has been produced to the level of, for example, A. Weiss's *After Stonewall* and *Blood and Roses: Under the Spell of the Lesbian Vampire*. Vera Productions, the Leeds based co-operative, manages to negotiate the divides between women's lesbian and community production.

(21) J. Copjec considers the idea that the gaze is 'a single cognitive position from which it is not only possible but necessary to look' to be supported by 'a partial misreading of Lacan'. ('Cutting Up' in T. Brennan, 1991, p 244, n 4)

(22) See G. Spivak (1990), p 50. My position is similar to hers when she says of reading that 'the political element comes out in the transaction between the reader and the texts.' A problem with American reader-response, about which she is talking, is its failure to look at the sociopolitical production of communities. This is highly relevant to theorising cinema, especially as the 'transaction between reader and texts' is so much more mediated, and thus more complex in its imbrications with dominant and hegemonic positions and politics.

(23) De Lauretis (1991) comes close to implying something like this when she finds J. Stacey's reading of *Desperately Seeking Susan* as addressing 'the specifically homosexual pleasures of female spectatorship ingenuous or perhaps ingenious.' Though I would agree with de Lauretis that this film is about identification rather than desire, I do not think that invalidates Stacey's overall thinking around lesbian spectatorship or the need for a more careful consideration of the meanings of 'identification'. (See also notes 18 and 22)

(24) On identification and its definitions see J. Stacey (1991) and her discussion of female audiences' relations to female stars, an expansion of her earlier arguments (Stacey, 1987).

(25) On 'male identification' see notes 11 and 18.

(26) For a discussion of the 'sexed body' see J. Butler (1990), p 128 *et seq*.

(27) *LA Story, Welcome Home Rosie Carmichael* and *Times Square* are all examples, according to *We've been Framed*.

(28) J. Copjec argues against the understanding 'by which the subject is thought to recognise itself in representations' in favour of the 'unruliness of the image that *resists* interpretation' (p 229).

(29) The videos were: *Peril or Pleasure – Feminist Produced Pornography* (Torrice, 1989); *Sweet Dreams* (Cottrell, 1979); *Current Flow* (Carlomusto and Bordowitz, 1989); *Joystick Blues* (Ginsburg and Goralsky, 1989); *Nancy's Nightmare* (Nurudin); *The Snatch Tape* (Brave and Light, 1990).

(30) C. Smyth seems to accept this by contrasting the representability of male arousal (the erect penis, spilled semen) with 'the mystery of female pleasure, which remains hidden' (pp 155–6). Though she hopes for a break with 'dominant patterns of filming sex' (p 159), she seems not to challenge the idea that the active gaze is a 'masculine' spectator position.

(31) This documentary includes clips from recent 'feminist porn' and explores the activities and controversies around women pornographers making pornography for women and for the existing 'straight' market.

(32) It is still rare. S. Sonderburg's widely distributed independent film *Sex, Lies and Videotape* (1989) is about the only example of male sexuality and voyeurism portrayed as problematic in itself – as opposed to pathologising, symbolising or individualising it – that I can think of. S. Seidelman's *Making Mr Right* (1987) does not seem to have received wide theatrical distribution.

(33) A. Severson's *Near the Big Chakra* (1972) shows 37 close-ups of the vulvas of women from 3 months to 56 years. It lasts 17 minutes and has no sound. S. MacDonald observes, 'For many filmmakers the body was a territory in need of liberation' (p 18). For me, seeing the film in the early 1980s at an all women screening was very important in going beyond the restrictive ways of seeing representations of women's bodies.

(34) S. McLaughlin observed that 'there are a lot of taboos that feminists still hold onto, and if we don't confront them, we're limiting the possibilities of understanding our own sexuality and desire' (Butler, 1987, p 27). I am sure it is right that holding on to taboos will limit us; equally, it will arrest discussion to disallow interrogation of the sexually explicit. The question remains whether the abolition of taboos means anything goes, anytime, because there is no such image as an oppressive image at any given historical moment. I do not think so; but neither do I advocate censorship.

(35) Adams's adherence to the basics of the Freudian account leads her to the odd finding that in contrast to the SM lesbian, the 'traditional homosexual' woman is 'fundamentally similar to the traditional heterosexual woman in that she bears the burden of maintaining a reference point which cannot give her her bearings.' (p 263)

A programme of radical German work was showcased at the Tyneside Cinema in 1987 (presented by Ulrike Zimmermann and including her *Tourists*). It included *Hyena's Breakfast* (1984) a film about masochistic fantasies, and *Bondage* (1983) which centres on a statement by a lesbian sado-masochist.

(36) The director of *Desert Hearts*, Donna Deitch, has a background in independent film. Deitch was sure it was time for a lesbian feature in a popular idiom and, having secured the film rights for *Desert of the Heart* from writer Jane Rule, spent three years fundraising for it. In an unpublished interview with me, she said that her sources were outside the usual film finance system. It seems they were more like a sophisticated version of women's usual ways of raising money: through lesbian networks, friends, fundraising events. It was not until after the film was made that the machinery of the industry came in, with distribution by the relatively mainstream Palace Pictures. Together with the censorship of lesbianism in other mainstream movies (except, still, where it is somehow neutralised) this funding history illustrates in practical terms some of the ways lesbian material is prevented from reaching the big screens from the earliest part of the production process onwards.

(37) J. Mayne takes up these issues of form and representability and refers to M. Merck's assessment of the structure of *Desert Hearts* as both heterosexual and stereotypical (in D. Fuss, 1991, pp 180–1). Maintaining hierarchies of form advances nothing, however. The history of the male avant-garde in all cultural practice often requires careful and subtle scrutiny in relation to its role in the construction of lesbians or women in general despite its innovatory achievements. The issues raised are far from straightforward and require careful re-articulation.

(38) The point at which any text may be inserted into the mainstream is becoming increasingly complicated to understand. Especially since television, the notion of an 'average' viewer or 'mass' audience has looked insufficient. Yet it is much used within the dominant film industry to justify restrictive and anti-gay practices.

(39) C. Tookey in *The Sunday Telegraph*. Thanks to Jane Arthurs for her extensive selection of quotations from the reviews of the film.

(40) Buddy movies in general do not seem to have been read in terms of homosexual desire, though I have not made a study of them. Female buddy movies listed in *We've been Framed* are: *Nine to Five* (1980), *Steel Magnolias* (1989), *Silkwood* (1983), *Outrageous Fortune* (1987), *Bagdad Café* (1987), *Desperately Seeking Susan* (1985), *Times Square* (1980), *Thelma and Louise* (1991). *The Color Purple* (1985) was 'disappointingly closet'.
Crocodiles in Amsterdam (1989) and *Times Square* (1980) were programmed at the 1992 London Lesbian and Gay Film Festival under a section entitled 'Just Good Friends: The Female Buddy Movie.'

(41) R. Schnickel, *Time Magazine*. Dora, too, has been interpreted as acting out of revenge (Forrester, 1990, p 56).

(42) The only substantial objection on feminist grounds is that Thelma sleeps with another man soon after the attempted rape. If the telescoped timescale of the film is taken into account, this can be read within the meanings set up by the film as another example of Thelma's inexperienced trust of men which results repeatedly in betrayal and danger. But as a comment on the actual effects of rape it remains false and unacceptably trivialising, and I would not wish to minimise the force of criticism such as E. Bader's in *Spare Rib* to the effect that it 'totally' negated the previous trauma, and offensively trivialises the seriousness of rape and its effects.'

(43) For a feminist view of the popular cop genre with women in the main roles, see S. Botcherly and R. Garland (1991). There has been no space here to deal with TV as well as film, so I have not mentioned other popular forms as exemplified by the BBC's *Oranges are Not the Only Fruit* (see H. Hinds, 1991) and *Portrait of a Marriage*, or the lesbian soap *Two in Twenty*.

(44) This is also the trajectory of *Coup de Foudre (At First Sight*, 1983) which is an autobiographical account of the director's mother's relationship with another woman as becomes clear at the (happy) end. Mayne discusses this film in relation to its authorial signature (at the end the spectator is returned to the point of view of the girl-child, the film-maker herself) and to 'the permeable boundaries between female bonding and lesbianism.' (Mayne in D. Fuss, 1991, pp 173, 175)

Chapter 8: Lesbians and Popular Music: Does It Matter Who Is Singing?

(1) Arguably the ideology of 'rock' has tried to square this illusion in its striving for 'authenticity' and in its belief in a 'romantic' notion of art as existing outside commercial circuits (Frith and Horne, 1987). In its material practices,

rock endeavoured to combine the multiple functions of the modern song-recording process into one 'authorial', and inevitably male, figure (Dylan, Jagger, Prince). Music of 'other' genres and communities (women, blacks) has, in a sense, been able to be more honest about its commercial situation, and has hence been more radically deconstructive of the notion of 'the author', in the development of a complex division of labour in musical and recording practices (cf. Dyer, 1991, on multiple authorship in film). Nevertheless, there is still a sense in which in everyday listening we hear the singer (often, actually, singers) as a sort of authorial presence in the song, a practice which feeds into, but which is not determined by, the creation of 'stars' in the multiple textual practices which surround popular music.

(2) In an article on Madonna's songs, I have argued that her perceived control over men is achieved materially through a use of *maternal* language (Bradby, 1992).

(3) The quote is from Fuss, 1989, pp 44–5.

(4) In demonstrating what she saw as 'the flip side of the whole Madonna stuff in lesbian community stuff', Amanda told a story of going to a lesbian dance with a woman who is 'really into Madonna and the body beautiful'. For Amanda, 'it was really traumatising, and she made so many comments about fat people that I was obliged to say something.'

(5) The song 'Justify My Love' appeared on the LP *Immaculate Collection* but not on the videotape of the same name. The video of the single, though not, as far as I know, played on mainstream television in Europe, was played on MTV Europe after midnight, which made it easy access in Ireland, and from where pirate tapes were made.

(6) This is not to support the widespread elitist notion that the popular song itself is meaningless (see Green, 1989, for an interesting discussion of musical meaning in popular song, and the distinction between 'inherent' and 'delineated' meanings). But, as I have tried to show elsewhere in looking at pre-teen girls' reception of Madonna, the discursive possibilities provided by songs are (only) resources that will be in competition with other discourses on the terrain of everyday interaction (Bradby 1991). In the present case, the shared feeling that a performer 'is' or 'might be' a lesbian needs validation in 'hearings' of songs, if it is to be sustained.

(7) Carol Warren discusses insider/outsider distinctions in researching gay subcultures in the context of a review of how gender affects the role of the field researcher (1988, pp 18, 32–3).

(8) The song Joni is referring to is in fact called 'The Girl is Mine' and appeared on the Michael Jackson *Thriller* album. The song portrays a 'good-humoured', 'bantering' style argument between the two men over a 'girl'.

(9) Compare the account by Weston and Rofel of the operation of class and sexual identities in a lesbian workplace (1984).

(10) See Pavletich for more discussion of style and politics in the American women's music movement (1980, pp 253–61).

(11) In my interview with Joni I tried to introduce this idea of a positive sense of 'appropriation' and she responded by producing an example of a song

that was very popular at one stage in the club, and the use of which she recognised as fitting my sense of 'appropriation'. This was the Crystal Gayle song 'Talking in Your Sleep' which was in the US charts in 1978 and which is addressed to a 'you', conventionally heard as male, who has been talking in his sleep about his present lover. As Joni put it, 'the "you" is intended to be male, but it's appropriated by lesbians'.

(12) What seems misguided is a search for solutions somehow *outside* the music industry and its social relations – the authors end up recommending a search through 'indie' music, having rejected almost all other current lesbian taste. While agreeing that there are some remarkable female performers to be encountered within this genre (and see Bloomfield 1993 for an exposition of the work of some of these female singers), I would nevertheless argue that it is an illusion to see such music as 'overlooked by the music industry' (Ainley and Cooper, 1992, p 15). There is a long history of popular musicians seeing their work as 'art', and as above 'commerce' and commodity forms, which is closely linked in with the sociology of British art colleges in the post-war world, but this illusion has been exposed elsewhere (Frith and Horne, 1987).

(13) As k.d.lang's album *Ingénue* appeared shortly before I embarked on this research, there was quite a bit of press coverage of her during this period. I make no claim to have read everything, but Patricia, who is a fan, lent me several press cuttings. Most interviews and articles do not mention sexuality at all, and I have so far seen only one that mentions the word 'lesbian'. An interview with k.d.lang in *Vox* magazine in May 1992 put to her the criticism that 'her sexuality and androgyny had been used to her own benefit and not to that of any gay movement; in short that she contrived her image' (Peachey, 1992, p 47). In reply she said:

> I wouldn't do anything just to get a reaction. I'm an alternative thinking artist, I fight the system and stereotypes, but that isn't just to become popular ... Androgyny comes to me naturally, it is my natural state. I suppose it's no different to the prejudices other people have to deal with, but there was a time when my image overshadowed my art ... I don't mind being a lesbian icon, or gay icon, a gay role model if that happens. I don't talk about my sexuality because, although it influences what I am as an artist, it's not the final product of what I am. It's an ingredient, but not the whole. I don't wanna use it as a political or artistic vehicle' (Peachey, 1992, p 47).

See also Brendan Lemon's interview with k.d.lang, entitled 'K.d. – a quiet life', in *The Advocate* 605 (16 June 1992) pp 33–46.

(14) I have not dealt with the use of male gay music in lesbian clubs in this paper.

Bibliography

Aaron, J. and S. Walby, eds *Out of the Margins: Women's Studies in the Nineties* (London: Falmer Press, 1990).

Abel, E., ed. *Writing and Sexual Difference* (Brighton: Harvester, 1982).

Abel, E., M. Hirsch and E. Langland, eds *The Voyage In: Fiction of Female Development* (Hanover: University of New England Press, 1983).

Abbott, S. and B. Love. *Sappho Was a Right-On Woman* (New York: Stein and Day, 1972).

Adams, P. 'Of Female Bondage' in T. Brennan, ed., *Between Feminism and Psychoanalysis*, pp 247–66.

Adelman, M., ed. *Long Time Passing: Lives of Older Lesbians* (Boston: Alyson Publications, 1986).

Ainley, R. and S. Cooper, 'Who's Conning Who?', *Trouble and Strife: the Radical Feminist Magazine* (1992), No. 23.

Alexander, K. 'Lesbian Reading' in *Gossip: A Journal of Lesbian Feminist Ethics* 6, pp 37–43.

Alther, L. *Other Women* (Harmondsworth: Penguin, 1977).

Arnold, J. *Sister Gin* (Plainfield, Vt: Daughters Inc., 1975).

Atwood, M. *The Handmaid's Tale* (London: Cape, 1986).

Bad Object Choices, eds *How Do I Look? Queer Film and Video* (Seattle: Bay Press, 1992).

Bannon, A. *Journey to Woman* (Tallahassee: Naiad Press, 1986).

—, *Odd Girl Out* (Tallahassee: Naiad Press, 1986).

—, *Women in the Shadows* (Tallahassee: Naiad Press, 1983).

Barry, K. *Female Sexual Slavery* (New Jersey: Prentice Hall, 1979).

Becker, E., M. Githen and J. Lesage. 'Lesbians in Film' in P. Stevens, ed. *Jump Out: Hollywood Politics, Counter Cinema* (1985).

Berger Gluck, S. and D. Patai, eds *Women's Words: The Feminist Practice of Oral History* (London: Routledge, 1991).

Bloomfield, T. 'Resisting Songs: Negative Dialectics in Pop', *Popular Music,* vol. 12, no. 1 (Cambridge University Press, 1993, forthcoming).

Bobo, J. and E. Seiter. 'Black Feminism and Media Criticism: "The Women of Brewster Place"' in *Screen 32/3* (Autumn 1991).

Boffin, T. and J. Fraser, eds *Stolen Glances* (London: Pandora, 1991).

Bond, P. 'Tapioca Tapestry' in M. Adelman, ed. *Long Time Passing: Lives of Older Lesbians* (Boston: Alyson Publications, 1986), pp 164–76.

Bowie, M. *Lacan* (London: Fontana, 1991).

Bradby, B. 'Do Talk and Don't Talk: the Division of the Subject in Girl-Group Music', in S. Frth and A. Goodwin, eds *On Record: a Rock and Pop Reader* (New York: Pantheon, 1990; London: Routledge, 1990).

—, 'Freedom, Feeling and Dancing: Madonna's Songs Traverse Girls' Talk', in *OneTwoThreeFour,* no. 9 (Los Angeles: 1991).

—, 'Like a Virgin-Mother?: Materialism and Maternalism in the Songs of Madonna', *Cultural Studies,* vol. 6, no. 1 (London: Routledge, 1992).

Brady, M. 'Insider/Outsider Coming of Age' in K. Jay and J. Glasgow, eds *Lesbian Texts and Contexts: Radical Revisions,* pp 49–58.

Brennan, T., ed. *Between Feminism and Psychoanalysis* (London: Routledge, 1989).

Brittain, V. *Raddyffe Hall: A Case of Obscenity?* (London: Femina Press, 1968).

Brossard, N. 'Lesbians of Writing Lore' in C. McEwan and S. O'Sullivan, eds *Out the Other Side: Contemporary Lesbian Writing* (London: Virago, 1988), pp 149–51.

Brown, R.M. *Rubyfruit Jungle* (New York: Bantam, 1977).

Bruford, W.H. *The German Tradition of Self-Cultivation* (London: Cambridge University Press, 1975).

Brunsdon, C. 'Pedagogies of the Feminine' in *Screen 52/4* (Winter 1991), pp 364–82.

Buckley, J.H. *Season of Youth: The Bildungsroman from Dickens to Golding* (Cambridge, Mass.: Harvard University Press, 1974).

Burgess, M. 'A Fantastic Picture of Female Success' in *The Independent* (10 April 1989), p 13.

Butler, A. 'She Must Be Seeing Things (Interview with Sheila McLaughlin)' in *Screen 28/4* (Autumn 1987).

Butler, B., ed. *Ceremonies of the Heart: Celebrating Lesbian Unions* (Washington: Seal Press, 1990).

Butler, J. 'Imitation and Gender Subordination' in D. Fuss, ed. *Inside/Out,* pp 13–31.

—, *Gender Trouble* (London: Routledge, 1990).

Butler, S. *Erewhon* (London: Penguin, 1970).

Califa, P. *Macho Sluts* (Boston: Alyson Publications, 1988).

Callenbach, E. *Ecotopia* (Berkeley: Banyon Books, 1975).

Carola, E. 'Women, Erotica, Pornography – Learning to Play the Game' in G. Chester and J. Dickie, eds *Feminism and Censorship: The Current Debate.* (Dorset: Prism Press, 1988), pp 168–77.

Chandler, R. 'The Simple Art of Murder' in *Pearls are a Nuisance* (Harmondsworth: Penguin, 1964), pp 181–89.

Chapkis, W. *Beauty Secrets: Women and the Politics of Appearance* (London: Women's Press, 1988).

Carbonneau, C. and L. Winer. 'Lesbians in Nice Films' in *Jump Cut,* 24/25 (1981), pp 27–30.

Charnas, S. McKee. 'A Woman Appeared' in M. Barr, ed. *Future Females: A Critical Anthology* (Bowling Green, OH: Bowling Green State University Press, 1981), pp 103–8.

—, *Motherlines* (London: Gollancz, 1980).

—, *Walk on the Edge of the World* (London: Gollancz, 1979).

Chodorow, N. *The Reproduction of Mothering: Psychoanalysis and the Sociology of Gender* (Berkeley: University of California Press, 1980).

Christian, B. *Black Feminist Criticism: Perspectives on Black Women Writers* (New York: Pergamon Press, 1985).

—, *Black Women Novelists: The Development of a Tradition 1892–1976* (Westport: Greenwood Press, 1980).

Chughtai, I. 'The Quilt' in *The Quilt and Other Stories* (London: Women's Press, 1991).

Clayton, S. 'Notes on Teaching Film' in *Feminist Review 14* (Summer 1983).

Cole, S.G. *Pornography and the Sex Crisis* (Toronto: Amanita Enterprises, 1989).

Cook, B.W. 'Women Alone Stir My Imagination: Lesbianism and the Cultural Tradition' in *Signs 4/4* (Summer 1979), pp 718–39.

Copjec, J. 'Cutting Up' in T. Brennan, ed. *Between Feminism and Psychoanalysis*, pp 227–47.

Couzyn, J. ed. *The Bloodaxe Book of Contemporary Women Poets: Eleven British Writers* (Newcastle upon Tyne: Bloodaxe Books, 1985).

Coward, R. *Female Desire: Women's Sexuality Today* (London; Paladin, 1984).

Coward, R. and L. Semple. 'Tracking Down the Past: Women and Detective Fiction' in H. Carr, ed. *From My Guy to Sci Fi: Genre and Women's Writing in the Postmodern World* (London: Pandora, 1989), pp 39–57.

Cruikshank, M., ed. *Lesbian Studies: Present and Future* (New York: Feminist Press, 1982).

Crow, C. *Miss X or The Wolf Woman* (London: Women's Press, 1990).

Daly, M. *Gyn/Ecology* (London: Women's Press, 1979).

Davies, K., J. Dickey and T. Stratford, eds *Out of Focus: Writings on Women and the Media* (London: Women's Press, 1987).

Davis, M. and E. Lapovsky Kennedy. 'Oral History and the Study of Sexuality in the Lesbian Community' in M. Duberman *et al*, eds *Hidden from History*, pp 426–40.

Delaney, S. *Babel–17* (London: Gollancz, 1967).

de Lauretis, T. 'Guerrilla in the Midst: Women's Cinema in the 80s' in *Screen* 31/1 (Spring 1990), pp 6–25.

—, *Alice Doesn't: Feminism, Semiotics, Cinema* (London: Macmillan, 1984).

DeLynn, J. *Don Juan in the Village* (London: Serpent's Tail, 1991).

D'Emilio, J. 'Gay Politics and Community in San Francisco Since World War II' in Duberman, M. *et al*, eds *Hidden from History*, pp 456–73.

Dickey, J. 'Heterosexism and the Lesbian Image in the Press' in K. Davies, J. Dickey and T. Stratford, eds *Out of Focus*, pp 81–8.

Dickson, L. *Radclyffe Hall at The Well of Loneliness: A Sapphic Chronicle* (London: Collins, 1975).

Dinnerstein, D. *The Mermaid and the Minotaur: Sexual Arrangements and the Human Malaise* (New York: Harper and Row, 1976).

Doane, M.A. 'Woman's Stake: Filming the Female Body' in *October 17* (1981), pp 23–6.

Dollimore, J. *Sexual Dissidence – Augustine to Wilde, Freud to Foucault* (Oxford: Clarendon Press, 1991).

Dreher, S. *Stoner McTavish* (London: Women's Press, 1987).

Duberman, M., Vicinus, M. and G. Chauncey, eds *Hidden from History: Reclaiming the Lesbian and Gay Past* (Harmondsworth: Penguin, 1991).

Duncker, P. *Sisters and Strangers: An Introduction to Contemporary Feminist Fiction* (Oxford: Blackwell, 1992).

—, 'Reading Genesis' in E. Hobby and C. White, eds *What Lesbians Do In Books*, pp 205–25.

DuPlessis, R. *The Pink Guitar: Writing as Feminist Practice* (London: Routledge, 1990).

—, 'For the Etruscans' in E. Showalter, ed. *The New Feminist Criticism*, pp 271–91.

Dyer, R. 'Believing in Fairies: The Author and the Homosexual' in D. Fuss, ed. *Inside/Out: Lesbian Theories, Gay Theories*, pp 185–204.

—, *Now You See It: Studies in Lesbian and Gay Film* (London: Routledge, 1990).

—, *Gays and Film* (London: British Film Institute, 1977).

Ehrenreich, B. *The Hearts of Men: American Dreams and the Flight from Commitment* (London: Pluto, 1983).

Elgin, S. Haden. *Native Tongue* (London: Women's Press, 1985).

Ettorre, E.M. *Lesbians, Women and Society* (London: Routledge & Kegan Paul,1980).

Faderman, L. *Odd Girls and Twilight Lovers: A History of Lesbian Life in Twentieth Century America* (New York: Columbia University Press, 1991).

—, *Surpassing the Love of Men: Friendship and Love between Women from the Renaissance to the Present* (London: Junction Books, 1980; London: Women's Press, 1985).

Fairbairns, Z. *Benefits* (London: Virago, 1979).

—, 'On Writing *Benefits*' in Feminist Anthology Collective, ed. *No Turning Back* (London: Women's Press, 1981), pp 255–8.

Farr, S. 'The Art of Discipline: Creating Erotic Dramas of Play and Power' in Samois, ed. *Coming to Power: Writing and Graphics on Lesbian S/M* (Boston, Mass.: Alyson Publications, 1981), pp 188–9.

Felski, R. *Beyond Feminist Aesthetics: Feminist Literature and Social Change* (London: Hutchinson Radius, 1989).

—, 'The Novel of Self-Discovery: A Necessary Fiction?' in *Southern Review: Literary and Interdisciplinary Essays* 2 (July 1986), pp 131–48.

Firestone, S. *The Dialectic of Sex: The Case for Feminist Revolution* (New York: Morrow, 1979).

Fitting, P. 'A Guide to Reading Single-Sex Worlds' in *Women's Studies* 14 (1987), pp 101–17.

Forest, K.V. *Murder at the Nightwood Bar* (Tallahassee: Naiad Press, 1987).

—, *Daughters of a Coral Dawn* (Tallahassee: Naiad Press, 1984).

Forrester, J. *The Seductions of Psychoanalysis* (Cambridge: Cambridge University Press, 1990).

Foucault, M. 'What is an Author?' in D. Bouchard ed. *Language, Counter-Memory, Practice: Selected Essays and Interviews by Michel Foucault* (Oxford: Blackwell, 1977).

Franklin, S., C. Lury and J. Stacey, eds. *Off-Centre: Feminism and Cultural Studies* (London: Harper Collins, 1991).

Freedman, E.B. 'Missing Links' in *The Women's Review of Books* IX/1 (1991), pp 15–17.

Freud, S. *The Standard Edition of the Complete Psychological Works* (London: Hogarth Press, 1955–74).

—, 'Fragment of an Analysis of a Case of Hysteria' ('Dora') (1901/5) vol. 7.

—, 'The Psychogenesis of a Case of Homosexuality' (1920) vol. 18.

Friedan, B. *The Feminine Mystique* (Harmondsworth: Penguin, 1986).

Friedan, S. 'Shadowing/Surfacing/Shedding: Contemporary German Writers in Search of a Female Bildungsroman' in E. Abel *et al*, eds *The Voyage In*, pp 304–16.

Frith, G. *The Intimacy Which is Knowledge: Female Friendship in the Novels of Women Writers* (PhD dissertation, University of Warwick, 1989).

Frith, S. 'Anglo-America and its Discontents', *Cultural Studies,* vol. 5, no. 3 (London: Routledge, 1991).

Frith, S. and H. Horne, *Art into Pop* (London: Methuen, 1987).

Fuss, D., ed. *Inside/Out: Lesbian Theories, Gay Theories* (London: Routledge, 1991).

—, *Essentially Speaking: Feminism, Nature and Difference* (London: Routledge, 1989).

Gearhart, S. Miller. *The Wanderground* (Massachusetts: Persephone Press, 1980).

Gilbert, S.M. and S. Gubar. *The Madwoman in the Attic* (New Haven: Yale University Press, 1984).

Gilman, C. Perkins. *Herland* (London: Women's Press, 1985).

Gitlin, T. 'The Politics of Communication and the Communication of Politics' in J. Curran and M. Gurevich, eds *Mass Media and Society* (London: Edward Arnold, 1991), pp 329–41.

Gledhill, C., ed. *Stardom: Industry of Desire* (London: Routledge, 1991).

Grae, C. *Paz* (Chicago: Blazon Books, 1984).

Grahn, J. *The Work of a Common Woman* (London: Onlywomen Press, 1985).

—, *Another Mother Tongue: Gay Words, Gay Worlds* (Boston: Beacon Press, 1984).

Greer, G. *The Female Eunuch* (London: Paladin, 1971).

Greig, C. *Will You Still Love Me Tomorrow: Girl Groups from the 50s on* (London: Virago, 1989).

Grier, B. *The Lesbian in Literature* (Tallahassee: Naiad Press, 1981).

Griffin, G. '*The Chinese Garden*: A Cautionary Tale' in E. Hobby and C. White, eds., *What Lesbians Do in Books*, pp 134–54.

Griffin, S. 'Transformations' in *Sinister Wisdom* 1/2 (1976), pp 7–15.

Grimshaw, J. *Feminist Philosophers: Women's Perspectives on Philosophical Traditions* (Aylesbury: Wheatsheaf, 1986).

Gross, L. 'Out of the Mainstream: Sexual Minorities and the Mass Media' in M. Wolf and A. Kielwasser, eds *Gay People, Sex and the Media* (London: Haworth Press, 1991, pp 19–46.

Grosz, E. *Jacques Lacan: A Feminist Introduction* (London: Routledge, 1990).

—, *Sexual Subversions: Three French Feminists* (London: Allen & Unwin, 1989).

Grundberg, S. 'Deserted Hearts: Lesbians Making it in the Movies' in *Gossip: A Journal of Lesbian Feminist Ethics* 4 (1987), pp 27–39.

Hall, R. *The Well of Loneliness* (London: Virago, 1981).

Hall Carpenter Archives Lesbian Oral History Group. *Inventing Ourselves: Lesbian Life Stories* (London: Routledge, 1989).

Hamer, D. 'I am A Woman: Ann Bannon and the Writing of Lesbian Identity in the 1950s' in M. Lilly, ed. *Gay and Lesbian Writing*, pp 47–75.

—, 'Significant Others: Lesbianism and Psychoanalytic Theory' in *Feminist Review* 34 (Spring 1990).

Hansen, M. 'Messages in a Bottle? (Women's Cinema and Feminist Film Theory in West Germany.)' in *Screen* 28/4 (Autumn 1987), pp 30–9.

Harris, B. 'Notes Toward Defining the Nature of Lesbian Literature' in *Heresies* 3 (1977), pp 14–21.

Hastings, M. *Three Women* (Tallahassee: Naiad Press, 1985).

Hayward, S. 'Beyond the Gaze and into Femme-Filmécriture: Agnes Varda's *Sans Toit Ni Loi*' in S. Hayward and G. Vincendeau, eds *French Film: Texts and Contexts* (London: Routledge, 1990).

Hennegan, A. 'On Becoming a Lesbian Reader' in S. Radstone, ed. *Sweet Dreams: Sexuality, Gender and Popular Fiction*, pp 165–90.

Highsmith, P. *Carol* (London: Bloomsbury, 1990).

Hinds, H. '*Oranges are not the only fruit*: Reaching Audiences Other Lesbian Texts Cannot Reach' in S. Munt, ed. *New Lesbian Criticism*, pp 153–72.

—, 'Fruitful Investigations: The Case of a Successful Lesbian Text' in *Women: A Cultural Review* 2/2 (Summer 1991), pp 128–33.

Hirsch, M. 'The Novel of Formation as Genre: Between Great Expectations and Lost Illusions' in *Genre* 12/3 (Fall 1979), pp 293–311.

Hobby, E. and C. White, eds *What Lesbians Do in Books* (London: Women's Press, 1991).

Hokenson, J. 'The Pronouns of Gomorrha: A Lesbian Prose Tradition' in *Frontiers* 10/1 (1988), pp 62–9.

hooks, b. *Feminist Theory: From Margin to Centre* (Boston: South End Press, 1984).

—, *Yearning: Race, Gender, and Cultural Politics* (London: Turnaround, 1991).

Isabell, S. *Yesterday's Lessons* (Oakfield, California: Women's Press Collective, 1974).

Jackson, R. *Fantasy: The Literature of Subversion* (London: Methuen, 1981).

Jay, K. 'Coming Out as Process' in G. Vida, ed. *Our Right to Love: A Lesbian Resource Book* (Englewood Cliffs, N.J.: Prentice-Hall, 1978), pp 28–30.

—, 'Portrait of the Lesbian as a Young Dyke' in K. Jay and A. Young, eds *Out of the Closet: Voices of Gay Liberation* (New York: Douglas Books, 1972), pp 275–7.

Jay, K. and J. Glasgow, eds *Lesbian Texts and Contexts* (New York: New York University Press, 1990).

Jeffreys, S. *Anti-Climax: A Feminist Perspective on the Sexual Revolution* (London: Women's Press, 1990).

—, 'Does It Matter If They Did It?' in Lesbian History Group, eds *Not A Passing Phase*, pp 19–28.

—, *The Spinster and Her Enemies* (London: Pandora, 1985).

Jelinek, E.C. ed. *Women's Autobiography: Essays in Criticism* (Bloomington: Indiana University Press, 1980).

Kaplan, C. 'An Unsuitable Genre for a Feminist?' in *Women's Review* 8 (1986), pp 18–19.

Kaplan, E.A. 'Is the Gaze Male?' in A. Snitow, E. Stansell and S. Thompson, eds *Desire: The Politics of Sexuality*, pp 321–38.

Kaplan, S.J. 'Varieties of Feminist Criticism' in G. Greene and C. Kahn, eds *Making a Difference: Feminist Literary Criticism* (London: Methuen, 1985), pp 37–58.

Kate, Angie, Martine, Sandra and Caroline. 'Sex on Film – Lesbians' Personal Statements' in H. Robenson, ed., *Visibly Female* (London: Camden Press, 1987), pp 13–19.

Kauffman, L., ed. *Gender and Theory: Dialogues on Feminist Criticism* (Oxford: Basil Blackwell, 1989).

Kaufmann, T. and P. Lincoln. *High Risk Lives: Lesbian and Gay Politics After the Clause* (Bridgport, Dorset: Prism Press, 1991).

Keener, K.M. 'Out of the Archives and into the Academy: Opportunities for Research and Publication in Lesbian Literature' in *College English* 44/3 (March 1982), pp 301–13.

Kennard, J.E. 'Ourself Behind Ourself: A Theory for Lesbian Readers' in *Signs* 9/4 (Summer 1984), pp 647–62.

Kessler, C. Farley, ed. *Daring to Dream: Utopian Stories by United States Women 1836–1919* (Boston: Pandora, 1984).

Kitzinger, C. *The Social Construction of Lesbianism* (London: Sage, 1987).

Kitzinger, S. *Women's Experience of Sex* (London: Penguin, 1986).

Klein, Y.M. 'Myth and Community in Recent Lesbian Autobiographical Fiction' in K. Jay and J. Glasgow, eds, *Lesbian Texts and Contexts*, pp 330–8.

Knight, S. '"A Hard Cheerfulness": An Introduction to Raymond Chandler' in B. Docherty, ed. *American Crime Fiction* (Basingstoke: Macmillan, 1988), pp 71–87.

Kramerae, C. and P. Treichler. *A Feminist Dictionary* (London: Pandora, 1985).

Krieger, S. 'Lesbian Identity and Community: Recent Social Science Literature' in *Signs* 8/1 (Autumn 1982), pp 91–108.

Kuhn, A. *Women's Pictures* (London: Routledge, 1982).

Labovitz, E.K. *The Myth of the Heroine: The Female Bildungsroman in the Twentieth Century* (New York: Peter Lang, 1986).

Lahire, S. 'Lesbians in Media Education' in H. Robinson, ed. *Visibly Female*, pp 274–83.

Landau, P. 'Lesbians and the Soap Opera Life' in *Advocate* 34 (6 March 1984), p 5.

LeFanu, S. *In the Chinks of the World Machine: Feminism and Science Fiction* (London: Women's Press, 1988).

Lehman, D. 'Oh no, [de] Man Again!' in *Lingua Franca* 1/4 (1991), pp 26–33.

Lesbian History Group, eds *Not a Passing Phase: Reclaiming Lesbians in History* (London: Women's Press, 1989).

Lewis, E. 'The Death of the Author and the Resurrection of the Dyke' in S. Munt, ed. *New Lesbian Criticism*, pp 17–32.

Linden, R., D. Pagano, D. Russell and S.L. Star, eds *Against Sadomasochism: A Radical Feminist Analysis* (Palo Alto, CA: Frog in the Well, 1982).

Livia, A. 'Lesbian Sexuality: Joining the Dots' in G. Chester and S. Nielsen, eds *In Other Words: Writing as a Feminist* (London: Hutchinson, 1987), pp 73–7.

Lobel, K., ed. *Naming the Violence: Speaking Out About Lesbian Battering* (Seattle: Seal Press, 1986).

Lorde, A. *Zami: A New Spelling of My Name* (London: Sheba, 1984).

—, 'Scratching the Surface: Some Notes on Barriers to Women and Loving' in *Sister Outsider* (Trumansburg, N.Y.: Crossing Press, 1984), pp 45–52.

—, and S.L. Star. 'Interview with Audre Lorde' in R. Linden *et al*, eds *Against Sadomasochism*, pp 66–71.

Lovell, T., ed. *British Feminist Thought* (Oxford: Basil Blackwell, 1990).

Lynch, L. 'Cruising the Libraries' in K. Jay and J. Glasgow, eds *Lesbian Texts and Contexts*, pp 39–48.

Macdonald, S. 'Demystifying the Female Body. Interviews with Anne Severson and Yvonne Rainer' in *Film Quarterly* 45/1 (Fall 1991), pp 18–32.

MacNair, M. 'The Contradictory Politics of SM' in S. Shepherd and M. Wallis, eds. *Coming on Strong: Gay Politics and Culture* (London: Unwin Hyman, 1989), pp 147–62.

Manning, R. *A Time and a Time* (London: Calder & Boyars, 1971).

Marcus, J. ed. *Suffrage and the Pankhursts* (London: Routledge & Kegan Paul, 1987).

Marcus, L. 'Feminism and Film Theory' in *Women: A Cultural Review* 1/1 (1990), pp 50–2.

Martin, A. 'Chantal Ackerman: A Film Dossier' in *Feminist Review* 3 (1974).

Martin, D. and P. Lyons. *Lesbian/Woman* (San Francisco: Gilde Publications, 1972; New York: Bantam, 1983).

Mayne, J. 'A Parallax View of Lesbian Authorship' in D. Fuss, ed. *Inside/Out*, pp 173–84.

McGregor, I. *Death Wore a Diadem* (London: Women's Press, 1989).

McIntosh, M. 'Liberalism and the Contradictions of Sexual Politics' in L. Segal and M. McIntosh, eds *Sex Exposed: Sexuality and the Pornography Debate* (London: Virago, 1992), pp 155–68.

Medhurst, A. 'That Special Thrill: Brief Encounter, Homosexuality and Authorship' in *Screen* 32/2 (Summer 1991), pp 197–208.

Mellen, J. *Women and Their Sexuality in the New Film* (New York: Dell, 1973).

Mercer, K. 'Just Looking For Trouble: Robert Mapplethorpe and Fantasies of Race' in L. Segal and M. McIntosh, eds *Sex Exposed*, pp 92–110.

Merck, M. 'Difference and Its Discontents' in *Screen* 28/1 (Winter 1987), pp 2–9.

—, 'Lianna and the Lesbians of Art Cinema' in C. Brunsdon, ed. *Films for Women* (London: British Film Institute), pp 166–75.

Miller, N. *Getting Personal: Feminist Occasions and Other Autobiographical Acts* (London: Routledge, 1991).

—, 'The Text's Heroine: a Feminist Critic and Her Fictions', in M. Hirsch and E. Fox Keller eds *Conflicts in Feminism* (New York and London: Routledge, 1990).

Millett, K. *Sita* (London: Ballantine, 1985).

—, *Sexual Politics* (London: Abacus, 1972).

Milloy, J. and R. O'Rourke. *The Woman Reader* (London: Routledge, 1991).

Miner, V. 'An Imaginative Collectivity of Readers and Writers' in K. Jay and J. Glasgow, eds *Lesbian Texts and Contexts*, pp 13–27.

—, *Blood Sisters: An Examination of Conscience* (Trumansberg: Crossing Press, 1982).

Mitchell, J. *Feminism and Psychoanalysis* (Harmondsworth: Penguin, 1986).

Modleski, T. *Loving with A Vengeance: Mass Produced Fantasies for Women* (London: Routledge, 1990).

Moi, T. *Sexual/Textual Politics* (London: Methuen, 1985).

Moraga, C. and B. Smith, 'Lesbian Literature: A Third World Perspective' in M. Cruikshank, ed. *Lesbian Studies*, pp 55–65.

More, T. *Utopia* (New York: Henry Schuman, 1952).

Morris, W. *News from Nowhere* (London: Lawrence & Wishart, 1986).

Morrison, Toni. *Sula* (London: Chatto & Windus, 1980).

Mulvey, L. 'The Oedipus Complex. Beyond the Riddles of the Sphinx.' in J. Donald, ed. *Thresholds: Psychoanalysis and Cultural Theory* (London: Macmillan, 1991).

—, 'Visual Pleasure and Narrative Cinema' in *Screen* 16/3 (1975), pp 6–18.

Munich, A. 'Notorious Signs, Feminist Criticism and Literary Tradition' in G. Greene and C. Kahn, eds *Making a Difference*, pp 238–60.

Munt, S., ed. *New Lesbian Criticism* (Hemel Hempstead: Harvester Wheatsheaf, 1992).

—, 'Review Essay' in *Feminist Review* 40 (Spring 1992), pp 94–9.

—, 'The Inverstigators: Lesbian Crime Fiction' in S. Radstone, ed., *Sweet Dreams: Sexuality, Gender and Popular Fiction*, pp 91–119.

Nachman, E. *Riverfinger Women* (Plainfield, Vt.: Daughters Inc., 1974).

Namjoshi, S. *The Conversations of Cow* (London: Women's Press, 1985).

Neild, S. and R. Pearson. *Women Like Us* (London: Women's Press, 1992).

Nestle, J. *A Restricted Country* (London: Sheba, 1988).

—, 'Voices from Lesbian Herstory' in *A Restricted Country*, pp 110–19.

—, 'When the Lions write History' in *A Restricted Country*, pp 178–88.

Newton, E. 'The Mythic Mannish Lesbian: Radclyffe Hall and the New Woman' in *Signs* 9/4 (Summer 1984), pp 557–75.

Norman, P. 'Nazi Chic' in *Weekend Guardian* 30 May 1992, pp 4–6.

Offen, K., R Roach Pierson and J. Rendall, eds *Writing Women's History* (Houndsmill: Macmillan, 1991).

O'Rourke, R. *Jumping the Cracks* (London: Virago, 1987).

Palmer, J. *The Watcher* (London: Women's Press, 1986).

Palmer, P. 'The Lesbian Feminist Thriller and Detective Novel' in E. Hobby and C. White, eds, *What Lesbians Do in Books*, pp 9–27.

—, 'Contemporary Lesbian Feminist Fiction: Texts for Everyone' in L. Anderson, ed., *Plotting Change: Contemporary Women's Fiction* (London: Edward Arnold, 1990), pp 43–62.

—, *Contemporary Women's Fiction: Narrative Practice and Feminist Theory* (Hemel Hempstead: Harvester, 1989).

Patton, C. 'Visualising Safe Sex: When Pedagogy and Pornography Collide' in D. Fuss, ed. *Inside/Out*, pp 373–86.

Pavletich, A. *Sirens of Song: the Popular Female Vocalist in America* (New York: Da Capo, 1980).

Peachey, M. 'Lang Time Coming', *Vox* (May 1992).

Perverse Politics Issue Group. 'Perverse Politics: Lesbian Issues' in *Feminist Review* **34** (Spring 1990).

Piercy, M. *Woman on the Edge of Time* (London: Women's Press, 1979).

Ponse, B. *Identities in the Lesbian World: The Social Construction of Self* (Westport, Connecticut: Greenwood Press, 1978).

Radstone, S., ed. *Sweet Dreams: Sexuality, Gender and Popular Fiction* (London: Lawrence & Wishart, 1988).

Radway, J. *Reading the Romance* (London: Verso, 1987).

Rich, A. 'When We Dead Awaken: Writing as Re-Vision' in *On Lies, Secrets, Silence* (London: Virago, 1980), pp 33–49.

—, 'Compulsory Heterosexuality and Lesbian Existence' in *Signs* 5/4 (1980): pp 631–60; also in A. Snitow *et al*, eds *Desire: The Politics of Sexuality* (London: Virago, 1984).

Richards, D. *Lesbian Lists* (Boston: Alyson Publications, 1990).

Roberts, J.R. *Black Lesbians: An Annotated Bibliography* (Tallahassee: Naiad Press, 1981).

Rohrlich, R., and E.H. Baruch, eds *Women in Search of Utopia: Mavericks and Mythmakers* (New York: Schocken, 1984).

Rondot, J. 'Hysteria or Resistance? The Great Freudian Cover-Up Part II' in *Trouble & Strife* 15 (Spring 1989).

Rose, J. 'The Cinematic Apparatus' in *Sexuality in the Field of Vision* (London: Verso, 1986), pp 199–214.

—, 'Dora – Fragment of an Analysis' in *m/f* 2 (1978); rpt in *Sexuality in the Field of Vision*, pp 27–48.

Rule, J. *Memory Board* (London: Pandora, 1987).

—, *Desert of the Heart* (London: Pandora, 1986).

—, *Lesbian Images* (Freedom, CA: The Crossing Press, 1975).

Russ, J. *The Two of Them* (London: Women's Press, 1986).

—, *The Female Man* (London: Women's Press, 1985).

Russo, V. *The Celluloid Closet: Homosexuality in the Movies* (New York: Harper & Row, 1986).

Saxton, J. *Queen of the States* (London: Women's Press, 1986).

Schlesinger, T. *Putting 'Reality' Together* (London: Methuen, 1987).

Schulman, S. *After Dolores* (London: Sheba, 1990).

Scott, J. *I, Vampire* (London: Women's Press, 1986).

Scott, S. *Millenium Hall* (London: Virago, 1986).

Segal, L. and M. McIntosh, eds *Sex Exposed: Sexuality and the Pornography Debate* (London: Virago, 1992).

Shaw, P. 'Devastating Developments Are Hastening the Demise of Deconstruction in Academe' in *Chronicle of Higher Education* 37/13 (28 November 1990), II, pp b1–b2.

Sheldon, C. 'Lesbians in Film' in K. Davies *et al* eds *Out of Focus*, pp 89–94.

Shockley, A.A. 'The Mistress and the Slave Girl' in *The Black and White of It* (Tallahassee: Naiad Press, 1987), pp 105–14.

Showalter, E. ed. *The New Feminist Criticism* (London: Virago, 1986).

—, 'Critical Cross-Dressing: Male Feminists and the Woman of the Year' in A. Jardine and P. Smith, eds *Men in Feminism* (London: Methuen, 1987), pp 116–32.

—, *A Literature of Their Own: British Women Novelists from Brontë to Lessing* (London: Virago, 1984).

Smith, A.M. 'Which One's The Pretender? Section 28 and Lesbian Representation' in T. Boffin and J. Frazer, eds *Stolen Glances*, pp 128–39.

Smith, B. 'Sappho was a Right Off Woman' in G. Chester and J. Dickie, eds, *Feminism and Censorship*, pp 178–84.

—, 'Towards a Black Feminist Criticism' in E. Showalter, ed., *The New Feminist Criticism*, pp 168–85.

Smyth, C. 'The Pleasure Threshold: Looking at Lesbian Pornography on Film' in *Feminist Review* 34 (Spring 1990).

Snitow, A. Barr. 'Mass Market Romance: Pornography for Women is Different' in *Radical History Review* 20 (Spring/Summer 1979), pp 141–61.

Spivak, G.C. *The Post-Colonial Critic* (London: Routledge, 1990).

Stacey, J. 'Feminine Fascinations' in C. Gledhill, ed. *Stardom: Industry of Desire*.

—, 'Desperately Seeking Difference' in *Screen* 28/1 (Winter 1987), pp 48–61.

Stanley, J. 'Lesbian Relationships and the Vision of Community' in *Feminary* 9 (Spring 1978), quoted from J.L. Hoagland, *Lesbian Ethics: Toward New Value* (California: Institute of Lesbian Studies, 1988), p 146.

Steward, S. and Garratt, S. *Signed, Sealed and Delivered: True Life Stories of Women in Pop* (London: Pluto, 1985).

Stimpson, C.R. 'Reading for Love: Canons, Paracanons, and Whistling Jo March' in *New Literary History* 21 (1990), pp 957–76.

—, 'Zero Degree Deviancy: The Lesbian Novel in English' in *Where the Meanings Are: Feminism and Cultural Spaces* (London: Routledge, 1989), pp 97–110.

Straayer, C. 'The She-man: Postmodern Bi-Sexual Performance in Film and Video' in *Screen* 31/3 (Summer 1990), pp 262–80.

—, 'Lesbian/Feminist Audience' in *Jump Cut* 29 (1984), pp 40–44.

Strachey, R. *The Cause* (London: Virago, 1978).

Sulter, M. 'Black Codes: The Misrepresentation of Blacklesbians in Film' in *Gossip: A Journal of Lesbian Feminist Ethics* 5 (1987), pp 29–36.

Symons, J. *Bloody Murder: From the Detective Novel to the Crime Novel – A History* (Harmondsworth: Penguin, 1972).

Taylor, V. *Return to Lesbos* (Tallahassee: Naiad Press, 1982).

Tate, C. *Black Women Writers at Work* (New York: Continuum, 1983).

Taylor, H. 'Romantic Readers' in H. Carr, ed., *From My Guy to Sci-Fi*, pp 58–77.

Tyler, C.A. 'Boys Will Be Girls: The Politics of Gay Drag' in D. Fuss, ed., *Inside/Out*, pp 32–70.

Uszkurat, C.A. 'A Classic Mistake' in *Trouble & Strife* 18 (Spring 1990), pp 42–6.

—, 'Process, Perspective, Politics and Meaning: The Search for a Way to Read Lesbian Romantic Paperback Fiction 1950–1990'. Unpublished paper given to the Women's Studies Network conference (London, 1990).

Walker, A. *The Color Purple* (London: Women's Press, 1988).

Ware, V. *Beyond the Pale: White Women, Racism and History* (London: Verso, 1992).

Warren, C. *Gender Issues in Field Research* (London: Sage, 1988).

Weed, E., ed. *Coming to Terms: Feminism, Theory, Politics* (London: Routledge, 1989).

Weeks, J. *Coming Out – Homosexual Politics in Britain from the Nineteenth Century to the Present* (London: Quartet, 1983).

—, 'Questions of Identity' in P. Caplan, ed., *The Cultural Construction of Sexuality* (London: Tavistock, 1987), pp 31–51.

Weiss, A. 'A Queer Feeling When I Look at You' in C. Gledhill, ed. *Stardom: Industry of Desire*.

Weiss, A. and G. Schiller. *Before Stonewall: The Making of a Lesbian and Gay Community* (Tallahassee: Naiad Press, 1983).

Weston, K. and L. Rofel, 'Sexuality, Class and Conflict in a Lesbian Workplace', *Signs*, vol. 9 (University of Chicago Press, 1984).

White, P. 'Female Spectator, Lesbian Specter: *The Haunting*' in D. Fuss, ed. *Inside/Out*, pp 142–72.

Whitelaw, L. 'Lesbians of the Mainscreen' in *Gossip: A Journal of Lesbian Feminist Ethics* 5 (1987), pp 37–46.

Whitford, M. *Luce Irigaray: Philosophy in the Feminine* (London: Routledge, 1991).

Williams, L. 'Pornographies On/Scene, or Diff'rent Strokes for Diff'rent Folks' in L. Segal and M. McIntosh, eds, *Sex Exposed*, pp 233–65.

Wilson, A. 'Investigating Romance: Who Killed the Detective's Lover?' unpublished paper given at the Fifth Annual Lesbian and Gay Studies Conference, Rutgers University, Nov. 1–3, 1991.

—, 'Lesbian Gumshoes' in *Bay Windows* 6/7 (18–24 February 1988), pp 1–2.

Wilson, B. *Gaudí Afternoon* (London: Virago, 1991).

—, *The Dog Collar Murders* (London: Virago, 1989).

—, *Sisters of the Road* (London: Women's Press, 1987).

—, *Murder in the Collective* (London: Women's Press, 1984).

Wilson, E. 'Tell It Like It Is: Women and Confessional Writing' in S. Radstone, ed., *Sweet Dreams*, pp 21–46.

—, *What is to be Done About Violence Against Women?* (Harmondsworth: Penguin, 1983).

—, 'I'll Climb the Stairway to Heaven: Lesbianism in the Seventies' in S. Cartledge and J. Ryan, eds, *Sex and Love: New Thoughts On Old Contradictions* (London: Women's Press, 1983), pp 180–95.

Wilson, E. with A. Weir. *Hidden Agendas: Theory, Politics and Experience in the Women's Movement* (London: Tavistock, 1986).

Wilton, T. 'Sisterhood in the Service of Patriarchy: Heterosexual Women's Friendships and Male Power' in C. Kitzinger, S. Wilkinson and R. Perkins, eds, *Heterosexuality: Special Issue of Feminism and Psychology* 2/3 (1992). London: Sage.

Wings, M. *She Came in a Flash* (London: Women's Press, 1988).

—, *She Came Too Late* (London: Women's Press, 1986).

Winterson, J. 'Interview' in *Spare Rib* 209 (1990), pp 26–9.

Wittig, M. 'The Straight Mind' in S. Hoagland and J. Penelope, eds *For Lesbians Only*, pp 431–8.

—, *The Lesbian Body* (New York: Avon Books, 1975; Boston: Beacon Press, 1986).

Yamaguchi, L. Fletcher and A. Saks, eds. *Lavender Lists* (Boston: Alyson Publications, 1990).

Young, L. 'Representation and British "Racial Problem" Films' in *Women: A Cultural Review* 2/1 (1991), pp 40–51.

Zimmerman, B. *The Safe Sea of Women: Lesbian Fiction 1969–1989* (Massachusetts: Beacon Press, 1990).

—, 'What Has Never Been: An Overview of Lesbian Feminist Criticism' in E. Showalter, ed., *The New Feminist Criticism*, pp 200–58.

—, 'The Politics of Transliteration: Lesbian Personal Narratives' in *Signs* 9/4 (Summer 1984), pp 663–82.

—, 'Exiting from Patriarchy: The Lesbian Novel of Development' in E. Abel *et al*, eds, *The Voyage In*, pp 244–57.

—, 'One Out of Thirty: Lesbianism in Women's Studies Textbooks' in M. Cruikshank, ed., *Lesbian Studies*, pp 128–31.

Notes on Contributors

Sonya Andermahr is a postgraduate research student at Warwick University, writing a PhD thesis on contemporary lesbian genre fiction. She also teaches English Literature and Women's Studies in higher and adult education.

Barbara Bradby teaches Sociology and Women's Studies at Trinity College, Dublin. She started writing on women and popular music when her daughter became a 'Blondie' fan at the age of seven. She has worked with textual approaches to popular songs, and with qualitative sociological approaches to audience research. She is on the editorial board of the journal *Popular Music*.

Penny Florence is an independent scholar and film-maker. She is author of *Mallarmé, Manet and Redon: Visual and Aural Signs and the Generation of Meaning* (Cambridge UP, 1986). She has also published on film, contemporary women's science fiction and on painting. Her next publication (with Dee Reynolds) will be a collection of essays, *Feminist Methodologies: Towards a New Critical Praxis*.

Gabriele Griffin teaches English and Women's Studies at Nene College, Northampton. Her research focuses on twentieth century women's writing. She is author of *Heavenly Love? Lesbian Images in Twentieth Century Women's Writing* (Manchester University Press, 1993). Together with Elaine Aston she has edited two volumes of plays by contemporary women's theatre groups entitled *Herstory* (Sheffield Academic Press, 1991). Other publications include chapters in Gina Wisker, ed, *Insights into Blackwomen's Writings* (Macmillan, 1992), Elaine Hobby and Chris White, eds, *What Lesbians Do In Books* (Women's Press, 1991), and Ann Thompson and Helen Wilcox, eds, *Teaching Women* (Manchester University Press, 1989).

Nicki Hastie recently completed an MA in the English Department at the University of Leicester, and is now a research assistant at Nene College, Northampton, where she is working on her PhD on the construction of lesbians as readers.

Celia Kitzinger is author of *The Social Construction of Lesbianism* (Sage, 1987), co-author (with Sheila Kitzinger) of *Talking With Children About Things That Matter* (Pandora, 1989), and co-author (with Rachel Perkins) of *Changing Our Minds: A Radical Lesbian Analysis of Psychology and its Dangers* (Onlywomen

Press, forthcoming 1993). In addition to many chapters and articles on lesbian and feminist issues, she recently guest edited (with Sue Wilkinson and Rachel Perkins) a special issue of *Feminism and Psychology: An International Journal* (October 1992, 2/3) on 'Heterosexuality'. She teaches Social Psychology and Women's Studies at the University of Loughborough.

Jenny Kitzinger is based at the Glasgow University Media Group where she is researching the media coverage of sexual violence against children. Her previous work includes examining audience understandings of media messages about AIDS, exploring adults' experiences of childhood abuse and investigating how young women 'manage' sexual reputation.

Paulina Palmer teaches an undergraduate course on 'Feminist Approaches to Literature' at the University of Warwick and contributes to the MA in Women's Studies. Her publications include *Contemporary Women's Fiction: Narrative Practice and Feminist Theory* (Harvester Wheatsheaf, 1989), an essay on 'Lesbian Fiction' in Linda Anderson, ed, *Plotting Change: Contemporary Women's Fiction* (Edward Arnold, 1990), a lesbian feminist reading of Antonia White's *Frost in May* in Susan Sellers, ed, *Feminist Criticism: Theory and Practice* (Harvester Wheatsheaf, 1991), and an essay on 'The Lesbian Thriller and the Detective Novel' in Elaine Hobby and Chris White, eds, *What Lesbians Do in Books* (Women's Press, 1991). She is a member of Cambridge Lesbian Line.

Carol Ann Uszkurat began study as a mature student at Bristol Polytechnic in 1985. She is now engaged in a part-time research degree into lesbian paperback romances which were published 1950–70 under the auspices of the Graduate School of Interdisciplinary Women's Studies at Warwick University. She has devised and taught evening classes on lesbian and gay history/literature and is active in both lesbian and disability movements as a singer/songwriter. She has a British working class past, a lesbian present and is registered as disabled due to increasing deafness.

Index